THE IMMORTAL COMMONWEALTH

In the midst of intense religious conflict in the late-sixteenth and early-seventeenth century, theological and political concepts converged in remarkable ways. Incited by the slaughter of French Protestants in the Saint Bartholomew's Day Massacre, Reformed theologians and lawyers began to marshal arguments for political resistance. These theological arguments were grounded in uniquely religious conceptions of the covenant, community, and popular sovereignty. While other works of historical scholarship have focused on the political and legal sources of this strain of early modern resistance literature, *The Immortal Commonwealth* examines the frequently overlooked theological sources of these writings. It reveals how Reformed thinkers such as Heinrich Bullinger, John Calvin, Theodore Beza, and Johannes Althusius used traditional theological conceptions of covenant and community for surprisingly radical political ends.

David P. Henreckson is Assistant Professor of Theology at Dordt College, and serves as Director of the Andreas Center for Reformed Scholarship and Service. His research interests include early modern religion and politics, resistance theory, secularity, and Christian ethics. His work has appeared in peer-reviewed journals such as the *Journal of the Society of Christian Ethics*, *Studies in Christian Ethics*, and the *Journal of Reformed Theology*, as well as magazines such as *Comment* and *Political Theology Today*. He is a contributing editor at *Comment*.

LAW AND CHRISTIANITY

Series Editor

John Witte, Jr., Emory University

Editorial Board:

Nigel Biggar, University of Oxford
Marta Cartabia, Italian Constitutional Court / University of Milano-Bicocca
Sarah Coakley, University of Cambridge
Norman Doe, Cardiff University
Rafael Domingo, Emory University / University of Navarra
Brian Ferme, Marcianum, Venice
Richard W. Garnett, University of Notre Dame
Robert P. George, Princeton University
Mary Ann Glendon, Harvard University
Kent Greenawalt, Columbia University
Robin Griffith-Jones, Temple Church, London / King's College London
Gary S. Hauk, Emory University
R. H. Helmholz, University of Chicago
Mark Hill QC, Inner Temple, London / Cardiff University
Wolfgang Huber, Bishop Emeritus, United Protestant Church of Germany /
Universities of Heidelberg, Berlin, and Stellenbosch
Michael W. McConnell, Stanford University
John McGuckin, Union Theological Seminary
Mark A. Noll, University of Notre Dame
Jeremy Waldron, New York University / University of Oxford
Michael Welker, University of Heidelberg

The Law and Christianity series publishes cutting-edge work on Catholic, Protestant, and Orthodox Christian contributions to public, private, penal, and procedural law and legal theory. The series aims to promote deep Christian reflection by leading scholars on the fundamentals of law and politics, to build further ecumenical legal understanding across Christian denominations, and to link and amplify the diverse and sometimes isolated Christian legal voices and visions at work in the academy. Works collected by the series include groundbreaking monographs, historical and thematic anthologies, and translations by leading scholars around the globe.

Books in the Series

The Immortal Commonwealth: Covenant, Community, and Political Resistance in Early Reformed Thought David P. Henreckson
Great Christian Jurists in American History edited by Daniel L. Dreisbach and Mark David Hall

The Immortal Commonwealth

COVENANT, COMMUNITY, AND POLITICAL
RESISTANCE IN EARLY REFORMED THOUGHT

DAVID P. HENRECKSON
Dordt College

CAMBRIDGE
UNIVERSITY PRESS

CAMBRIDGE
UNIVERSITY PRESS

University Printing House, Cambridge CB2 8BS, United Kingdom

One Liberty Plaza, 20th Floor, New York, NY 10006, USA

477 Williamstown Road, Port Melbourne, VIC 3207, Australia

314–321, 3rd Floor, Plot 3, Splendor Forum, Jasola District Centre, New Delhi – 110025, India

79 Anson Road, #06–04/06, Singapore 079906

Cambridge University Press is part of the University of Cambridge.

It furthers the University's mission by disseminating knowledge in the pursuit of education, learning, and research at the highest international levels of excellence.

www.cambridge.org
Information on this title: www.cambridge.org/9781108470216
DOI: 10.1017/9781108556378

First published 2019

Printed and bound in Great Britain by Clays Ltd, Elcograf S.p.A.

A catalogue record for this publication is available from the British Library.

Library of Congress Cataloging-in-Publication Data
NAMES: Henreckson, David P., 1985– author.
TITLE: The immortal commonwealth : covenant, community, and political resistance in early reformed thought / David P. Henreckson.
DESCRIPTION: Cambridge ; New York, NY : Cambridge University Press, 2019. | Includes bibliographical references and index.
IDENTIFIERS: LCCN 2018060983 | ISBN 9781108470216 (alk. paper)
SUBJECTS: LCSH: Covenant theology – History of doctrines. | Covenants – Religious aspects – Reformed Church. | Christianity and justice – Europe – History – 16th century. | Christianity and justice – Europe – History – 17th century. | Protestantism – Political aspects. | Reformation – Europe.
CLASSIFICATION: LCC BT155 .H46 2019 | DDC 231.7/6–dc23
LC record available at https://lccn.loc.gov/2018060983

ISBN 978-1-108-47021-6 Hardback

Contents

Acknowledgments

God willed to train and teach human persons not through angels, but through our fellows. For the same reason, God distributed his great gifts diversely throughout humanity. He did not confer all things to one person, but some to one and some to others, so that you have need for my gifts, and I for yours.

Johannes Althusius, *Politica* 1.26

When I look back on the past decade, I am astounded by how many communities welcomed me into their midst and by how many conversations I was able to join. These are the sorts of common goods you cannot demand or fully anticipate in advance.

In their own distinctive ways, Eric Gregory, Jeff Stout, John Bowlin, and John Witte have shepherded this project to its completion. Eric has been a constant source of intellectual inspiration and moral support. Intellectual historians have an affinity for the minutiae of life, but we sometimes struggle to explain *why* the details matter; Eric never lacks for this sort of explanation. Jeff's drive for clarity, his insistence on interpretive charity, and the pastoral intensity of his care for students – all these traits characterize Jeff's life and work. One could spend several decades as a teacher and a scholar trying to figure out how he managed to do all this at once. John Bowlin and his Thomas have been my constant companions since I first arrived in Princeton. This was true even when Thomas was partially obscured by my early readings of dear old Karl. John's scholarship and mentorship reminded me why I wanted to be a theological ethicist in the first place. John Witte entered the game in the final innings, but has been an absolutely vital contributor to the book project. I am deeply grateful for his generous feedback, and for the great privilege of being part of his well-curated Law and Christianity series at Cambridge University Press.

Intellectual communities on both sides of Alexander Street in Princeton provided me with all sorts of support in the early stages of writing. At the University, the Religion and Critical Thought Workshop simply *is* the core of the graduate program. It was this workshop that structured my weeks, my years, my writing, and my local friendships. I am tempted to name and thank every person who passed through during my time in the workshop, but the following litany will have to suffice: Molly Farneth, Joseph Clair, Clifton Granby, Sam Goldman, Shira Billet, Alda Balthrop-Lewis, Gustavo Maya, Joseph Naron, Daniel May, Brian Lee, Raissa von Doetinchem de Rande, and Toni Alimi. I am grateful to each of them for time taking to care about what I cared about, and for asking me to take an interest in what they cared about. I could say similar things about several individuals outside the workshop, including Michael Lamb – one of my earliest sources of encouragement – Beth Stroud, Michael Dann, and Tim Benedict. At the Seminary, my involvement was less formal but still incredibly formative. Whether through class or through caffeine-fueled conversation, my work is what it is thanks to my friendships with Adam Eitel, Emily Dumler-Winckler, Anthony Bateza, Sarah Stewart-Kroeker, Derek Woodard-Lehman, Jeff Skaff, and Daniel Pedersen.

Beyond Princeton, I also want to express my gratitude to Jamie Smith, Brad Littlejohn, Cathy Kaveny, Neil Arner, David Decosimo, Jennifer Herdt, Jerry McKenny, Justin Bailey, Rebekah Earnshaw, and – most importantly – my parents, parents-in-law, and siblings for the various ways they supported me along the way. I also owe a great deal to Richard Oosterhoff, for countless late night conversations about late medieval and early modern history, and also for his copyediting and consultations on Latin translations.

I owe thanks to several sources of institutional and financial support. These include fellowships and grants from Princeton's Department of Religion, the University Center for Human Values, the Center for the Study of Religion, and the Office of Research and Scholarship at Dordt College (now University). These sources of support made possible many discussions and relationships that I would not have enjoyed otherwise. I am grateful for the feedback I received on early chapter drafts at the Society of Christian Ethics, AAR's Political Theology Workshop, and the Wheaton Workshop in Political Thought. I would also like to express gratitude to my faithfully rigorous editors at *Comment* magazine, where some early portions of the fifth chapter were published as "Not Trained By Angels" (Fall 2017).

Lastly, my deepest debt of gratitude goes to Kate, my dearest and most constant partner in all endeavors. She has edited my writing with the meticulousness of Jeff Stout. She has inquired into my broader scholarly aims with the farsightedness of Eric Gregory. She has pressed me on my conceptual fuzziness with the earnestness of John Bowlin. This work exists because of her.

Introduction

With a linguistic history reaching back to ancient Hebrew writings, Roman law, and medieval jurisprudence, the concept of covenant has shaped Western notions of law and justice like few others. In its barest sense, it is a contract or agreement between parties. It establishes or recognizes the terms by which a relationship among persons is preserved or set right, and is often ratified by some ritual or sacrifice. It promises rewards for the fulfillment of obligations, and punitive consequences for the breach thereof. It involves the exchange of goods, rights, or services, according to some specified norm. In a fuller sense, a covenant is the founding or recognition of a common project, or fellowship, by which individuals pursue goods that they could not in isolation.

Christian theologians, from Augustine of Hippo (354–430) to John Calvin (1509–1564) to Karl Barth (1886–1968), have made great use of this concept to describe the relations both between God and humanity, and among human persons. Political theorists have also recognized the usefulness of covenantal language to explain the ways that individuals come together in voluntary forms of political association. This is notably true of modern political theory. During the early modern era, there are few political thinkers who did *not* employ some conception of covenant. The writings of Hugo Grotius (1583–1645), Thomas Hobbes (1588–1679), John Milton (1608–1674), Samuel Pufendorf (1632–1694), John Locke (1632–1704), Christian Thomasius (1655–1728), and Jean-Jacques Rousseau (1712–1778) are just the most prominent examples.

Many works of scholarship have told some story about the significance of covenantal language during the early modern period. Many works of scholarship have pointed out that the concept of covenant was marshaled for projects of political resistance around the turn of the seventeenth century, in particular. But few works of scholarship have intentionally accounted for the political *and* the theological valence of the concept in its traditional form. Further, much of contemporary Anglophone scholarship has focused on the alleged

secularizing aspects of covenantal thought – since it is bound up with voluntary contracts and agreements as the normative foundations for political life
and authority. These ostensibly secular elements are often abstracted from the
medieval and early modern theological context that gave them their original
expression.

Secularist narratives of this sort elide the theological out of the genesis of
modernity. It is this elision that I will expose and correct in subsequent
chapters. In one respect, this book asks a single question: How would we
understand the early modern context – and the development of early modern
theories of resistance – differently if we accounted for both the theological and
political valence of covenantal thought? By attending to the theological
sources and taking their biblical, doctrinal, and ethical commitments seriously, I will argue that we have a deeper, richer, less blinkered view of early
modern political thought.

My approach to these topics builds on the insights of scholars such as Eric
Nelson,[1] Oliver O'Donovan,[2] and – in a more oblique manner – Giorgio
Agamben.[3] In their own very distinctive ways, each of these scholars has
criticized secularist narratives of early modern politics. Nelson argues that
the transformation of early modern European political theory was not the
result of secularization, but rather the opposite, as political thinkers increasingly turned to the Hebrew Bible to find new and better models of political
order. Likewise, O'Donovan makes the case that modern – ostensibly secular –
political theory has failed to recognize its own origins and its own delimited
theological charter. In fact, he argues, the rise of early modern constitutionalism was the logical culmination of the project of premodern Christendom.
Agamben, working within a genre of his own making, has spent the past several
decades performing theological excavations of some of the central concepts of
modern political life and thought. Recently, he went so far as to suggest, "it is
certain that the political philosophy of modernity will not be able to free itself
of its contradictions if it does not become aware of its theological roots."[4]

---

[1] Eric Nelson, *The Hebrew Republic: Jewish Sources and the Transformation of European Political Thought* (Cambridge, MA: Harvard University Press, 2010).

[2] Oliver O'Donovan, *The Desire of the Nations: Rediscovering the Roots of Political Theology* (Cambridge: Cambridge University Press, 1996); *The Ways of Judgment* (Grand Rapids, MI: Eerdmans, 2006).

[3] Agamben's recent forays into this field include *The Kingdom and the Glory: For a Theological Genealogy of Economy and Government*, trans. Lorenzo Chiesa (Stanford, CA: Stanford University Press, 2011) and *Leviathans Rätsel*, trans. Paul Silas Peterson (Tübingen: Mohr Siebeck, 2014).

[4] Agamben, *Leviathans Rätsel*, 60.

My work does not rely explicitly on any of these particular, and sometimes controversial, interpretations of early modern politics. However, it does bear a formal similarity, insofar as my historical work argues for the centrality of theological commitments within early modern political thought. Like Nelson, O'Donovan, and Agamben, I will argue in subsequent chapters that theological sources and commitments cannot be rewritten out of the genesis of political modernity without doing injustice to the history. Unlike these fellow skeptics of secularization, however, my work focuses on what may seem a surprising set of figures: radical French, Dutch, and German Protestant theorists of resistance. It is here, at the turn of the seventeenth century, among the zealous, theologically trained, king-killing Calvinists of northwestern Europe that we encounter a strain of political thought that is both profoundly traditional and theological in its sources and shape, and yet distinctively modern in its practical implications.

SITUATING THE PROJECT

If you were to look at many historical surveys of modern political thought, you would likely find a narrative that begins either with sixteenth-century reformation theologians like John Calvin and Martin Luther (1483–1546), or with ostensibly secular mid-seventeenth-century theorists like Grotius and Hobbes. Few pay much attention to the decades in between. However, between the years 1574 and 1614, the idea of covenant began to emerge as a significant and almost ubiquitous concept in both theological and radical political writings.

My work addresses the ways that prominent Protestant thinkers during this transitional period used conceptions of the covenant to articulate uniquely theological views of political life, law, and the common good. In particular, I analyze the ways in which Reformed theologians and lawyers marshaled theological conceptions of covenant and law in order to justify political resistance to systemic injustice.

Set up on these terms, my project necessarily engages with two communities of historical scholarship that rarely interact: intellectual historians of political thought and historical theologians. Each community has an interest in early modern conceptions of covenant, but commonly under different terms and with respect to different figures and texts. The first of the scholarly communities attends to the way that covenantal and contractual language was developed by early modern political theorists. The second confines itself to the development of covenant theology in late-sixteenth- and seventeenth-century Reformed dogmatics. With few exceptions, the respective fields of study have remained separate. The historical theologians limit their analysis to early modern theological treatises on topics such as law and gospel, natural law, and intra-Protestant debates over the sacrament of baptism. The political historians skirt around these texts and focus instead on the political treatises of Protestant resistance theorists, or later thinkers such as Grotius, Hobbes, and Locke.

Unfortunately, this division of labor between the scholarly communities has produced narrow readings of the early modern context – both politically and theologically. My project aims, of historical necessity, to reintegrate the two fields of study. For the early modern Protestants I examine in subsequent chapters, the fields of politics and theology might be distinguished, but they could never be isolated. Most fundamentally, they were united because they were each ordered to the end of human happiness, whether in this life or the next. As a result, the overlap in normative sources for theology and politics was extensive. Therefore, while it is entirely appropriate to speak of distinct early modern genres of theology and politics – each pertaining to certain interests and ends – it would be erroneous to think they operated independently of each other. It would be even more problematic to assume that theology and political theory comprised two entirely different ways of conceiving of human existence – one "religious" and one not.

It is in fact the *contemporary* reader of these early moderns who may be tempted to treat the fields of theology, law, and politics in isolation from each other. This, at least, is a possibility that I will pursue with particular focus in chapters two, three, and five. I will look at readings of early modern covenant and law offered by historians such as Quentin Skinner, Anthony Black, Daniel Lee, and Brad Gregory. I will also examine the assumptions made by historical theologians and theological ethicists about the nature and ends of covenants and covenantal laws.

In situating my project against these particular works, it is useful to identify three influential interpretative strains in contemporary scholarship: The first strain emphasizes the disciplinarian function of early modern covenants and laws, the second their secularizing aspects, and the third their artificiality. Each of these interpretive strains claims to identify a distinct feature of early modern covenantal thought. These strains are not mutually exclusive. In fact, they are often complementary to each other, and it is common to find them woven together within a single historiographical account.

The *disciplinarian* reading takes the emergence of Protestant covenantal thought to be emblematic of an early modern rejection of a traditional or "teleological" social ethic oriented toward the common good. Brad Gregory offers perhaps the most forceful version of this interpretation in his polarizing book *The Unintended Reformation*. According to Gregory's narrative,

"Protestant rulers oversaw ethical regimes that were dominated not by habituation in Christian virtues but by the following of moral rules." These strict rules, expressly revealed in divine law, were practically impossible for the majority of citizens and congregants to keep. As a result, "conscientious authorities needed a clear-eyed strategy to maintain order commensurate with the depravity of human nature ... Hence the centrality of covenant theology in Reformed Protestantism." For the Reformed tradition, "public morality simply *was* following the rules stipulated by the restored church's leaders working with the political authorities established by God." On these terms:

> The most important social virtue among early Lutheran and Reformed Protestants, at every social level from disciplined individuals through patriarchal households to well-ordered regimes as a whole, was therefore not *caritas* but obedience—newly important given the sobering truth about human nature and the reality of a divided Christendom.[5]

While Gregory's account is polemically charged, he is not alone in emphasizing the disciplinarian features of early Reformed moral and political thought. We can trace similar views of early modern covenant and law back to many works of mid-twentieth-century historical theology. J. B. Torrance, under the influence of Anglophone scholarship on Puritanism and Karl Barth's theological critique of Protestant scholasticism, argued that mature covenant theology effectively turned the gospel of grace into a legal contract.[6] While the first generations of Protestants emphasized God's unconditional love for his people, Torrance argued, later Reformed theologians and jurists detached the concept of covenant from this gracious relationship. Alienated from this fellowship with God, covenants became contractual burdens, placing moral obligations on members of the Christian community that no one could ever fulfill.[7] For the greater part of the twentieth century, many

---

[5] Brad Gregory, *The Unintended Reformation: How a Religious Revolution Secularized Society* (Cambridge, MA: Harvard University Press, 2012), 209.

[6] James B. Torrance, "Covenant or Contract?" *Scottish Journal of Theology* 23:1 (February 1970): 51–76. German scholarship has also tended to emphasize the disciplinarian elements of Reformed thought, relating it to an entrenched thesis about early modern "confessionalization," the increasing popularity of neo-Stoicism, or both. See Gerhard Oestreich, *Neostoicism and the Early Modern State*, trans. David McClintock (Cambridge: Cambridge University Press, 1982); Heinz Schilling, *Religion, Political Culture, and the Emergence of Early Modern Society* (Leiden: Brill, 1992), and *Civic Calvinism in Northwestern Germany and the Netherlands* (Kirksville, MO: Sixteenth Century Journal Publishers, 1991); and Christoph Strohm, *Calvinismus und Recht* (Tubingen: Mohr Siebeck, 2008).

[7] Torrance writes that late-sixteenth and seventeenth-century Reformed theologians held that "imperatives of law and human obligations" exist prior to the recognition of any relationship.

theologians and historians of Christian doctrine shared this disciplinarian or legalistic reading of the early modern relationship between covenant and law.[8]

In one respect, the disciplinarian reading simply makes the concepts of covenant and law identical to each other: The covenant simply *is* the laws that obligate its members. Covenantal law exists independently of any antecedent relationship or moral order. On this view, covenants are the means by which individuals in positions of power issue commands to the community. In political terms, these powerful persons issue commands for the sake of maintaining social order. This social order is best maintained when individuals are prevented, under threat of force, from acting in accordance with their sinful nature. And in theological terms, God's covenants are reducible to a set of legal prescriptions – or positive laws – that individuals must obey in order to obtain divine favor. Failure to abide by these covenantal norms results in punitive consequences, either in this life (exile or excommunication) or, worse, the next.

The second reading of covenantal thought involves a distinction between religious covenants and secular contracts. What I will call the *secular republican* interpretation is particularly influential among historians of political thought. I will address two prominent representatives of this view, although subsequent chapters will delve deeper into some of the issues raised here.

Quentin Skinner and several political historians associated with the Cambridge school of historiography have argued that the concept of covenant underwent a process of secularization in the early modern era. In the conclusion of his classic two-volume work, *The Foundations of Modern Political*

___

As a result, they tried – problematically – "to articulate moral obligation in contractual terms," "Covenant or Contract?," 56.

[8] For important and representative accounts, see Karl Barth, *Church Dogmatics* IV/1 (Edinburgh: T&T Clark, 1956), esp. IV/1, 59–66. Perry Miller, *The New England Mind* (Cambridge, MA: Harvard University Press, 1982 [1939]); Holmes Rolston, "John Calvin Versus the Westminster Confession," *Scottish Journal of Theology* 23 (1970): 129–56; R. T. Kendall, *Calvin and English Calvinism to 1649* (Oxford: Oxford University Press, 1979); and David Weir, *The Origins of Federal Theology in Sixteenth-Century Reformation Thought* (Oxford: Oxford University Press, 1990). Over the past thirty years or so, scholars such as Richard Muller, Robert Letham, Andrew Woolsey, Jordan Ballor, Peter Wallace, Mark Beach, and others have argued that aspects of this mid-twentieth-century scholarship were built on faulty assumptions – persuasively, to my mind. The exemplary works on this topic are Muller's "The Covenant of Words and the Stability of Divine Law in Seventeenth-Century Reformed Orthodoxy," *Calvin Theological Journal* 29 (1994): 75–101, and Andrew Woolsey's comprehensive *Unity and Continuity in Covenantal Thought* (Grand Rapids, MI: Reformation Heritage Books, 2012). I will not retread Woolsey's extensive evaluation of the earlier scholarship here, but only note that any stringent juxtaposition of law and gospel, nature and grace, or covenant and contract ought to be viewed with suspicion in light of what recent theological scholarship has shown.

Thought, Skinner relates the concept to the very genesis of modern political theory. Through its emphasis on consent and mutual obligation, the idea of a political covenant was used by theorists such as Johannes Althusius (1563–1638) to "emancipate the study of 'politics' from the confines of theology and jurisprudence."[9] According to Skinner and several of his students, this emancipation provided an opening for thinking about political association and authority in a more republican manner. For Skinner, it is important to note, republicanism is itself a secularizing form of political life.

More recently, Martin van Gelderen has modified Skinner's original position. While acknowledging the role that covenant played in the early modern era, van Gelderen distinguishes among various species of early Protestant political thought. On one side, van Gelderen identifies Althusius and several of his colleagues not as forerunners of secular political theory, as Skinner does, but as covenantal theocrats. These "radical" covenantal theorists assumed that "the study of political institutions and constitutions was *intertwined* with religion and theology."[10] Althusius and the covenantal tradition looked to positive divine law – promulgated through God's covenants with humanity and published in sacred scripture – for God's directives concerning social order. Since the omnipotent divine sovereign issued the law of covenant, we are obligated to obey it. Covenantal law ought to serve as the basis for all human obligations – moral and political. While deviating from Skinner's interpretation of Althusius and covenantal thought, van Gelderen follows Skinner's general approach by distinguishing this *theological* conception of covenant and law from the *secular* republicanism of several of Althusius' Aristotelian contemporaries, including Althusius' student, Johann Heinrich Alsted (1588–1638).[11] According to van Gelderen, the secular Aristotelians

---

9   Quentin Skinner, *The Foundations of Modern Political Thought,* vol. 2 (Cambridge, Cambridge University Press, 1978), 341–42.

10 Martin van Gelderen, "Aristotelians, Monarchomachs and Republicans: Sovereignty and *respublica mixta* in Dutch and German Political Thought," in *Republicanism: A Shared European Heritage,* vol. 1 (Cambridge: Cambridge University Press, 2002), 205 (emphasis added).

11 van Gelderen also identifies Henning Arnisaeus (1570–1636) and Bartholomeus Keckermann (c. 1572–1609) as secular Aristotelians. The label is a strange one when applied to figures such as Alsted, Keckermann, and Arnisaeus. Alsted followed in the vein of Althusius' consociational thought, an association that will become more significant in chapter five. Howard Hotson even places him as a direct intermediary between Althusius and Leibniz, in Howard Hotson and Maria Rosa Antognazza, *Alsted and Leibniz: On God, the Magistrate and the Millennium* (Wiesbaden: Harrassowitz, 1999). Keckermann similarly defies the theologians versus the Aristotelians dichotomy; cf. Richard Muller, "*Vera Philosophia cum sacra Theologia nusquam pugnat:* Keckermann on Philosophy, Theology, and the Problem of Double Truth," *The Sixteenth Century Journal* 15:3 (Autumn 1984): 341–65. Even Arnisaeus cannot be described

rejected the "utopian dreams" of Althusius and instead believed that "the purpose of *politica* was to promote the *bonum commune*." For these thinkers, the study of political life did not rely on scriptural or theological norms, but was a "practical and secular science, devoted to the practical wisdom of *utilitas reipublicae*."[12]

While offering contradictory interpretations of Althusius (among others), Skinner and van Gelderen fundamentally agree that the difference between religious and secular conceptions of covenant has to do with law's *origin* and *end*. In the religious conception, they suggest, the source for society's law is the will of God expressed through divine positive law contained in scripture; for the secular conception, it is the mutual consent of the contracted individuals. With regard to law's end, the theological conception prioritizes conformity to God's providential rule as mediated by the established clerical and civil authorities. For the secular conception, law's end is the common good of *human* society, pursued through the fulfillment of contracted obligations – most importantly, the mutual obligations that exist between the ruler and the ruled. For the secular republican reading, it is the tension between these rival conceptions of covenant and law that provides the context for the emergence of modern secular political theory.

Finally, what I will call the *contractarian* reading seeks to identify the artificial character of covenantal norms and relations. Here, the emphasis has less to do with specific moral directives (as in the disciplinarian reading) or the abandonment of theological sources and aims (as in the secular republican reading), and more to do with the fact that covenantal norms are said to be the product of contingent human volition, detached from any prior relationship or moral order. Aspects of this reading can be traced back to Perry Miller's work on the Puritan tradition, Gerhard Oestreich's analysis of the rise of the early modern nation-state, as well as Carl Schmitt's work on Thomas Hobbes, among other sources.[13] Schmitt's description of the early modern covenant

---

as a secular republican according to van Gelderen's definition since Arnisaeus employs his own theological account of political authority, even if it differs from that of Althusius. Compare my discussion of Arnisaeus in chapter four with van Gelderen, "Aristotelians," 205. Horst Dreitzel adopts a view that is similar to van Gelderen's, distinguishing between two rival forms of Protestant political thought: the traditional form that advocated for vast socio-political reforms on biblical and theological principles, and the neo-Aristotelian form that tended "to emphasize the secularized autonomy of *politica*," Dreitzel, *Protestantischer Aristotelismus und absoluter Staat* (Wiesbaden: Steiner, 1970), 166.

12   Van Gelderen, "Aristotelians," 208.
13   Perry Miller, *The New England Mind*. Gerhard Oestreich, *Neostoicism and the Early Modern State*, Carl Schmitt, *The Leviathan in the State Theory of Thomas Hobbes*, trans. George

is particularly striking, as it presumes a radical break with the preceding scholastic tradition of Aquinas and his interlocutors:

[C]ovenant does not accord with medieval conceptions of an existing commonwealth forged by God and of a preexistent natural order. The state as order and commonwealth is the product of human reason and human inventiveness and comes about by virtue of the covenant. This covenant is conceived in an entirely individualistic manner. All ties and groupings have been dissolved. Fear brings atomized individuals together. A spark of reason flashes, and a consensus emerges about the necessity to submit to the strongest power.[14]

Schmitt connects this conception of covenant not only to Hobbes, but also to the Calvinist tradition as a whole, as we will see in chapter one. While Schmitt does not provide much textual evidence outside Hobbes' corpus, more recent scholarship has attempted to flesh out this covenant-as-artifice conception within the broader tradition of Reformed covenantal thought. Victoria Kahn's recent work *Wayward Contracts* centers on covenant and contract in the English Civil War, but her comments on the trans-Atlantic tradition of covenant theology are relevant. According to Kahn, over the early decades of the seventeenth century a new discourse of contract and covenant gradually replaced traditional Aristotelian notions of natural human sociality. While she acknowledges that traditional Aristotelian or Thomist conceptions of politics referred to the existence of social contracts, Kahn suggests that these contractual arrangements were limited in application by premodern commitments to the idea of an antecedent moral order or humanity's natural sociability. By contrast, early modern contractual theory viewed all social and political arrangements as "wholly artificial."[15] Individuals may choose to enter into whatever relationships or pacts they desire, and may end these relationships for any reason they choose. Kahn identifies multiple strands of this contractarian theory, one of which is Reformed covenant theology.

According to Kahn's narrative, the earliest forms of covenant theology – represented by the French and Dutch resistance theorists – advanced a notion of covenant that was still beholden to traditional and Aristotelian views of political order. They "did not yet conceive of the creation of the state as wholly

---

Schwab (Westport, CT: Greenwood Press, 1996 [1938]). Cf. David Zaret's contestable sociological analysis of colonial American covenant theology in *The Heavenly Contract: Ideology and Organization in Pre-Revolutionary Puritanism* (Chicago, IL: University of Chicago Press, 1985).

14 Schmitt, *Leviathan*, 33.
15 Victoria Kahn, *Wayward Contracts: The Crisis of Political Obligation in England, 1640–1674* (Princeton, NJ: Princeton University Press, 2004), 9–10.

artificial," but "conceived of political obligation as arising 'from the nature of things and the will of God.'" Nevertheless, Kahn argues, covenantal thought possessed resources for an "artificial" or fundamentally voluntarist conception of political life. Kahn suggests "at the extreme, covenant theology reimagined fixed status or, rather, the ontological relations of man and God, in terms of the voluntary relations of contract." This explains the early Protestants' "intense preoccupation with the artificial arrangements—or covenants—established by the voluntarist God of Calvinism." Further, this conception of covenant and covenantal norms would "have profound implications for the relation of subject and sovereign."[16]

For the contractarian reading, early modern covenant discourse is bound up with a specific voluntaristic conception of law and obligation. Just as the "voluntarist God of Calvinism" freely entered into contracts with his people, so human beings may create social covenants for whatever reason they choose. While the contractarian reading may acknowledge the theological prehistory of covenantal law, there is an assumption that the concept's secular kernel can shed its theological shell with little loss of meaning. The sacred covenant mutates into what Kahn calls the *nudum pactum*, and, correspondingly, the voluntarist God morphs into the voluntarist sovereign or collective of individuals. On these terms, once transposed out its original theological key, the law of the covenant could be viewed as a mere artifact – a happenstance of human ingenuity that was made in response to social distrust, division, and the contingencies of political life.[17]

I will say more about these three interpretative approaches in subsequent chapters. At present, I will offer only this promissory note: By attending closely to the theological sources, and showing how they shape radical Protestant political discourse from 1574 to 1614, I aim to complicate and correct the secularizing tendencies of contemporary scholarship on this historical context. Against the disciplinarian reading, I will show how covenantal thought interrelated covenants, covenantal laws, and the common goods of fellowship. Against the secular republican reading, I will show how early modern republican thought during this period drew explicitly and substantially from theological sources, principles, and arguments. And against the contractarian interpretive strain, I will show that many radical Protestant thinkers during this period believed that a covenant or law could *not* be arbitrary, or a *nudum pactum*, and still have normative authority.

---

[16]   Kahn, *Wayward Contracts*, 49.
[17]   Kahn, *Wayward Contracts*, 55–6, 78–9.

METHODOLOGY AND SCOPE

In a classic essay written four decades ago, Quentin Skinner addressed the need for historians to account for the *intentionality* of their objects of study. He argued that by examining the spectrum of conventional concepts or words available to an author it is possible to inquire about what he or she intended to do in writing. In other words, the shared vocabulary, assumptions, and criteria for making knowledge-claims help us to limit the possible range of things that the author may have intended to do in writing a particular text. To be in a position to carry out this work, intellectual historians cannot just read the canon. To understand their objects of study, they need to become acquainted with the conceptual world in which the canonical works came to be.

This contextualist approach to historiography informs my work on two levels. First, broadly speaking, I focus on one significant part of the early modern conceptual world that many political theorists have neglected in their focus on the canonical texts of Hobbes, Rousseau, Kant, and others. Each of these canonical thinkers inherits (and often transfigures) traditional conceptions of covenant and law.[18] In subsequent chapters, I examine the history of these concepts and argue that they retain much of their theological content even as early modern Protestants deployed them for new and sometimes radical ends.

The second application of the contextualist approach regards the scope and subjects of my study. My project does not concern a single figure. Rather, I am focused on what I would call a community – or *schola* – of Reformed scholars writing in northern continental Europe in the late-sixteenth and early-seventeenth centuries. As historians like Michael McGiffert and Robert Letham have pointed out, there was a "common pool of theological thought" shared by Reformed scholars across England, Scotland, and modern-day Switzerland, Germany, and the Netherlands.[19] This Calvinist republic of letters provided conditions for an astonishing degree of intellectual exchange. Because of this phenomenon, no singular figure stands out as the originator of

---

[18] Hobbes, it has been argued recently, was quite familiar with Althusius and was frustrated by the persistent influence of Protestant Aristotelian thought in mid-seventeenth-century England. Rousseau talks of the Genevan Calvinist school of thought and used Grotius as a foil for his own views on political order. In the culmination of his treatise *On Perpetual Peace*, Kant himself makes an important distinction between the *foedus pacificum* and a *pactum pacis* – distancing himself from a tradition of political thought that he traces back to Grotius and Pufendorf.

[19] Michael McGiffert, "From Moses to Adam: The Making of the Covenant of Works," *The Sixteenth Century Journal* 19:2 (Summer 1988): 134; cf. David Weir, *The Origins of Federal Theology*, 2.

covenantal thought in theology or politics. Rather, the work of scholars such as Girolamo Zanchi (1516–1590), Theodore Beza (1519–1605), and Althusius must all be read with (and, on occasion, against) each other.

The writings of these figures display a patchwork of influences – ancient, medieval, scholastic, and early modern. The rapid publication and dissemination of political and doctrinal treatises allowed these thinkers to remain abreast of contemporaneous scholarship.[20] In addition to these considerations, it is important to remember that many of these thinkers were working in territories that had recently rejected old jurisprudential structures of canon law, episcopal authority, and – in some cases – Catholic empire. The various treatises published over these few decades were, in many respects, contributions to a coordinated project of significant social and legal reformation, and sometimes even armed resistance.

In fact, it is this idea of covenantal resistance that provides a thematic unity for the figures and texts that I have brought to the forefront of my work. Many early modern Protestants wrote about covenants and covenantal laws during this period. Since this project is not intended to be an exhaustive survey of this conceptual history, some of these figures play proportionately smaller roles in my narrative. In fact, some fascinating figures – e.g. David Pareus and Franciscus Junius – barely make their way out of my footnotes. However, I have chosen to concentrate on influential Reformed theologians and political thinkers who were central to the application of the theological conception of covenant to theories of political resistance. Figures like Pareus and Junius, while they have noteworthy things to say about political life and order, do not trade in covenantal concepts to the extent that figures like Mornay and Althusius do.

Following this principle, my narrative has three primary stages. First, I look at late-sixteenth-century *theological* writings on covenant and law that explicitly influenced later theorists of political resistance. Second, I examine late-sixteenth-century Protestant *political* writings on covenant, law, and resistance in the immediate wake of political crises in France and the Netherlands. Third, I turn to Johannes Althusius' *Politica* (1603, 1610, and 1614), one of most comprehensive products of early-seventeenth-century Reformed political thought. Many aspects of Althusius' political thought can be traced to his theological contemporaries or immediate antecedents. For example, his discourse on natural and positive law very closely follows the work of Girolamo Zanchi. His later chapter on resistance to tyranny draws on

---

[20] In the 1614 edition of his *Politica*, Althusius included numerous references to the works of Hoen, Keckermann, and Arnisaeus (some of which had appeared only a couple of years prior).

the late-sixteenth-century resistance treatises of Beza, George Buchanan (1506–1582), and Mornay (1549–1623). Althusius also offers a crucial perspective on the ways in which the disciplines of theology, jurisprudence, and political philosophy were related in his day.[21]

Since I have described the international and porous boundaries of early modern Protestant thought, I need to explain the rationale behind the specific delimitations I have chosen to set up. The first concerns geography. While the "common pool" covers both the European continent and the British Isles, this book will focus on the continental development of Reformed covenantal thought. It is true that English, Scottish, and continental Calvinists were highly conversant with each other during this period. This is especially the case regarding doctrinal matters. The development of covenant theology, particularly during the late-sixteenth century, is a phenomenon that impacts both shores of the English Channel. However, when it comes to the *political* application of the covenant, the English and Scottish context remains rather distinct from the continent. For Dutch and French Protestants, the covenant became an important political concept fairly early on (certainly after the St. Bartholomew's Day Massacre) as each community struggled to define itself against an entrenched Catholic regime.[22] For the English and Scottish Calvinists, political use of the covenant became more prominent during the English Civil War. In both contexts a period of crisis seems to have generated, or at least intensified, the political use of covenant.[23] I will explore this point in chapters three and four.

As for scope, I have chosen to focus on the years between 1574 and 1614 for the following reasons. While I analyze some theological prehistory in chapters

---

[21] Although his appointment at Herborn was to the faculty of law, he was at home in both the worlds of Reformed dogmatics and political thought. He engaged in theological debates from the beginning to the end of his career. (In fact, his primary contestation with Hugo Grotius seems to have been sparked by the latter's views on ecclesiology.)

[22] English and Scottish Calvinists also existed under Catholic regimes for a brief time in the mid-sixteenth century. Political tracts by the Marian exiles John Knox, Christopher Goodman, and John Ponet were published between 1556–1558 (not to mention George Buchanan's seminal work). However, these tracts did not employ the political concept of covenant in the manner or to the same extent that continent thinkers did. (E.g. John Knox, "The Appellation from the Sentence Pronounced by the Bishops and Clergy," [1558]; and "A Godly Letter of Warning or Admonition to the Faithful," [1553].) These tracts also quickly fell out of favor after the end of Mary's reign in 1558, as the Protestant Elizabeth took the throne. It seems to be only later, on the eve of the English Civil War, that they gained a second audience.

[23] For instance, the influential Scottish Presbyterian Samuel Rutherford made great use of Althusius in his 1644 treatise *Lex Rex*. It is also interesting to note that, decades earlier, Althusius' main Scottish interlocutor was the *royalist* theorist William Barclay, whose views on sovereignty and political authority prompt some of Althusius' most direct polemics.

one and two, my narrative of political history picks up in the years after the Saint Bartholomew's Day Massacre in 1572, perhaps the most pivotal moment in the development of Protestant resistance theory.[24] In 1574, following this seminal event, Beza published his *De jure magistruum*, and Philippe de Mornay most likely penned the first draft of the *Vindiciae contra tyrannos*.[25] In 1614, Althusius published the final – and significantly expanded – edition of his *Politica*, drawing widely from earlier Protestant theological and political sources, including the theologians I examine in chapters one and two, and the political thinkers I examine in chapters three and four. This forty-year window provides us with a perspective on the ways that Protestant political thought drew on traditional theological commitments to develop innovative accounts of covenanted political life, mutual accountability, and the legitimacy of popular resistance.

PREVIEWING THE NARRATIVE

My engagement with early modern sources may initially prove disorienting to contemporary historical theologians and political historians for opposite reasons. In the first two chapters, I approach a series of texts in the theological genre by asking questions that are more common to the genre of political thought and history. In the remaining chapters, I turn the tables and ask theological questions of texts in the political genre. For the reader's sake, it is important that I make this clear: I believe I am licensed to treat these texts in this way because this is precisely what the early moderns are doing themselves. For instance, early modern authors of theological treatises commonly analogize political concepts of rule, authority, and tyranny to talk about the relationship between God and humanity and God's governance of the world. Likewise, writers of political treatises analogize standard doctrinal *loci* such as creation, law, and covenant to make sense of public life and the *communicatio* of rights and goods.

With that in mind, this is a roadmap to what lies ahead: Chapter one addresses the nature of covenantal authority, showing how early Protestant theologians adopted covenantal language to speak about the relationship between the divine sovereign and his subjects. I address and counter the previously mentioned scholarship that associates covenantal thought with strains of so-called voluntarist thought. Chapter two addresses theological

---

[24]   See, for example, Harro Höpfl and Martyn Thompson, "The History of Contract as a Motif in Political Thought," *The American Historical Review* 84:4 (Oct. 1979): 929.

[25]   I address controversy surrounding the *Vindiciae*'s authorship in chapter three.

conceptions of covenant and law in the late-sixteenth century. Specifically, I look at some of the most influential treatises on the nature of law and the ways in which early Protestants related law to the theological themes of covenant, creation, and the common good. Chapter three turns more directly to Protestant political writings – specifically, late-sixteenth-century treatises that advocated resistance to tyranny. I pay particular attention to the theological commitments that undergird – and make coherent – these early defenses of political resistance. Chapter four engages with representative writings of the critics of Protestant resistance theory. I demonstrate that the debates between the so-called monarchomachs and absolutists were profoundly theological – and even biblically exegetical – in nature. Chapter five arrives at Johannes Althusius and his *Politica*. Contrary to the assumptions of much of German and Anglophone scholarship, I argue that Althusius' innovative consociational account of political life, and his argument for political resistance, cannot be properly understood or appreciated without attending to his theological sources and commitments. Finally, in chapter six, I delve deeper into Protestant arguments for resistance and suggest that this earlier tradition offers important resources for contemporary political theology and social ethics.

* * * * *

In the preface to the third edition of his *Politica*, Althusius argued against some of his detractors that "all arts are unified in practice." This is an assumption that would drive some of Althusius' own students to publish some of the first encyclopedias ever assembled. It is also an assumption that animates my own project.

Althusius believed that the work of the theologian, the jurist, and the political philosopher ought to be coordinated to the shared ends of the community. Coordination of this sort can be difficult, since it requires specialists to listen to – and sometimes be corrected by – exemplars in other fields. For Althusius, it was vitally important that the disciplines of theology, politics, and law did not exist in isolation from each other. They ought to inform, correct, and submit to each other according to their respective purview and purposes.

In what lies ahead, I will show how this interdisciplinary approach motivated some of the most original and important political thought of the early modern period. Further, my hope is that this book is itself a demonstration of the ways in which contemporary scholars should approach the integrated fields of theology, political history, and social ethics.

1

The Covenanting God

Theological Models for Authority and Power

The God of early modern Reformed theology has sometimes been described as a leviathan: all-powerful, unaccountable, and utterly free in his dealings with humanity. His chief end is the increase of his own glory. His covenants are made apart from any prior recognition of goodness or merit, depending solely on his sovereign whim. Theologians, political theorists, and historians of early modernity have all contributed to this construal of the tradition. In his classic work *The Divine Right of Kings*, John Neville Figgis analogized Thomas Hobbes' political Leviathan with the "Deity of Calvinism," since both possessed power that was "unchecked by law, justice or conscience."[1] Several decades later, Carl Schmitt seized on this historical parallel in one of his lesser known – but most revealing – works, marking it as a prime example of how our most important political ideas are, at root, secularized theological concepts.[2] The source of God's covenant with humanity cannot be traced to anything like the essential goodness or love of God, since, as Schmitt reads Hobbes, "God is above all a power, not wisdom or justice." In turn, the human rationale for obeying God according to the terms of his covenant derives, in Hobbes' language, not from "gratitude for his benefits; but from his irresistible power."[3] God entered into covenant with humanity simply *because*. No further explanation or justification is needed. There is no possible standard by which to evaluate the goodness of the covenantal relationship or its terms. To put it in

---

[1] John Neville Figgis, *The Divine Right of Kings*, second edition (Cambridge: Cambridge University Press, 1914 [1896]), 325.
[2] Carl Schmitt, *The Leviathan in the State Theory of Thomas Hobbes*, trans. George Schwab (Westport, CT: Greenwood Press, 1996 [1938]), 32.
[3] Schmitt, *Leviathan*, 38n2.

simple terms, the divine Leviathan of the Calvinists begat the human Leviathan of the early modern nation-state.[4]

Schmitt may be one of the few theorists of the past century who finds this secularized account of divine power agreeable for modern politics. However, he is far from the only one who assumes that the emergence of the early modern nation-state owes something to the Reformed doctrines of God and the covenants. At the very least, the Deity of Calvinism[5] shares with Leviathan the attribute of absolute power. The label *voluntarism* gets bandied about with disconcerting ease. While the substance of the label shifts in unpredictable ways, a common charge is that the God of the Reformed tradition commands and covenants arbitrarily, apart from any antecedent standard of goodness, justice, wisdom, or love. In his oft-cited work on natural law, Alexander d'Entreves related the Reformed doctrine of divine sovereignty to the "voluntarist bent" of Protestant political thought. Like many others, d'Entreves suggested that it was the voluntarism of early modern Protestant thought that fostered a peculiar reverence for the "positive law of the State conceived as ultimately grounded upon the will of God." It is "certainly significant," he continued, that "the 'divine right of kings' is a typical product of this age."[6]

[4] A similar, more recent version of this historical narrative can be found in Brad Gregory's *The Unintended Reformation: How a Religious Revolution Secularized Society* (Cambridge, MA: Harvard University Press, 2012).

[5] To avoid confusion, I should note some things about my use of the terms "Protestant," "Reformed," and "Calvinist." Regarding the last term, nineteenth- and early-twentieth-century scholarship commonly referred to Calvinism as a synecdoche for the entire Reformed tradition. Implicit in this use of terms was the belief that John Calvin was the sole, or at least the most significant, fountainhead of the Reformed tradition. This assumption has been effectively challenged over the past several decades. While Calvin was certainly an important second-generation reformer, he was one among many voices. He receives no unique treatment among his peers or even his immediate successors. Other significant progenitors of the tradition – e.g. Martin Bucer, Ulrich Zwingli, Heinrich Bullinger, Peter Martyr Vermigli, and Johannes Oecolampadius, to name a few – ought to be considered as having similar authoritative weight in early Reformed Protestantism. For this reason, I will use the term Reformed even when many of my secondary sources refer to Calvinism. I should also note that calling first-generation reformers like Zwingli and Oecolampdius "Reformed" is itself something of an anachronism, since the label is applied retrospectively a few generations later. Like most contemporary scholars, however, I find this anachronism to be necessary and useful. While the identity of various Protestantisms became clearer in the mid- to late-sixteenth century, important differences between Lutherans and the Reformed were evident by 1520, particularly on matters relating to the sacraments and the doctrines of justification and sanctification. See Christoph Strohm on the origin of the term "Calvinism" in "Methodology in Discussion of 'Calvin and Calvinism'" in *Calvinus Praeceptor Ecclesiae*, ed. Herman Selderhuis (Geneva: Librairie Droz, 2004), 67.

[6] Alexander D'Entreves, *Natural Law: An Introduction to Legal Philosophy* (New Brunswick, NJ: Transaction Publishers, 2009 [1951]), 70–1.

More recent theologians and moral philosophers have kept this voluntarist reading of early Protestant thought alive and well. Reverence for the leviathan-like God of Luther, Calvin, and their followers led, by various routes and over the course of centuries, to many of the perceived ills of modernity – in particular, political absolutism and the disciplinary state.[7] In his early writings, Alasdair MacIntyre described the early Protestant view of humanity's relationship with God as a state of absolute subjection, wherein we hope for divine favor despite "our inability to obey the arbitrary fiats of a cosmic despot."[8] John Milbank likewise labels the entirety of mainline Protestant thought as "voluntarist from beginning to end."[9]

It is not only Protestantism's critics that advance this reading of the early tradition. Many contemporary Protestant scholars are likely to accept this account of the voluntarist God as foundational to their own tradition. While shying away from the more radical statements of Hobbes or Schmitt, theologians such as Richard Mouw and David Little have ascribed some form of voluntarism to the early tradition. Mouw, for instance, defines the Reformed conception of the covenantal relationship between God and humanity as "a revelatory encounter in which a naked divine will issued legal commands to a naked human will."[10]

Constrained by all these historical and theological assumptions, the social and political ramifications of covenantal discourse seem almost preordained. There is a golden causal chain connecting vicious theological conceptions of God and his covenants with some of the most illiberal elements of modern political thought.

---

[7] Examples of this sort of account include: William Cavanaugh, "A Fire Strong Enough to Consume the House: The Wars of Religion and the Rise of the State," *Modern Theology* 11:4 (Oct. 1995): 397–420; and Brad Gregory, *The Unintended Reformation: How a Religious Revolution Secularized Society* (Cambridge, MA: Belknap, 2012).

[8] Alasdair MacIntyre, *A Short History of Ethics* (London: Routledge and Kegan Paul, 1967), 123.

[9] John Milbank, "Radical Orthodoxy and the Radical Reformation," *The Conrad Grebel Review* 23:2 (Spring 2005): 45.

[10] Richard Mouw, *The God Who Commands* (Notre Dame, IN: University of Notre Dame Press, 1991), 97. Mouw tempers his statement by emphasizing other ameliorating aspects of the Reformed tradition, but his initial concession already grants too much, as I will argue below. See also the descriptions of Reformed "voluntarism" in part two of David Little's *Religion, Order, and Law* (Chicago, IL: University of Chicago Press, 1984), and John Witte's rather different use of the term in *God's Joust, God's Justice* (Grand Rapids, MI: Eerdmans, 2006), 148. Stephen Grabill's account of Protestant attitudes toward natural law and voluntarism after Karl Barth is a helpful survey, although his reading of Barth is limited by Grabill's focus on Barth's rejection of natural law rather than his reworking of covenant theology. See *Rediscovering the Natural Law in Reformed Theological Ethics* (Grand Rapids, MI: Eerdmans Publishing, 2006), 38–53.

This narrative, however, suffers from being too tidy and too provincial. The theological and political use of the concept of covenant runs deeper and in more interesting – perhaps unexpected – directions than many of the received accounts acknowledge. For one, as we will see in later chapters, it utterly fails to account for the emergence of resistance theory in the allegedly totalitarian soil of early modern Calvinism.

The primary task of this chapter, therefore, is to inquire into how (and why) early modern Protestants, and particularly continental Reformed theologians and polemicists, used the concept of covenant to reflect on the identity of the divine sovereign and the nature of his relationship with his subjects. In what sense, and for what reasons, does God promise and obligate himself to his own creatures and creation? I will begin with a discussion of early Protestant views of the nature of the covenanting God, addressing the ways that the early Reformed tradition in particular described the relationship between God's power and his goodness, justice, and love. Framed by this discussion, I will then address specific ways in which early Reformed theologians theorized the covenant in order to describe humanity's relationship with the sovereign God.

Several of the matters that I will address, particularly in these first two chapters, touch on doctrinal *loci* that historical and confessional theologians have focused on over the past several decades. While I make use of much of this scholarship, the questions that I will raise often arise from a different set of concerns. For instance, recent scholarship on covenant theology has addressed questions such as: Which theologians first made covenant the "central dogma" of their doctrinal system? Did John Calvin's theology contain one covenant (of grace), or two (one of works and one of grace)? Is Karl Barth's critique of covenant theology in his *Church Dogmatics* a fair appraisal of the tradition? While I recognize the significance of many of these questions for historical and doctrinal disputes, I am more concerned with addressing how the covenant was used by the early Reformed to describe the nature of the relationship between rulers and the ruled, between relations and norms, and the nature and work of law in the context of covenanted communities.

WHAT SORT OF GOD ENTERS INTO COVENANT WITH HUMANITY?

As one of the early modern heirs to medieval scholasticism, the Reformed tradition was concerned to find ways to address a central lingering theological tension: Why did the sovereign God, who lacks nothing in himself, enter into relationship with humanity, obligating himself to his creatures and securing their salvation at such great cost to himself – that is, the sacrifice of his son? Within this overarching question, there are also a number of related issues that touch on the origin and ends of the divine covenant. Does God's covenant with humanity reveal something about who God is, what he loves, and what he hates? And how do human beings come to recognize him as their sovereign lord? Or, in fact, are these questions irrelevant to understanding the nature of the covenantal relationship, since it consists entirely in the imposition of the will of an absolute sovereign upon creatures who simply must obey the whims of the "cosmic despot"?

References to the medieval precursors can be overgeneralized, and run the risk of anachronism, since charges of voluntarism and nominalism are almost always retrospective.[11] Even so, to understand the range of views available in the early modern setting, it is worthwhile to identify two distinctive schools of thought on these matters among medieval theologians. The first, often associated with Thomas Aquinas, held that it was not strictly necessary for God to create the world or to order it in any single particular manner. However, while the divine act of creation is gratuitous – strictly speaking – it is also a consistent expression of God's own nature. The God who has revealed himself by various means would not – and could not – will something that is in any way contrary to who he is. And if we believe that God is perfect in his wisdom, goodness, and love, we may trust that his providential ordering of the world and the particular nature of his relations to humanity manifest this perfect character.

Among late medieval scholastics, there arose another school of thought, retrospectively called voluntarism, which was concerned to reinforce God's absolute freedom to will whatever he wants with respect to his creation and the moral order. Outlined in broad terms, the voluntarist answer to the questions posed above about the nature of God's act of creation and relationship to humanity is that nothing of explanatory value can be said about why God entered into covenant with humanity beyond that *he so willed*. Among prominent scholastics such as William of Ockham, Duns Scotus, and Gabriel Biel there was some internal debate over the contingency of God's promises and the laws he gave to humanity – for example, could God "dispense" with certain moral laws that he had previously issued without being guilty of an injustice or deceit?[12] For now, however, it is enough to identify this late

---

[11] For an extensive analysis of the preceding context, see Bonnie Kent, *Virtues of the Will: The Transformation of Ethics in the Late Thirteenth Century* (Washington, DC: Catholic University of America Press, 1995). Cf. Tobias Hoffmann, "Intellectualism and Voluntarism," in *The Cambridge History of Medieval Philosophy*, ed. Robert Pasnau (Cambridge: Cambridge University Press, 2010), 414–27.

[12] Further, as David Steinmetz has shown, figures like Scotus and Johannes von Staupitz were also concerned to emphasize that, after deciding to make a covenant with his creatures, God would – of his own free will – be faithful to his own promises. Cf. David Steinmetz, *Luther and*

medieval theological form of voluntarism with the central affirmation that "the divine will alone is the first rule of all justice."[13] Consideration of whether God's actions, or his relationship with humanity, correspond with the goodness of his nature are immaterial.

Up until the past few decades, it was almost generally assumed that, insofar as Protestant Christianity was influenced by medieval Christianity – and not simply a radical break with the preceding tradition, as some early-twentieth-century scholarship assumed – it fell into the voluntarist rather than the Thomist camp. There are some reasons for this, beginning with the fact that much of the scholarship has focused on Luther and Calvin as singular representatives of the early Protestant tradition. The writings of Luther, in particular, offer plenty of prima facie evidence to conclude that Protestantism is the direct descendant of medieval voluntarism. Taking one infamous example from his early exchange with Erasmus:

> If any rule or standard, or cause or ground, existed for it, it could no longer be the will of God. What God wills is not right because He ought, or was bound, so to will; on the contrary, what takes place must be right, because He so wills it. Causes and grounds are laid down for the will of the creature, but not for the will of the Creator – unless you set another Creator over him![14]

Luther is always happy to take the path of most terrifying theological consistency, no matter where it may lead. As John Rist once put it, where previous theologians approached these questions with trepidation bordering on contradiction, Luther, "looking for consistency, inclines to plump."[15] Calvin, on the other hand, is typically less volatile – despite his distorted popular image as a hard-hearted heretic-burning predestinarian. Even so,

Staupitz: An Essay in the Intellectual Origins of the Protestant Reformation (Durham, NC: Duke University Press, 1980) and *Calvin in Context*, second edition (Oxford: Oxford University Press, 2010), esp. 40–53; Heiko Oberman, "Some Notes on the Theology of Nominalism," *Harvard Theological Review* 53 (1960): 47–76; Denis Janz, "Late Medieval Theology," in *The Cambridge Companion to Reformation Theology*, eds. David Bagchi and David Steinmetz (Cambridge: Cambridge University Press, 2004), 5–14.

13   From Gabriel Biel's *Collectorium circa quattuor libros Sententiarum*: "God can do something which is not just for God to do; yet if he were to do it, it would be just that this be done. Wherefore the divine will alone is the first rule of all justice, and because he wills something to be done, it is just that it be done, and because he wills something not to be done, it is not just that it be done," I.43. Translation from Janine Marie Idziak, "In Search of 'Good Positive Reasons' for an Ethics of Divine Commands: A Catalogue of Arguments," *Faith and Philosophy* 6.1 (1989): 53.

14   Martin Luther, *The Bondage of the Will*, trans. J. I. Packer and O. R. Johnston (Grand Rapids, MI: Baker Academic, 2012 [1525]), 209.

15   John Rist, *Augustine Deformed: Love, Sin, and Freedom in the Western Moral Tradition* (Cambridge: Cambridge University Press, 2016), 181.

Calvin, too, has been charged with voluntarism on the basis of several passages, usually selected from his *Institutes of the Christian Religion*. In his discussion of the justice of God's decision to save only part of humanity, Calvin writes:

> God's will is so much the highest rule of righteousness that whatever he wills, by the very fact that he wills it, must be considered righteous. When, therefore, one asks why God has so done, we must reply: because he has willed it. But if you proceed further to ask why he so willed, you are seeking something greater and higher than God's will, which cannot be found. Let men's rashness, then, restrain itself, and not seek what does not exist.[16]

To fill out the picture, we might also turn to some of the early statements of first- and second-generation reformers such as Girolamo Zanchi and Wolfgang Musculus. Zanchi, in his treatise on predestination, holds that the will of God is "the rule by which He goes in all His dealings with His creatures, since nothing out of God (i.e. exterior to Himself) can possibly induce Him to will or nill one thing rather than another."[17] In his *Common Places*, Musculus likewise states that God "has free and absolute power over his own affairs. He does not owe anything to anyone."[18] Like Calvin, Musculus warns his Christian readers that pious minds (*pii mentiae*) should not try to pry into the divine will.[19]

Taken in isolation, statements such as these could seem to present a strongly voluntarist picture of the divine sovereign. God apparently willed to create and enter into relationship with humanity for no reason, without reference to any prior intention, judgment, or recognition of goodness. Before accepting this representation of the covenanting God, however, two matters need to be addressed.

The first has to do with our definition for what counts as a "voluntarist" conception of the covenanting God. Sometimes, the label is used, rather imprecisely, to describe theologians who place an *emphasis* on the divine will over and against the justice, wisdom, or love of God.[20] But defining

---

[16] John Calvin, *Institutes of the Christian Religion* (1559), III.23.2.

[17] From Augustus Toplady's translation of Zanchi's *Tractatus de Praedestinatione Sanctorum*, pos. 7 (New York, NY: George Lindsay, 1811).

[18] From Jordan Ballor's translation of locus fifty of Musculus' *Loci Communes* (Basel: 1564 [1560]) in Ballor, *Covenant, Causality, and Law: A Study in the Theology of Wolfgang Musculus* (Gottingen: Vandenhoeck & Ruprecht, 2012), 126.

[19] See Jordan Ballor's excellent survey of Musculus on this matter, *Covenant*, 122–3.

[20] For example, Stephen Strehle's rather Latinate definition of voluntarism as "an undue accentuation upon the will of God which neglects and even negates in its desiderations other divine attributes, especially the righteousness of God," Strehle, *Calvinism, Federalism,*

voluntarism as an emphasis on one divine attribute over others – as if such a thing could be measured out – does not tell us much of substance. Others have applied the label to those theologians who affirm that God is utterly free to choose A or –A, or in Zanchi's phrase, "to will or nill one thing rather than another." However, in its technical sense, a voluntarist account of the will does *not* simply posit that an agent has the capacity to choose freely between A and –A. Rather, it supposes that an agent's choice of A or –A are in no way dependent on some antecedent willing or judgment. The choice is wholly arbitrary.[21] A voluntarist account of divine agency would therefore hold that when God acts, his choice to act in one way and not another must have been made apart from any antecedent standard, judgment, or recognition of some good in another or even in himself. Further, a strictly voluntarist account of the covenanting God would hold that no feature or characteristic of God or humanity – no prior love, intention, or knowledge – could give God reason to enter into covenant with his creatures.

This leads to the second matter that must be addressed before applying the voluntarist label. If the God of the covenants is properly described in voluntarist terms, we could assume that when early Reformed theologians talk about the *voluntas Dei*, they make no attempts to ground it, relate it, or otherwise make it intelligible in light of the wisdom, goodness, justice, or love of God.

When we return to the writings of the early Reformed in light of these considerations, the voluntarist charge becomes substantially more difficult to maintain, both formally and materially. Regarding the former, Richard Muller has shown that there is a preponderance of evidence, stretching all the way back to second-generation reformers like Calvin (if not Luther), that theological reflection on the will of God is grounded in our understanding of the wisdom of God. Muller points out that in the more systematic writings of the Reformed Orthodox, especially, this conceptual prioritization of the divine wisdom to the divine will only grows more pervasive.[22] If we are to understand the early Reformed account of the divine *voluntas*, we must understand this concept in relation to corresponding accounts of God's perfect wisdom, goodness, or love.

---

and *Scholasticism: A Study of the Reformed Doctrine of Covenant* (Bern: Verlag Peter Lang, 1988), 2.

[21] In this strict sense, voluntarism pertains to the relation of intellect and will. However, a further question may be raised about the *inscrutability* of the intellect's judgment about what is good or desirable. In what sense can an agent be held accountable by others for their judgment about what is good and about the proper means of attaining that good? This question will become relevant to a subsequent distinction between the authority of divine and human agents, particularly in Chapter 3.

[22] Richard Muller, *Post Reformation Reformed Dogmatics*, vol. 3 (Grand Rapids, MI: Baker Academic, 2006), 444.

Cherry-picking statements about God's absolute power or freedom leads to an impoverished understanding of the nature and character of the God of the early Reformed tradition.

What then should we make of the seemingly voluntaristic statements of Luther, Calvin, Zanchi, and Musculus, among others? It is likely that little can be done to shift Luther away from core aspects of the voluntarism that he picked up as a student at Erfurt,[23] although some have managed to bring out counterpoints in Luther's own writings.[24] Calvin, however, is in many ways a more interesting case. For while he certainly makes statements that sound voluntarist in nature (according to the technical definition I am using), he also emphasizes, unlike Luther,[25] that it would be "profane and impious" to divorce God's justice from his power.[26] All God's judgments, he insists, accord with equity.[27] Calvin even refers to the notion of God's "absolute power" as a "devilish blasphemy forged in hell, for it ought not once to enter into a faithful man's head."[28]

In fact, the hell to which he refers appears to have been created by the scholastics of the Sorbonne, whom Calvin believed encouraged all sorts of impious speculations about the nature and power of God.[29] Calvin argues that Job's complaint against God is based on a misbegotten absolutist view of divine power. Job thinks that the divine being is someone who says: "I am God, I will do what I wish, although there be no order of justice in it but plain lordly overruling." In this, Job "blasphemes God, for although God's power be infinite, yet to imagine it to be so absolute and lawless is as much as to make

---

[23]   For material on Luther's scholastic training see Heiko Oberman's important works, *The Dawn of the Reformation: Essays in Late Medieval and Early Reformation Thought* (Grand Rapids, MI: Eerdmans, 1992) and *Luther: Man Between God and the Devil*, trans. Eileen Walliser-Schwarzbart (New Haven, CT: Yale University Press, 2006). Cf. Berndt Hamm's nuanced contextualist reading of Luther in *The Early Luther: Stages in a Reformation Reorientation*, trans. Martin Lohrmann (Grand Rapids, MI: Eerdmans, 2014).

[24]   For instance, Paul Hinlicky, *Paths Not Taken: Fates of Theology from Luther Through Leibniz* (Grand Rapids, MI: Eerdmans, 2010); Anthony Bateza, "Becoming a Living Law: Freedom and Justice in the Ethical Writings of Martin Luther" (PhD diss., Princeton Theological Seminary, 2017).

[25]   E.g. *Bondage of the Will*, section lxiv: "But God hidden in majesty neither deplores, nor takes away death, but works life and death and all things: nor has He, in this Character, defined Himself in His Word, but has reserved unto Himself, a free power over all things."

[26]   Calvin, *Institutes*, I.7.2.

[27]   Calvin, *Institutes*, III.23.9.

[28]   Calvin, *Sermons on Job* 23:1–7, trans. Arthur Golding (London: George Bishop and Thomas Woodcocke, 1580), 413b–14a (I have modernized the spelling). For an account of Calvin's complex relationship to scholasticism, see Muller, *The Unaccommodated Calvin: Studies in the Foundation of a Theological Tradition* (Oxford: Oxford University Press, 2010), 47.

[29]   Calvin, *Sermons on Job*, 415a.

him a tyrant, which were utterly contrary to his majesty. For our Lord will not use might without right, neither is he less rightful than powerful: his rightness and power are inseparable things."[30]

Calvin is less clear when it comes to defining what he means by saying that all God's judgments accord with "equity."[31] He also does not provide much of a defense for his sharp rejection of the voluntarist separation of divine justice and power, that is, beyond charging this position with impiety. However, this charge is notable itself. While there are ambiguities in Calvin's discussions of the divine will, what remains clear is that he cannot abide any account of divine power that leaves God open to the charge of tyranny. God is not beyond the law (*ex lex*): "We, however, give no countenance to the fiction of absolute power, which, as it is heathen, so it ought justly to be held in detestation by us. We do not imagine God to be lawless."[32] God's governance of the world is for our good, as Calvin affirms many times. At the same time, he often goes on to warn fallible human beings against demanding an account of God's reasons for governing in one way and not another. Once again, he says this would be an impiety. "We deny that [God] is bound to give an account of his procedure; and we moreover deny that we are fit of our own ability to give judgment in such a case." The logic is fairly straightforward: There are reasons to demand the accountability of a tyrant for the judgments he makes, but the perfect God is no tyrant, and because of our own moral corruption we have no standing to question him.[33] As we will see, this logic provides a crucial launching point for later Reformed theorization of resistance to tyrants.

Calvin's desire to avoid the charge of divine tyranny, on one hand, and to uphold the freedom of the divine will, on the other, is also present in the writings of Musculus, which are particularly notable for two reasons. The first is chronological, since Musculus offers us the earliest discrete *locus* on the covenant written by a Reformed theologian as part of a wide-ranging theological system.[34] The second thing to note is that Musculus is generally recognized as one of the early Reformed theologians most influenced by Scotus and

---

[30]   Calvin, *Sermons on Job*, 413b–14a.

[31]   See Irena Backus, "Calvin's Concept of Natural and Roman Law," *Calvin Theological Journal* 38 (2003): 7–26.

[32]   Calvin, *Institutes*, III.23.2.

[33]   Steinmetz's judgment seems apt: Calvin is very much at home in the world and language of Scotus, yet shrinks back from a particular form of late medieval thought that endorses an *ex lex* view of God's governance of the world. "Calvin and the Absolute Power of God," *Journal of Medieval and Renaissance Studies* 18.1 (Spring 1988): 65–79. The best recent analysis of whether Calvin ought to be labeled a voluntarist is found in Paul Helm's *John Calvin's Ideas* (Oxford: Oxford University Press, 2005), 312–46.

[34]   Ballor, *Covenant*, 15–17.

the voluntarist tradition.[35] Perhaps unsurprisingly, then, Musculus makes strong statements about divine freedom, power, and the priority of the divine *voluntas*.[36] Yet, also like Calvin, Musculus repudiates the notion that God is *ex lex*, stressing that the sovereignty (*maiestas*) of God is not separable from his other attributes, particularly his goodness and his love. Interestingly, Musculus begins his discussion of the love of God by drawing attention to the fact that, considered abstractly, it would seem that the love of God and the sovereignty of God are incompatible attributes. Divine sovereignty, after all, admits of nothing abject or servile, nor does it appear to permit for God to be bound to another.[37] Love, by contrast, is in operation when a lover is "wholly drawn into the service" of the beloved, such that the lover seems to be part of the beloved more than their own self.

Musculus' solution unfolds in this way: The sovereignty of God admits of no base thing, no vile servitude, yet we know from scripture that God simply *is* love. Here, he references classic Johannine texts. Therefore, the love that is essential to God must not be characterized as base or servile, but rather as something most excellent and praiseworthy. In fact, Musculus continues, just as it is proper to say that it is more excellent to love than to be the object of love, so God – who is love himself – overflows with love toward his creatures, like a virtuous king toward his subjects. Correspondingly, because we were loved first and perfectly, human beings rightly respond with love for God because of his excellence, goodness, and sovereignty. In the same way, Musculus argues that the love of God and the goodness of God are naturally and indivisibly conjoined (*naturalem et indivulsam connexionem*), since the former arises from the latter. Returning to the question of divine tyranny, Musculus concludes by stressing that we must consider the goodness, love, and sovereignty of God jointly, since it is extremely fitting "for the good God and prince of all to love his subjects."[38] By contrast, he describes tyranny as sovereignty conjoined with malice, which is manifest when rulers act out of hatred for their subjects, rather than justly loving them.

With this discussion in the background, we can turn to Musculus' discussion of the source or rationale (*ratio*) of God's covenantal relationship with humanity. As with his discussion of the love of God, Musculus prefaces his statements about the reason of the divine covenant by noting that it is "clearly

---

[35] Muller, *Post Reformation Reformed Dogmatics*, vol. 3, 444; Ballor, *Covenant*, 111–66.
[36] See Heinrich Heppe, *Reformed Dogmatics*, trans. George Thomson (London: George Allen & Unwin, 1950 [1861]), 93–4, and the lengthy citations from 92 to 103 that provide context for the non-voluntarist accounts of most of Musculus' theological contemporaries and successors.
[37] "nihil humile, nihil abiectum, nihil servile et cuipiam obstrictum."
[38] Musculus, *Loci Communes*, "De Philanthropia Dei" (Basil, 1560), 590.

marvelous" (*stupendum plane est*) that the sovereign God, "whose will and power is rightly most free" would "vouchsafe to bind and constrict himself to the norms of covenants." After all, Musculus writes, God was not driven to the covenant by external necessity, nor allured by the prospects of any personal advantage. He lacks nothing. Certainly, Musculus writes, God is good, but it still seems unclear why he would act in this manner. Musculus might have left matters here in order to avoid speculation, but he ventures a judgment. God makes covenant with us, he says, promising himself to us for our own benefit. Through the covenant, we have our trust confirmed in God. And through this confirmation of our trust and God's subsequent fidelity to his covenant,[39] we are "made partakers forever of the goodness of God" (*ut diviniae bonitatis in sempiternum participes efficiamur*). Therefore, he ventures, the "chief reason" why the infinite, sovereign, and everlastingly good God wanted to enter covenant with us is so that we – his subjects – could participate in his own goodness.

It is worth underscoring the fact that Musculus, while initially feinting toward the expected voluntarist position, actually takes a strikingly different path, one which leads him to say that the *ratio* for the covenant is God's love for his creatures, and that the principal end of the covenant is humanity's participation in God's own goodness. Human beings partake in the goodness of God and return love to their divine sovereign because he, out of the goodness of his own nature, loved his creatures first.

The emphasis on God's natural inclination to favor his creatures is in evidence throughout early Reformed writings. The first-generation Swiss reformer Ulrich Zwingli held that the "supreme good, which is God, is by nature kind and bountiful." God's goodness, he writes, "is limitless and loves to impart itself."[40] Zwingli's successor in Zurich, Heinrich Bullinger, also straightforwardly states that "God is said to be good naturally"[41] and "that he should be good of necessity."[42] Consequently, it is in God's nature to be "bountiful and liberal [and] just" to his creatures.[43] Throughout his sermons, compiled and widely distributed in English as *The Decades*, Bullinger affirms

---

[39] Musculus adds that God must be faithful because he is incapable of lying (Titus 1:2; 2 Timothy 2:13).

[40] Ulrich Zwingli, *Commentary on True and False Religion*, eds. Samuel Jackson and Clarence Heller (Eugene, OR: Wipe and Stock Publishers), 70–1.

[41] Heinrich Bullinger, *Sermonum Decades Quinque* (Zurich, 1557), 163b; cf. the English edition provided by the Parker Society, *Decades*, 3.10 [vol. 2] (Cambridge: Cambridge University Press, 1851), 366.

[42] "Nam necessitate fuisset bonus," Bullinger, *Sermonum Decades Quinque*, 165b; cf. *Decades*, 3.10, 375.

[43] Bullinger, *Sermonum Decades Quinque*, 165b; cf. *Decades*, 3.10, 375.

that "it does not befit God to act against himself."[44] He exercises his will and power in a manner that is fitting to who he is. Other Reformed theologians echo this belief. Zanchi, for instance, argues that "we take no power from God nor weaken it at all if we say God cannot sin," because such things "are directly repugnant to the truth of God and simply impossible." After all, "neither is any thing taken away from the power of God in that he cannot bring to pass, but that he must be good, just, wise, seeing he cannot be God unless he be such as the scriptures describe him."[45]

In the late-sixteenth and early-seventeenth century, this emphasis becomes even more pronounced among the Reformed.[46] Caspar Olevianus, whose work was so central to the development of covenant theology at both Heidelberg and Herborn, argued that God's decision to enter into a loving relationship with humanity was premised on God the Father's antecedent (and eternal) love for his Son, such that all God's consequent actions were performed to satisfy the norm of "perfect justice," which is so essential to his nature that "he can no more deny it than he can deny himself."[47] The Heidelberg-trained theologian Marcus Friedrich Wendelin held that the power of God "is that by which God is able to do whatever is not alien to his nature and truth."[48] God is the most perfect and desirable good in himself (*in se*), and is the source for all that is good and desirable outside himself (*extra se*).[49] Related to this account of divine goodness, Wendelin qualifies any description of divine power by stressing that God's power is always exercised in accordance with his just and merciful nature. Here, Wendelin has in mind certain (unnamed) late medieval scholastics who separated divine justice and power (*quia justitiam eius ab imperio separant*) – and also Luther himself. In fact, Wendelin cites the erstwhile Augustinian

---

[44] "Non quod omnia non possit, sed quod id nolit quod contra naturam eius est, neque deceat, ut contra semetipsum agat," *Sermonum Decades Quinque*, 371b; cf. *Decades*, 5.9 [vol. 4] (Cambridge: Cambridge University Press, 1852), 452.

[45] Girolamo Zanchi, *De Religione Christiana Fides*, eds. Luca Baschera and Christian Moser (Leiden: Brill, 2007), 673.

[46] The emphasis on the natural justice and goodness of God is especially clear in the Reformed response to Socinian theologians, who argued that God's decision to exercise punitive justice operates free of his nature. The Socinians held that God could choose to punish or withhold punishment however he willed. See Muller, *Post Reformation Reformed Dogmatics*, vol. 3, 481–2.

[47] Caspar Olevianus, *De substantia foederis gratuiti inter Deum et electos* (Geneva, 1585), 30–1.

[48] "Absoluta est, qua Deus potest facere, quaecunque a natura et veritate divina aliena non sunt, seu, quae contradictoria non sunt." Wendelin, *Christianae theologiae* (Hanover, 1634), 1.1.27, 83.

[49] Wendelin, *Christianae theologiae*, 1.1.20, 77. Like many of his Reformed contemporaries, Wendelin adopts the Aristotelian maxim that "the good is what all desire," adding that God, as the highest good, is *maximus perfectus et appetibilis*.

friar as saying that God has the absolute right to subject the innocent to eternal suffering, regardless of whether the judgment was merited or not.[50] Muller has pointed out that Wendelin misattributes the quote to Luther (it actually belongs to an anonymous interlocutor in Calvin's treatise on divine providence). But this detail is noteworthy in itself, since Wendelin – who engages in anti-Lutheran polemics throughout his work – assumes that this is exactly the sort of thing that Luther *would say*, and that it is enough of a commonly held opinion among the Lutherans that it required repudiation.

As in Heidelberg, the theologians at Herborn affirm that God's power and will are not diminished simply because they operate in accordance with God's good, loving, and righteous nature. Johannes Piscator, Althusius' colleague at Herborn, says of divine justice: "God does some things by a natural necessity, because by nature he cannot do otherwise."[51] Similarly, Matthias Martinius, who was Althusius' colleague both at Herborn and later in Emden, links God's infinite power together with his infinite wisdom, so that both are operative in God's creation and governance of the world. God is able to do all things insofar as they are agreeable with his holy nature.[52] In his aid for theological teaching, Johann Heinrich Alting, one of Althusius' students at Herborn, echoes Martinius, defining divine *potentia* as that which God effects in agreement (*convenientia*) with his nature.[53] And since God is righteous and good, it follows that all that he wills, does, and approves is likewise righteous and good.[54]

As we will see in more detail later, Althusius will appeal to this non-voluntarist *theological* account of power to argue that if absolute power is "wicked and prohibited" for the divine sovereign, it is doubly so for human sovereigns. Even "almighty God is said not to be able to do what is evil and contrary to his nature."[55] This is no impiety, Althusius argues, since it is not as if the *jus et potestas* of divine or human sovereigns is "diminished" when they are exercised in accordance with justice. As he repeats in his addendum on "Tyranny and Its Remedies," "even God is not thought to be less powerful

---

[50] This citation appears in a latter 1657 edition of *Christianae theologiae* published in Amsterdam, 1.1.2, 91.

[51] As cited in John Owen's *Dissertation on Divine Justice* (1652) in *The Works of John Owen*, vol. 10, ed. William Goold (New York, NY: Robert Carter and Brothers, 1852), 604. Owen draws from the *amica collatio* between Piscator and Vorstius, published in Herborn in 1613.

[52] Matthias Martinius, *De gubernatione mundi commentaries* (Bremen, 1613), 1.16.

[53] Johann Heinrich Alting, *Methodus theologiae didacticae* (Amsterdam, 1656), locus III.

[54] See the discussion of the *voluntas Dei* in locus III (De Deo) of the *Methodus*. "Estque Bona voluntas, qua ea quae bona sunt, vult, facit, et approbat."

[55] Johannes Althusius, *Politica methodice digesta* (Herborn, 1614), 19.11.

because he is intrinsically unable to sin."[56] There are strikingly radical political implications to this theological doctrine, as we will see later.

Non-voluntarist accounts of divine wisdom, power, goodness, and love can be traced through the work of later Reformed theologians, including Hermann Witsius,[57] Benedict Pictet,[58] Johann Heinrich Heidegger,[59] and Francis Turretin.[60] The influence of these thinkers extended across continental European, British, and later American traditions – notably in the academies and seminaries.[61]

While there is diversity in subsequent scholastic disputes among the Reformed and their interlocutors, there is sufficient evidence to conclude that the Reformed tradition as a whole cannot be identified in any substantial sense as voluntarist. There is too much evidence to the contrary, much of it surrounding the concern – traced all the way back to Calvin – that God might be described as a tyrant. None of these Reformed theologians wanted to concede such an impiety. Rather, they hold that the God who wills something

---

[56] Althusius, *Politica*, 38.71–2.

[57] Witsius writes that God's governance of the world is "founded not in the mere arbitrary good will and pleasure of God, but in his unspotted nature. For if it is necessary that God should therefore prescribe a law for man, because himself is the original holiness; no less necessary is it, he should prescribe a law, which shall be the copy of that original. So that the difference between good and evil, ought to be derived not from any positive law, or arbitrary constitution of the divine will, but from the most holy nature of God himself," *The Economy of the Covenants Between God and Man* (1677), 1.3.12.

[58] In particular, see Pictet's account of the goodness and justice of God in *Theologia Christiana* (Geneva, 1696), 2.7–8.

[59] Heppe translates: "The further question now arises as to the source from which flows the promise mentioned of eternal and heavenly life for man, if he fulfills the law. Is it of the sheer *eudokia* and judgment (*arbitrium*) of the divine will, or of *theoprepeia* of the virtues proper to God's nature, such as principally His goodness and holiness? Those who affirm the former rely on the principle that God is free either to present the innocent creature with life or to annihilate, punish, torture it eternally. This is the hypothesis of most Scholastics. Our view then must clearly be that it becomes God to return the love of the creature who loves Him, and that since a loving God cannot not wish and do well to one beloved, He must give and impart Himself entire to be enjoyed. Love is an affect of conjunction; as proceeding from Himself, God cannot fail to approve it as good or to desert it as bad," *Corpus theologiae christianae* (Zurich, 1732), locus 9.57, 321.

[60] See Stephen Spencer, "Francis Turretin's Concept of the Covenant of Nature," in *Later Calvinism: International Perspectives* (Kirksville, MO: Sixteenth Century Journal Publishers, 1994), 71–92; James Bruce, *Rights in the Law: The Importance of God's Free Choices in the Thought of Francis Turretin* (Gottingen: Vandenhoeck & Ruprecht, 2013); Peter Wallace, "The Doctrine of the Covenant in the Elenctic Theology of Francis Turretin," *Mid-America Journal of Theology* 13 (2002): 143–79.

[61] See for example the wide range of essays on their influence and connections in Carl Trueman and R. Scott Clark, eds., *Protestant Scholasticism: Essays in Reassessment* (Carlisle: Paternoster, 1999); and Willem van Asselt, ed., *Introduction to Reformed Scholasticism* (Grand Rapids, MI: Reformation Heritage Books, 2011).

freely is the God who *is* wisdom, and also goodness, justice, and love – attributes that are identical to the divine being.[62] Figures like Calvin and Musculus will say that fallible human creatures may not always know *why* God wills A rather than –A, but that does not mean that God does not have reasons – that is, that his willing of A has no relation to his nature. God acts in certain ways because of who he is, what he loves, and what he hates.

These were significant concerns of the tradition in which covenantal discourse came to figure so prominently. We can now begin to anticipate that covenantal theology, formed in certain ways by these theological commitments and concerns, had particular resources to address the nature of sovereign power, and the terms by which a ruler ought to acquire the recognition and love of his subjects. Further, as I will argue next, the concept of covenant provided these early Reformed thinkers with a distinct set of conceptual tools – in addition to those of will, power, and sovereignty – which allowed them to address not only the nature of the covenanting God, but the various modes in which individuals relate to God and those other human beings with whom they find themselves in covenant.

A COVENANTED PEOPLE

Early Protestant reflections on God's sovereignty and the nature of his relationship with humanity help us understand more about the intellectual context of the theologians, polemicists, and jurists who employed covenantal language in the early modern era. It is important to note, however, that the earliest Protestant use of the concept of covenant did not occur in systematic works of theology or jurisprudence. Nor did the concept initially serve as an organizing principle, either for narrating all of salvation history, or for describing various modes of human sociality. Rather, covenantal discourse developed over the course of several decades in response to specific exegetical, doctrinal, and social concerns – particularly among theologians in Zurich and in Reformed centers throughout the Palatinate.[63]

---

[62] In this, the Reformed simply stand in continuity with ancient and medieval Christian beliefs about the simplicity of God.

[63] The genealogy could easily be traced to the British Isles, primarily through Cambridge scholars such as Dudley Fenner, William Perkins, and William Ames. A Scottish line also exists quite early on, notably in the work of Robert Rollock, who, as Robert Letham has noted, self-consciously trained his Edinburgh students "in the catechism of the Palatinate" as early as 1583. See Robert Letham, "The *Foedus Operum*: Some Factors Accounting For Its Development," *The Sixteenth Century Journal* 14.4 (Winter 1983): 457–67; Michael McGiffert, "From Moses to Adam: The Making of the Covenant of Works," *The Sixteenth Century Journal* 19:2 (Summer 1988).

Mid-twentieth-century theological scholarship often attempted to find a single, unified explanation for the remarkable rise of covenantal thought between 1520 and 1585. David Weir suggested that it developed as a sort of Reformed theodicy in the wake of criticisms of Calvin's doctrine of predestination. Theologians such as Jurgen Moltmann and Brian Armstrong incorporated covenant theology into a narrative about a broadly Reformed countermovement that "liberated theology from the grasp of philosophy," namely, all forms of "scholasticism."[64] Others presumed that the spread of covenant theology was largely an Anglophone phenomenon, as Perry Miller did with regard to colonial Puritanism and James Torrance did with British Calvinism. In most cases, however, there was an assumption that covenant theology introduced a rift, or constituted a countermovement, within the Reformed tradition or even Western Christianity as a whole.

By the end of the twentieth century, this narrative of discontinuity had fallen apart, thanks in large part to the scholarship of Heiko Oberman and his intellectual heirs: David Steinmetz, Susan Schreiner, Richard Muller, and Lyle Bierma, among others.[65] Rather than hunting for a single, unified explanation, scholarship over the past several decades has paid attention to the diverse sources and contexts of covenantal thought.[66] In what follows, I will build on this revisionist scholarship, but venture out into political waters that the historical theologians have generally left uncharted.[67]

---

[64] Jürgen Moltmann, "Zur Bedeutung des Petrus Ramus für Philosophie und Theologie im Calvinismus," *Zeitschrift für Kirchengeschichte* 68 (1957): 317. Cf. similar approaches in Brian Armstrong, *Calvinism and the Amyraut Heresy: Protestant Scholasticism and Humanism in Seventeenth-Century France* (Madison, WI: University of Wisconsin Press, 1969); and Charles McCoy and Wayne Baker, *Fountainhead of Federalism* (Louisville, KY: Westminster John Knox Press, 1991).

[65] A third generation of scholars has also emerged in the work of historical theologians such as Carl Trueman, Jordan Ballor, Mark Beach, Brian Lee, James Bruce, Peter Wallace, and Christopher Cleveland. Cf. Trueman and Clark, eds., *Protestant Scholasticism*; Ballor, *Covenant, Causality, and Law*; Mark Beach, *Christ and the Covenant: Francis Turretin's Federal Theology as a Defense of the Doctrine of Grace* (Gottingen: Vandenhoeck & Ruprecht, 2007); Brian Lee, *Johannes Cocceius and the Exegetical Roots of Federal Theology* (Gottingen: Vandenhoeck & Ruprecht, 2009); Bruce, *Rights in the Law*; Wallace, "The Doctrine of the Covenant"; and Christopher Cleveland, *Thomism in John Owen* (Burlington: Ashgate, 2013).

[66] Muller, for instance, holds that specific exegetical issues along with the early Protestants' renewed interest in the Hebrew language and scriptures, were prominent sources of covenantal thought. He strongly disagrees with the attempt to set these biblical concerns at odds with a boogeyman called "scholasticism." Much of the recent scholarship supports Muller's thesis. See Martin Klauber's early appraisal, "Continuity and Discontinuity in Post-Reformation Reformed Theology: An Evaluation of the Muller Thesis," *Journal of the Evangelical Theological Society* 33.4 (December 1990): 467–75.

[67] For instance, Andrew Woolsey recently published an expansion of his 1988 dissertation, which remains the most comprehensive work on the development of Reformed covenant theology

Covenantal terms such as *pactum, promissio, testamentum*, and *foedus*, were embedded in Western theological, political, and legal discourse long before they became central to the early modern Reformed tradition. This can lead to overly simple readings of the history. For instance, the presence of these terms in late- medieval voluntarist theology has led some scholars to assume that early Reformed covenant theology straightforwardly imported late medieval (voluntarist) conceptions of covenant into its own framework.[68] Yet, as we have seen, while these late medieval conceptions were certainly part of the sixteenth- and early-seventeenth-century intellectual landscape, it is not at all clear that they played a direct or predominant role in the earliest Reformed discussions of covenant. Bierma notes the "absence of any clear ties to the medieval theological tradition" of voluntarists like Scotus and Biel among the first generation of covenant theologians.[69] While this does not mean that the early covenant theologians were unfamiliar with the use of covenantal language by voluntarist theologians, it should at the very least suggest that the late medieval reasons for using covenant might be substantially different than the reasons of early Reformed theologians.

until the Westminster Assembly (1643–53). Midway through his work, he briefly touches on the possible political implications of covenant theology. He suggests that while theological and political conceptions of the covenant "provided support for each other," they developed independently, *Unity and Continuity in Covenantal Thought: A Study in the Reformed Tradition to the Westminster Assembly* (Grand Rapids, MI: Reformation Heritage Books, 2012), 192–4. To support his relegation of political thought, he cites a century-old essay which argued that theorists like Althusius confined their covenantal teaching to "the political or legal sphere," August Lang, "The Reformation and Natural Law," trans. J. Gresham Machen, *The Princeton Theological Review* 7:2 (April 1909). In short, Woolsey contends, the dogmaticians and political theorists may have coexisted in the same confessional and institutional spaces, but had little to say to each other.

68   Some late-twentieth-century scholars, including Oberman, Strehle, Courtenay, and Francis Oakley, suggest that there may be some possible influence, but do not spell it out. Aaron Denlinger attempts to make the connection more explicit through the mediating work of the counter-reformation theologian Ambrogio Catarino, *Omnes in Adam ex pacto dei* (Gottingen: Vandenhoeck & Ruprecht, 2010). It is striking to note, however, that Denlinger's evidence for Catarino's direct influence on Reformed covenant theology is largely circumstantial, and even that evidence is limited to possible connections between very late-sixteenth-century sources. While it is important to note that certain voluntarist uses of covenant were live options in the sixteenth century, it is equally important to note that they were not the only uses of covenant, and that they were generally not made explicit in early Reformed theology. As Ballor notes, Musculus' *Loci Communes* (1560) may present a stronger case for a connection. Even so, it was not Musculus, but the Zurich, Heidelberg, and Herborn strands of covenant theology that quickly came to predominate in the tradition. Cf. Bierma's comparison of Musculus and Ursinus in *German Calvinism in the Confessional Age: The Covenantal Theology of Caspar Olevianus* (Grand Rapids, MI: Baker, 1996), 61–2.

69   Bierma, *German Calvinism*, 168–73; cf. Bierma's critical review of Strehle in *Sixteenth Century Journal* 21 (Summer 1990): 269–71.

Rather than restricting the scope of covenantal thought to one particular late medieval source, it is worthwhile to acknowledge that terms like *pactum* and *foedus* had a significant social cache in late medieval and early modern life. Even apart from specific doctrinal and biblical exegetical issues, covenantal language could be used to describe the baptismal promises made by an initiate to the Christian faith,[70] a last will and testament (*testamentum*), the relationship between feudal lords and vassals, the relationship between the pope and his ecclesiastical subjects,[71] or a social partnership that depends on mutual consent and the communication of goods among its members.[72] Once again, it seems clear that early Reformed theorization of covenant should not be tied to just *one* of these precedents. Better to acknowledge the concept's multiple valences, and inquire instead into the particular ways in which the early Reformed themselves began to employ it.

One of the most traditional distinctions made among covenantal terms was one that can be traced back to the eminent patristic authority of Jerome: A *testamentum* pertained to the dead, and a *pactum* or *foedus* to the living. That is to say, a *testamentum*, which Jerome translated from the Greek *diatheke* in the Latin Vulgate, had to do with the arrangement and disposal of goods in the event of a testator's death. By distinction, a *pactum* or *foedus*, which Jerome most often translated from the Hebrew *berith*, involved some sort of mutual agreement and obligation among the (living) parties to the relationship.[73]

Luther, like many of the reformers, was quite familiar with the traditional distinction between a *testamentum* and a *pactum* or *foedus*, although he often uses the terms interchangeably when discussing the relationship between God and humanity in biblical texts. In certain instances, however, Luther makes a sharp distinction between the covenant or testament associated with God's evangelical promise to save his people and other forms of covenantal

---

[70]   See Stanley Chodorow's discussion of medieval conceptions of "The Church as a Juridical Community" in *Christian Political Theory and Church Politics in the Mid-Twelfth Century* (Berkeley: University of California Press, 1972), 65–95. In particular, note Chodorow's analysis of the reasons why orthodox medieval theologians emphasized the priority of the ecclesial community to the individual's act of faith in determining the sacramental efficacy of baptism, 79–82.

[71]   Antony Black, "The Juristic Origins of Social Contract Theory," *History of Political Thought* 14.1 (Spring 1993): 57–76.

[72]   Black, "The Juristic Origins," 66.

[73]   Brian Lee has pointed out the interpretive difficult introduced by Jerome's choice of translation, since many Greek New Testament passages quote from Hebrew scriptural passages that talk of God's *berith* with his people. In the New Testament, this term was translated as *testamentum*, while its correlate in the Hebrew scriptures would be translated as *foedus* or *pactum*. Lee, *Johannes Cocceius*, 27–31.

relationship, which entail obedience according to particular norms and the recognition of individual merit. Luther described God's evangelical covenant with the patriarch Abraham in the account of Genesis 15 as an example of the former type, noting that "a testament is not a law; it is a gift. For heirs do not look for laws or for enforcement; they look for an inheritance from a testament.... It was not laws that were handed down to [Abraham], but a testament about a spiritual blessing."[74]

Luther's reference to the covenant with Abraham raises a question, however, since the biblical account also mentions that male circumcision was required of Abraham and his descendants by God as form of ritual obedience in the relationship. As Peter Lillback has chronicled, Luther attempts to solve this problem by making a strong distinction between "spiritual" covenants that do not contain stipulations or laws and "temporal" covenants that do. God's first covenant with Abraham, detailed in Genesis 15, was spiritual in nature, since it contained only promise and no norms or conditions. God's second covenant, described in Genesis 17, included the law of circumcision, and was therefore temporal in nature. Luther contends that no Christian should imagine that they are burdened by the latter temporal type of covenant. In fact, he goes so far as to warn Christian readers that the account in Genesis 17 presents a "danger" to them, since they will be tempted to think that their covenant with God entails a particular performance.[75] In line with many of his other (even more odious) statements against the Jewish people, Luther writes that they are proud "beyond measure" because of this carnal covenant; they even falsely imagine that it is an *eternal* covenant.[76] In reality, he argues, only the spiritual covenant, which has no particular conditions or norms, is an expression of God's eternal favor for his people.

Inasmuch as Luther was a biblical theologian and exegete, it was impossible for him to avoid talking in terms of covenant. Yet the sort of covenant that he preferred, and which he consistently related in sacramental terms to the "new testament" of Christ's body and blood, was a covenant of promise. That is, it was the testament or declaration of the good will of a sovereign God toward a people in need of salvation. It entailed no mutual obligation. It stood in

---

[74] Martin Luther, *Lectures on Galatians 1535, Luther's Works*, vol. 26, trans. and ed. Jaroslav Pelikan (St. Louis, MO: Concordia, 1963), 298.

[75] D. *Martin Luthers Werke* [LW], ed. J. C. F. Knaake et al. (Weimer: Hermann Bohlaus Nachfolger, 1911), vol. 42, 603.

[76] Of course, the biblical text *does* repeatedly indicate the eternality of this covenant (17:7, 8, 13, 19), but Luther dismisses this reading by highlighting the fact that God appends the caveat that the covenant is everlasting "throughout the generations to come." Luther takes this to mean that the temporal covenant is "eternal" as long as the Jews continued to inhabit the Promised Land.

opposition to other forms of covenant embraced by the rival religious traditions of the Jews and Catholics, which, as he saw it, were erroneously based on law and works-righteousness.

Judaism and Catholicism were not the only traditions that Luther faulted for clinging to the wrong sort of covenantal relationship with God. By 1530, he had also begun cataloging the errors of his fellow reformers, notably Zwingli and Johannes Oecolampadius, charging them with "defecting from Christ to Moses."[77]

Luther's contentious relationship with the emerging Reformed party (first called Zwinglians, not Calvinists) has been covered well in other places.[78] Here it is merely important to note that the early rift between Luther and his Reformed counterparts develops along lines that pertain directly to the nature of the covenant between God and the people of God. Luther generally employed the biblical concept of covenant to set up an opposition between relationships of law and promise. In doing so, he criticized Jews, Catholics, and the emerging Reformed party for – as he saw it – believing that specific moral duties or ritual performances were entailed for human parties as terms of the covenantal relationship.

First-generation Reformed writings describe the divine covenant in rather different terms and use it for distinct purposes. In his 1525 commentary on Isaiah, Oecolampadius associates the divine covenant (interchangeably called a *pactum* or *foedus*) with God's self-revelation to the Hebrew patriarchs. By revealing himself – specifically, by revealing his various names to ancient patriarchs – God shows himself to be their faithful lord. God desired to be in fellowship with the patriarchs and their descendants, and so entered into covenant with them in order that they (and we) can call him father.[79] Later, Oecolampadius notes that this intimate covenantal fellowship first arises from the covenant (*pactum*) that the Father shared with his own Son. Just as the Father is covenantally faithful to his Son, even raising him from the dead, we ought to be assured that God's covenant with us will be everlasting.[80] In entering into covenant with humanity, God places his law in our hearts. We, in turn, recognize that he is our God. It is important to note that for

---

[77] "Sic fiunt meri Legistae et Mosaistae, a Christo ad Mosen deficientes . . . " LW, vol. 40, 250.

[78] E.g. Bruce Gordon, *The Swiss Reformation* (Manchester: Manchester University Press, 2002), 146–90; Peter Lillback, "The Early Reformed Covenant Paradigm," in *Peter Martyr Vermigli and the European Reformations*, ed. Frank James (Leiden: Brill, 2004); W. P. Stephens, *The Theology of Zwingli* (Oxford: Oxford University Press, 1986); Mark A. Garcia, *Life in Christ: Union with Christ and Twofold Grace in Calvin's Theology* (Carlisle: Paternoster, 2008).

[79] Oecolampadius, *In Iesaiam* (Basel, 1525), 200b.

[80] Oecolampadius, *In Iesaiam*, 268a.

Oecolampadius the death and resurrection of the Son serve as a testament of God's faithfulness, both as the *sacrifice* by which God binds his people to himself, and also as *surety* of his fidelity and mercy toward us (*summa fide misericors tibi erit*).[81] The God who has the power to raise Jesus from the dead is the same God who will save his people from suffering anything they cannot bear to endure.[82] Elsewhere in his commentary, Oecolampadius writes that, although the princes of this age perish, "it is impossible for the covenant of God to be destroyed since he has entered into it with us in his Son."[83]

Lillback notes that for Oecolampadius the love of God is what binds the divine sovereign and his covenanted people together. The reformer writes: "we are united with God, insofar as we are loved by him and are moved to love in return."[84] This reciprocating love arises naturally in us because God has written his law on human hearts, so that his creatures incline themselves toward the source of all goodness and love – that is, God's own self. Oecolampadius calls this law – or rather, this inclination toward relationship with the good God – a "blessed bond" or "obligation" (*felix nexus*), which prompts us to cling to our sovereign and to be his people.[85] Human obedience to the sovereign is in this sense anything but arbitrary; it is for our wellbeing. While the specific terms, rites, and sacraments that God requires of his human creatures may change according to time and context, the substance of his covenant remains the same.[86] After all, the covenant is the expression of God's eternal favor toward us, which itself flows constantly out of God the Father's love and faithfulness toward his Son.

The emphasis on the eternality of covenant predates the controversy that soon erupted between the Swiss Brethren (later called Anabaptists) and what we now think of as the magisterial reformation – that is, Luther, Zwingli, Bullinger, and the later Lutheran and Reformed traditions.[87] Yet within a few

---

[81] The sacrificial aspect is mentioned on 265b (Woolsey mistakenly cites 268a); the surety aspect is mentioned on 268a.

[82] Oecolampadius, *In Iesaiam*, 268a.

[83] Oecolampadius, *In Iesaiam*, 265b.

[84] Oecolampadius, *In Epistolam Ioannis Apostoli Catholicam primam* (Basel, 1525), 28a.

[85] Oecolampadius, *In Epistolam Ioannis*, 28a.

[86] The "eternal covenant is one with God, which He arranges differently in various times," quoted in Peter Lillback, *The Binding of God: Calvin's Role in the Development of Covenant Theology* (Grand Rapids, MI: Baker Academic, 2001), 112.

[87] Lillback, *The Binding of God*, 83. Interestingly, as Hughes Oliphant Old shows, several of the early Anabaptist leaders had been trained in the *via moderna* of Scotus and Biel, *The Shaping of the Reformed Baptismal Rite in the Sixteenth Century* (Grand Rapids, MI: Eerdmans Publishing, 1992), 94–5.

years, Reformed defenses of infant baptism began to employ the concept of covenant in more expansive (and often polemical) ways.[88]

In the initial years after his break with Rome, Zwingli had been attracted to Anabaptist arguments against the practice of infant baptism – a fact that certain Anabaptist leaders liked to remind him of in their debates. By December of 1524, however, Zwingli had made a decisive break with the Swiss Brethren, and instead allied himself to Oecolampadius, Bucer, Bullinger, and other magisterial reformers. Lillback has noted that the initial spate of anti-Anabaptist polemics did not immediately rely on the concept of covenant. However, by the end of 1525, both sides began to relate the controversy over baptism to rival conceptions of covenant, and what it means to be a member of the covenantal fellowship.[89] The Anabaptists contended that the ability to consent to the terms of the covenant was a prerequisite for membership. Therefore, no children should be permitted to undergo baptism (a ritual of covenantal initiation) until they were sufficiently instructed – and able to accede to – the articles of faith. Zwingli, by contrast, argues that the covenantal relationship itself is antecedent to all attendant signs, sacraments, or rites:

> For by nature being of the body precedes bearing the mark of the body … The grace of the spirit by which we are admitted into union with the church precedes the sign of union. For no one is sealed unless he has first been enrolled in the army or service.[90]

Zwingli argues that infants and adults who are intellectually disabled are by no means cut off from participating in God's covenant. Rather, when God covenants with his people, he gives them a sure sign of the relationship (namely, the sacrament of baptism) "from the least to the greatest." Those who cannot yet understand the terms of the relationship, or as of yet fully comply with the subsequent commands of the divine sovereign, are nevertheless members of the fellowship with God. That is to say, God gives signs,

---

[88]   See Old, *The Shaping of the Reformed Baptismal Rite*, 177. Old also notes the integral relationship between early covenant theology and the development of Reformed sacramental theology, 285–6.

[89]   In a classic older work, *Gottesreich und Bund im alteren Protestantismus* (Gütersloh: 1923), Gottlob Schrenk argued that the Reformed adopted the language of covenant from the Anabaptists. Even apart from considering just how pervasive the concept was in multiple contexts in the early-sixteenth century, more recent scholarship has indicated that the earlier Reformed use of covenantal language predates the controversy with the Swiss Brethren. See Andrew Woolsey's review of historiography in *Unity and Continuity in Covenantal Thought*, 103–58.

[90]   Ulrich Zwingli, *Refutation of the Tricks of the Catabaptists*, in *Selected Works*, ed. Samuel Macauley Jackson (Philadelphia, PN: University of Pennsylvania, 1901), 223.

sacraments, and delivers his commands to those with whom he is already in relationship. These external marks are pledges or "public signs" meant to preserve, and display commitment to, a common life.[91]

Zwingli's theorization of the covenant is suggestive, but remains undeveloped. Over the next few decades, however, Reformed theologians began to reflect on the concept more precisely, piecing apart the constitutive elements of what makes a covenant, and the divine covenant in particular. Zwingli's own successor in Zurich, Heinrich Bullinger, developed his mentor's position in his seminal treatise *On the One and Eternal Testament or Covenant of God* (*De Testamento seu foedere dei unico et aeterno*, 1534).[92]

As was the case for many subsequent treatises on covenant theology, Bullinger begins with an extensive etymology of the terms *testamentum*, *pactum*, *foedus*, and their correlates in Greek and Hebrew. Trained as a humanist at Cologne, Bullinger pays particular attention to the various ways that Roman jurists, Latin grammarians, and biblical writers had employed a range of covenantal terms. He distinguishes between three primary senses of covenant: the covenant as a last will or testament, as an oath or promise, and as a covenant proper.

In this latter type of covenant, Bullinger notes that there is a common structure, involving promulgation, proper authority, and often some ratifying sacrifice (he points out that Latin grammarians had written that *foedus* derives from the Romans' "grotesque" [*foede*] ritual slaughter of a pig). Throughout various times and cultures, Bullinger posits that certain formal elements were common to these covenantal relationships: There was an agreement among consenting parties and a recognized authority who was entrusted with arbitrating specific terms; the agreement was ratified by words or ceremonies; and the terms of the covenant were made public in a suitable manner. All these conditions were instituted to protect the relationship: Although the covenant "puts forth proposals for harmony and fellowship, yet it is still entered into solemnly and with special ceremonies and conditions."

This is the bare sense of the covenant (*foedus*). Bullinger notes how remarkable it is that the sovereign God would "follow human custom" by entering into this sort of covenantal relationship with his creatures. However, Bullinger

---

[91] Cf. Zwingli's description of the human covenant of marriage, which he says serves as an analogy of Christ's covenantal love for the church. Marriage, as Zwingli says in *De Vera et Falsa Religione* (Zurich, 1525) is a "covenant of life" (*foedus vitae*) that involves a sharing of all possessions and a common venture."

[92] In an imaginative passage, Bullinger goes so far as to compare his mentor's recovery of the concept of covenant, after the dark times of the papacy, to Josiah's rediscovery of the deuteronomic law. Lillback, *The Binding of God*, 98.

goes on to fill out this bare definition of covenant with content relating to the particular history of God's relationship with humanity. He describes "the one and eternal covenant of God" as an expression of the antecedent goodness of God. The very articulation of covenantal terms is a gracious expression of the "mystery of the unity and fellowship with the divine by a human custom." This relationship comes into existence, not on account of human merit, but rather as a pure natural expression (*impulsus*) of God's goodness.[93]

In this sense, before the recognition of specific legal or contractual terms, there must first be recognition of the goodness of a relationship – in this case, one that is constituted by the eternal favor of the divine sovereign toward his people. The people of the covenant, in turn, recognize that the just and merciful actions of the divine sovereign are excellent and praiseworthy. Much like Zwingli, Bullinger frames his critique of the Anabaptists by insisting that we not focus primarily "on the conditions of the covenant," but rather the grace that underlies it. God entered into covenant with all the descendants of Abraham, including those young children still unable to comprehend its terms. Bullinger takes this to be a true statement of all God's covenants with humanity. Heirs to the covenant are participants in its goodness before they are conscious of it or capable of voluntary accession. Voluntary accession is necessary for the perfection of the relationship, but it does not establish it. Further, as Bullinger argues, the capacity to understand and appreciate the nature of the covenantal relationship is personal and historical process. Through God's constant self-revelation to us within the covenantal relationship, "we are able to gain a full understanding that this God is the highest good, that he is our God."[94] The specific conditions of the covenant – to walk uprightly with God and neighbor – are naturally consequent to the recognition of this highest good and all the goods that overflow from the divine nature.[95]

In his sermons, Bullinger expounds this matter, noting that all the formal features of the divine covenant "serve to this end," namely "that God would be in covenant with man, and have men bound to him, and all his goods communicated to us." As in the human covenant of marriage, God "will have communion with the faithful," and as a testament to this, he has "given a pledge of faith and perpetual friendship," that is, the sacramental rites and

---

93 Bullinger, *De Testamento seu foedere dei unico et aeterno* (Zurich, 1534), 6b.
94 Bullinger, *De Testamento*, 13b.
95 Bullinger's discussion of the *conditiones foederis* follows his discussion of the history of God's self-revelation to his people.

his own Spirit.[96] The parallels between divine and human covenants are explicit intentional on God's part. Bullinger claims:

> God, in establishing covenants, applies himself to our capacities as he does in all other things, and imitates the mores and practices of human beings. Through covenants, human beings, though most sure and steadfast bonds (*vincula*), bind themselves to the society and fellowship of one body or people. For their wellbeing … they mutually communicate (*communico*) both their lives and fortunes … [97] Therefore, when God wished to declare his favor (*gratia*) to humankind, and to communicate all of himself and his goodness, by pouring himself out upon us for our benefit, he entered into covenant with humanity.[98]

A similar approach to the covenantal relationship and its conditions can be found later in the writings of the Heidelberg theologians. In his commentary on the Heidelberg Catechism (of which he was the principle author), Ursinus defines a covenant along the same lines as Bullinger.[99] It is a mutual agreement between two parties, "in which the one party binds itself to the other to accomplish something, upon certain conditions, giving or receiving something." It is "accompanied with certain outward signs and symbols," which serve to confirm the covenant, to the end that is it "kept inviolate."[100] He later notes that these external signs and practices, which are instituted for the preservation of the relationship, renew the loyalty and fidelity of the participants in the covenant.[101]

---

[96] Bullinger, *A Hundred Sermons upon the Apocalypse of Jesus Christ*, sermon 82 (London: John Day, 1561), 564 (I have modernized the spelling).

[97] The Parker Society edition notably appends the phrase "the one in defense of another's freedom" to the end of the statement. It is not in the original Latin edition, *Decades* [vol. 2], 169.

[98] Cf. Bullinger's similar comments about the biblical account of the Noahic covenant and the rainbow as a sacramental token: "Therefore the rainbow puts us in remembrance of the God's grace, and that God which by his providence governs all things, has bound himself in league to mankind, to whom he wishes well. That league is still green, and always of force. The goodness of God towards men is perpetual. For though he should fall, and although that out of this throne should proceed most grievous thunderbolts, and calamities fall upon us like a storm: yet is God in league with us, and loves us dearly." Bullinger, *A Hundred Sermons*, sermon 23, 142.

[99] Another matter which links Bullinger and Ursinus together is their common affinity for more Thomistic language about God's natural inclination to covenant with humanity in creation. As Bierma has noted, this feature marks them as distinct from Musculus' more Scotist emphasis on the (Noahic) covenant as a divine command or revelation, Bierma, *German Calvinism*, 61–2.

[100] Zacharias Ursinus, *Commentary on the Heidelberg Catechism*, trans. G. W. Williard (1851), reprint of second American edition (Columbus: Scott & Bascom, 1852), 196.

[101] Cf. John Farthing's discussion of the *symbola externa foederis* in Jerome Zanchi, "Foedus Evangelicum: Jerome Zanchi on the Covenant," *Calvin Theological Journal* 29 (1994): 162.

Again, much like Bullinger, Ursinus proceeds from the bare, or what he calls "general," definition of the covenant to describe in much fuller terms the particular covenantal relationship between God and humanity. Ursinus places special emphasis on the fact that, after humanity's fall into sin, reconciliation becomes a necessary element of the covenant. In fact, the relationship between God and fallen humanity can rightly be called a covenant of reconciliation. This type of relationship requires a mediator – that is, a person who has standing to oversee the reconciliation between parties that are in conflict for some reason.[102] After humanity's fall, Ursinus continues, God out of his own mercy and faithfulness promised that he would accomplish all that was necessary to reconcile humanity to himself, offering a mediator in the person of Jesus, forgiving sins, and bestowing all manner of gifts to his people. In turn, human parties bind themselves to this covenant by walking uprightly in faith in gratitude for all God's gifts.[103] As members of the covenant, human beings also acquire a responsibility to protect the fellowship from those who would subvert it. It would "profane the covenant" to "recognize as con-federates" those who are enemies of God.[104] Put in different terms, this conception of the covenant presupposes the necessity of distinctions and judgments about what constitutes the right ordering of the relationship, and – conversely – what sorts of persons or practices would destroy its very foundation.

By the time that the Heidelberg theologian Caspar Olevianus wrote his work *De substantia foederis gratuiti inter deum et electos* (1585), the basic contours of the Reformed doctrine of covenant were fairly well set. Olevianus' influential work, which is generally considered the touchstone of late-sixteenth-century covenant theology, follows many of the patterns set by Bullinger and his colleague Ursinus. As noted above, Ursinus describes the divine covenant as a consequence of God the Father's love for his Son and for his people. God enters into relationship with humanity according to the demands of the "perfect justice," which is so "essential to himself [that] he can no more deny it than he can deny himself."[105]

---

[102] "It has been shown, that a Mediator is one who reconciles parties that are at variance, as God and men. This reconciliation is called in the Scriptures a Covenant, which has particular reference to the Mediator, inasmuch as every mediator is the mediator of some covenant, and the reconciler of two opposing parties. Hence the doctrine of the Covenant which God made with man, is closely connected with the doctrine of the Mediator," Ursinus, *Commentary*, q. 18.

[103] Ursinus, *Commentary*, q. 18.

[104] Ursinus, *Commentary*, q. 82.

[105] Olevianus, *De substantia*, 30. "The heavenly Father resolved so to execute the decree of His love as to satisfy perfect justice. As it is essential to Himself, He can no more deny it than He can deny Himself. So in the actual execution of the righteousness the greatness and strength

One rather notable feature of Olevianus' covenant theology is his adaptation of certain concepts from Roman jurisprudence. Before taking his post at Heidelberg, Olevianus had spent some years pursuing a doctorate in civil law at Orleans and Bourges during a period when Roman contract law was profoundly influential in humanist pedagogy.[106] As Bierma points out, the influence of Roman jurisprudence is particularly striking in Olevianus' discussion of the *naturalis obligatio* that obtained between God and his creatures: "In the Roman law of obligations this term *obligatio* denoted not merely the duty of one party to another, like the English word 'obligation,' but the whole relationship between the two parties."[107] Bierma explains that this is precisely the way in which Olevianus talks of the covenant between God and humanity. It is a "relationship of conformity between Creator and creature which involved certain rights and entitlements on the part of the former and certain duties or responsibilities on the part of the latter."[108]

Olevianus moved from Heidelberg to assume the post of rector at the newly formed Herborn Academy in 1584. His successors in the school of theology adopt much of his framework in their own treatments of the covenant. In his 1613 work *De gubernatio mundi* Matthias Martinius follows the traditional pattern set by Bullinger, providing a general definition of the covenant as an agreement or relationship among parties that entails some form of mutual obligation. Also like Bullinger, he offers a brief linguistic history of the use of covenantal terms, and mentions Jerome's distinction between *testamentum* and *foedus*. However, in a more systematic fashion than earlier covenant theologians, Martinius proceeds to use the concept of covenant to describe all sorts of social relationships (he describes certain relationships as *consociatio*). Some exist in the domestic or economic realm (e.g. marriage), other in politics (e.g. treaties to prevent injustice), and others are religious, namely, the covenant between God and humanity.[109] In all particular covenants, Martinius continues, there is some sort of mutual promise made. This promise is often strengthened and confirmed by some memorial or rite.[110] This element of mutual promise and obligation applies even to the covenant between God and humanity. Since God is naturally truthful, good, and just (*naturalis*

of His love in the Son and of His perpetual mercy sworn from the beginning had to shine forth," translation from Heinrich Heppe, *Reformed Dogmatics*, 373.

[106] Bierma, *German Calvinism*, 155.

[107] Bierma, *German Calvinism*, 155–6.

[108] Bierma, *German Calvinism*, 155–6.

[109] Matthias Martini, *De gubernatione mundi* (Bremen, 1613), VI.3.

[110] Some covenants, such as marriage, can be described as a *consociatio* – a term that, as we will see in chapter five, is so central the political thought of Martini's colleague Johannes Althusius, *De gubernatione mundi*, VI.10.

veracitas, bonitas, et justitia est), he promised to keep his human creatures from suffering any harm, for as long as they kept covenant with him.

In his groundbreaking *Encyclopedia,* Johann Heinrich Alsted theorizes the concept of covenant in a similar way, noting that humanity's participation in the covenant necessarily entails obligations of fidelity and obedience to the good and just commands of the sovereign God.[111] Elsewhere, Alsted rather strikingly explains that God always gives humanity his commands out of his own love, and he would not have given us these commands unless we were naturally able and inclined to love him in return: "by natural inclination we are swept up into his love, which we recognize as an estimable good (*bonum honestum*), and in this manner [or "in this covenant"; *et hoc pacto*] we come to recognize God."[112]

Although different terms and emphases are sometimes present, it becomes clear that the covenant theologians from Zurich, Heidelberg, and Herborn share a common set of concerns and commitments. In various ways, they want to answer two questions: How can God's covenantal relationship with humanity be eternal while the particular signs, terms, and commands that attend it mutate over time? And how is it that these particular conditions and practices arise out of humanity's relationship with a good and sovereign God? The eternal faithfulness of the sovereign God turns out to be a foundational matter for all the early Reformed covenant theologians. While sacraments and precepts may change over time, they necessarily take their form from the goodness, love, and righteousness of God.

COVENANTS MORTAL AND IMMORTAL

In his discussion of the natural covenant that existed between God and humanity in creation, Alsted makes an important distinction among the analogies and disanalogies that exist between God's covenant with humanity and covenants among human parties. The former, he notes, is not a covenant among equals; it has a *ratio* distinct from other covenants. That is to say, the particular form and terms of a covenant depend on the standing and character of the parties involved.

---

[111] See the locus "De foedere naturae," *Encyclopedia,* vol. V, lib. XXV, sec. III, locus xiii.

[112] "Quia naturae instinctu rapimur in eius amorem quod a nobis cognoscitur ut bonum honestum et hoc pacto Deus a nobis cognoscitur. Si naturaliter non possemus Deum creatorem amare, Deus non dedisset praeceptum de se diligendo, quod quam sit absurdum, quivis facile intelligit." *Encyclopedia,* vol. IV, lib. XXI, ch. XXV, sec. xlv. The Latin phrase *et hoc pacto* could be translated in a more colloquial fashion as above, but Alsted's use of the term *pactum* is very suggestive considering its theological valence in the rest of his work.

This disanalogy touches on an issue that appears throughout early Reformed covenantal discourse. It is one thing to say that the perfectly good, just, and loving God will be faithful to his covenanted people, governing the world and directing all things to their final blessed end. It is another thing to harmonize this account of the divine sovereign and his covenant with the ever-present reality that *human* powers and institutions constantly and often egregiously break covenant with their subjects and with God. Put in more urgent political terms: If God's covenant with his people is immortal and is stronger and more binding than any princely power, what should the response of an aggrieved people be to sovereign power that is tyrannical in nature?

However difficult, it is important to approach this matter with the perspective and concerns of the early Protestants in mind. We ought to remember that, in one sense, the very inception of the Protestant tradition as a whole was a response to a perceived instance of tyranny. Calvin spoke for many of his contemporaries when he defended breaking off ecclesial relations with Rome: "So at this day, when we resist the Papal priests, *we do not violate God's covenant*, that is, it is no departure from the order of the Church, which ought ever to remain sacred and inviolable."[113] Notice Calvin's crucial phrase at the end. His explanation for why Protestants are not covenant-breakers themselves, despite their resistance to the regnant order, is that he believes that there is, in some sense, an antecedent covenantal order to whatever ecclesial administration happens to exist. Calvin insists, on these terms, that the Protestants' ecclesial resistance to the bishop of Rome and his corrupt priests is an instance of obedience to an antecedent covenant with God. In short, for Calvin, the Protestants resist Rome so that right order might be restored.

There is a tension here, to be sure, particularly when we recall that figures such as Calvin and Musculus will not go so far as to endorse active *political* resistance, even though ecclesial resistance was already well underway.[114] The conceptual framework is available, but Calvin opts out of *direct* political

---

[113]   John Calvin, *Commentaries on the Twelve Minor Prophets*, vol. 5, trans. John Owen (Edinburgh: T. Constable, 1849), 520 (emphasis added).
[114]   I address Calvin's distinction between direct vs. indirect (or active vs. passive) resistance in "Rights, Recognition, and the Order of Shalom," *Studies in Christian Ethics* 27:4 (November 2014): 453–73. See also Ballor's chapter on Musculus' social doctrine, *Covenant*, 203; Matt McCullock, "Johannes Althusius' *Politica*: The Culmination of Calvin's Right of Resistance," *European Legacy* 11:5 (2006): 485–99; Robert M. Kingdon, "Calvinism and Resistance Theory, 1550–1580," in *The Cambridge History of Political Thought 1450–1700*, ed. J. H. Burns (Cambridge: Cambridge University Press, 1991), 193–218; Quentin Skinner, *The Foundations of Modern Political Thought*, vol. 2 (Cambridge: Cambridge University Press, 1978), 189–349.

resistance, claiming it would be an impiety worthy of judgment. As Matthew Tuininga writes, Calvin "denies that a ruler's failure to keep his side of the bargain relieves his subjects from their obligation of obedience." What is legitimate when resisting the pope is illegitimate when resisting the civil magistrate.[115]

This is precisely the point at which certain figures in the later tradition – notably, theorists and polemicists like Althusius and the anonymous authors of *Political Education* and the *Vindiciae contra tyrannos* – press the internal logic of covenant and right order one step further. For now, however, it is merely important to note that the tension between the immortal covenant of God and the all-too-mortal covenants of earthly authorities exists and that it was known to exist by these early Protestant theologians.

Before examining the particular ways in which early Reformed political thinkers used the concept of covenant to address this fundamental tension, it is important to engage in second-order reflection on the various layers, or modes, of the concept of covenant that we can already identify in the primary theological sources. As we have seen, many of the early Reformed proceed from discussing a bare definition of covenant, more closely resembling what we think of as a contract, to a fuller expression of the relationship between parties. The formal structure of this covenant-as-contract is useful for the theologians, particularly since it can apply to so many ordinary forms of human interaction. Yet, this use of covenant does not satisfactorily describe the nature of the particular relations that exist between God and humanity. While contractual elements are certainly present, God's covenantal relationship also has a unique history that involves persons with moral characteristics of a specific sort. The bare definition of covenant-as-contract cannot adequately account for all this.

Likewise, the mode of covenant-as-testament proves quite useful to the early covenant theologians, not least because of its biblical and linguistic history

---

[115] Matthew Tuininga, *Calvin's Political Theology and the Public Engagement of the Church: Christ's Two Kingdoms* (Cambridge: Cambridge University Press, 2017), 242. On this point, Tuininga and I disagree about which parts of the inconsistent Calvin we should reclaim. Tuininga sees Calvin's fledging doctrine of resistance as both secular in nature (88n105) and potentially illiberal – the implications of which were on full display in the disastrous Conspiracy of Amboise. Comparing Calvin with theorists such as Beza and (presumably) Althusius, Tuininga writes, "Calvin's theory of active resistance was much less defined and his personal proclivities were much more restrained than were the theories of later Calvinist writers" (351). I prefer to recover Calvin's more expansive doctrine of ecclesial resistance as well as the doctrine of political resistance articulated by these later, less restrained Calvinists. As for the idea that political resistance was motivated by secular reasons, I will address this claim in several subsequent chapters.

(complicated by its use in the Vulgate). This is a fact noted by figures spanning the entire tradition, from Bullinger to Martinius, all the way to Grotius and Witsius. While the early tendency was to see covenant and testament as synonyms, the tradition – at least as early as Bullinger – found reasons to distinguish among these concepts. Certainly, there must be a testamentary aspect to God's covenant with humanity. Promises are made, norms are promulgated, and – in fulfillment of Jerome's dictum – there is the death of a testator in the person of Jesus, who, through his death, disperses the goods of salvation to his people. At the same time, the mode of covenant-as-testament cannot fully account for the agency and responsibilities of either the divine or the human parties to the covenant. On one side, God does not merely decree or promise some good; he also takes on certain obligations to act faithfully, lovingly, and justly toward his covenanted people. On the other side, human parties to the covenant do not merely passively receive the promises of God; they are given responsibilities to uphold the covenant with God and neighbor and to prevent it from being destroyed by covenant-breakers.

Beyond the contractual and testamentary modes of covenant, the elements of reconciliation and sacrifice also acquire significance quite early on. As we saw in Ursinus, there is an important identification of God's relationship with sinful humanity as a covenant of reconciliation. Implicit or explicit in this conception of covenant is the idea that the paradigmatic divine covenant is one in which a good God sacrifices his son so that his people might be restored to fellowship with him. Various practices and sacramental rites can be explained in light of this reconciliation. That is, the sovereign God who reconciled his people to himself establishes various external signs of membership and renewal in order to confirm their trust in him and the grounds of covenantal fellowship. Observance of these practices and sacraments is owed to this sort of sovereign because he has already shown himself to be faithful to his people, even to the extent that he gave his own son, and raised him from the dead, for their eternal well-being.

Finally, by the late-sixteenth and certainly by the early-seventeenth century, we begin to find the early Reformed engaged in more extensive theorization of multiple forms of covenantal relations. Different relationships have different *ratio*, as Alsted pointed out. Covenants between equals or non-equals, existing in various domestic, commercial, political, and ecclesial contexts, may have distinct goods, ends, and conditions, even if they share a basic covenantal form. As we will see in more detail in subsequent chapters, this covenantal theorization plays a special role in Protestant political treatises and polemics around the turn of the seventeenth century – with the work of Johannes Althusius serving as the most sophisticated example.

The covenant considered solely in the mode of contract or testament cannot satisfactorily account for these various elements and relational modes. This realization, which is already present in the theological literature and becomes even more prominent in the writings of Althusius, is precisely why the tradition finds reasons to describe the covenant as a fellowship, a communion, or – in Althusius' term of art – a *consociatio*. Taken under these descriptions, the covenant is an antecedent relationship or a form of life-sharing in which individuals recognize themselves as participants in some common good (e.g. fellowship with God or neighbor). Just as distinct sacramental rites arise out of a prior covenantal fellowship with God, various social pacts and legal conditions arise out of the particular nature of the antecedent relationship. These conditions may change, as necessary, in order to preserve the good of the fellowship itself.

Even within the eternal covenant of God with his people, as we will see in the next chapter, there are different modes of relation and different norms that are made explicit in order to protect the common goods of the relationship. Most significantly, the irruption of sin into the world introduces a need for different relational and normative terms in the covenant between God and humanity. As in paradise, humanity is still called to participate in the goodness of fellowship with God and neighbor, but the presence of moral corruption and structural injustice means that many individuals will fail to enjoy the common good of fellowship. The perfect harmony of just rule and righteous obedience, the perfect coordination of sovereign authority with subjective agency, is spoiled by sinful domination. New measures are needed to address this inherent human tendency to dominate. Virtuous exemplars must be recognized. Prudent laws must be made. This is the matter to which we must turn next.

2

The Law of the Covenant

Relations and Norms in the Theological Context

"The republic is an example and image of eternal life."

Johann Heinrich Alsted, *Theologia Naturalis* (1615)

In early modernity, covenantal language could evoke biblical, theological, contractual, or political themes – often all at once. The boundaries between disciplines and realms of social life, as we will see, were far more porous for early modern theologians, lawyers, and political philosophers than late moderns usually assume. The task of this chapter is to show the distinctive theological shape of covenantal language, with an eye to the political application of covenant around the turn of the seventeenth century.

In the sixteenth century, covenantal terms such as *pactum, foedus,* and *testamentum* could refer to several species of relationships. I concluded the previous chapter with an outline of what I call the consociational model of covenant. A covenant of this sort refers to a particular sort of fellowship or form of life-sharing in which members participate in some common good through the communication of rights and services. While this conception of covenant is more than a mere contract or testament, it is not void of contractual, testamentary, or other legal characteristics. In fact, as I will argue over the course of the next two chapters, it is impossible to understand what a covenant-as-consociation actually *is* without recognizing the particular norms, conditions, penalties, and promises that might be attached to it.

In order to understand this early modern conception of covenant, we have to address several important questions. What role do specific species of law fulfill within a covenanted community? How is it that particular obligations become attached to particular covenantal relationships? And how might members of a covenantal relationship come to recognize the difference between just laws that direct individuals toward the common good and unjust laws that oppress?

LAWS OF THE COVENANT: NATURAL, HUMAN, AND DIVINE

The concept of covenantal law was significant for both Reformed theologians and political thinkers. For theologians, questions about the nature, terms, and ends of covenantal law were relevant to wide range of doctrinal *loci* – including discussions of creation, fall, and redemption, as well as doctrines such as justification and sanctification. Discussions of covenantal law also pervade early modern Reformed political writings, particularly treatises on resistance and in the genre that contemporary scholars identify as the *politicus*.[1] What is often overlooked in contemporary scholarship, however, is the way that specific early Reformed theological commitments informed political conceptions of covenantal relationships and the various species of law that protect them.

We have already looked at some ways in which covenantal discourse related to early Reformed views of the nature and power of God, the divine sovereign. By the latter half of the sixteenth century, many second- and third-generation Reformed theologians began applying the concept of covenant to a wider range of topics. Most notable for our purposes, theologians began using covenantal language to describe God's creation of humanity and the reasons for which God writes natural law upon the hearts and minds of all human beings. The relationship between these three concepts – covenant, creation, and natural law – is complicated and perhaps foreign to modern ears, but it is central to the intellectual context of early modern Protestant thought.

While Reformed theologians began applying covenantal language to discussions of natural law and creation in the 1560s,[2] we can find the concept of natural law throughout Protestant writings from the very beginning of the

---

[1] See Nicolai Rubinstein, "The History of the Word *Politicus* in Early-Modern Europe," in Anthony Pagden, ed., *The Languages of Political Theory in Early-Modern Europe* (Cambridge: Cambridge University Press, 1987); Robert von Friedeburg, "*Persona* and Office: Althusius on the Formation of Magistrates and Councilors," in *The Philosopher in Early Modern Europe* (Cambridge: Cambridge University Press, 2006); and Martin van Gelderen, "Aristotelians, Monarchomachs and Republicans: Sovereignty and *respublica mixta* in Dutch and German Political Thought," in *Republicanism: A Shared European Heritage*, vol. 1 (Cambridge: Cambridge University Press, 2002). In sum, the early modern genre of *politicus* refers to a body of texts written by figures such as Althusius as a scholastic guide, or manual of practical training, for a broader project of early modern Protestant social reformation. Politics was considered a distinct art or discipline that could foster excellence among its participants according to the teachings of various authoritative sources, tables, examples, and commonplaces. Horst Dreitzel includes a comprehensive list of works in the genre in *Protestantischer Aristotelismus und absoluter Staat* (Wiesbaden: Steiner, 1970), 413–14n26.

[2] See Michael McGiffert, "From Moses to Adam: The Making of the Covenant of Works," *The Sixteenth Century Journal* 19:2 (Summer 1988); David Weir, *The Origins of Federal Theology in Sixteenth-Century Reformation Thought* (Oxford: Oxford University Press, 1990); Robert Letham,

reformation. If we wish to understand the role of covenantal law in general, we first need to understand something about the role of natural law in particular within early Reformed theology.

Not that many years ago, it would have been difficult to find scholarship on Protestant conceptions of natural law – at least in a positive sense. Many twentieth-century historical theologians assumed that natural law was one of many medieval inheritances that the early reformers renounced. Over the past twenty-five years, however, historical theologians such as Susan Schreiner, Irene Backus, Paul Helm, Stephen Grabill, and others have pointed out that natural law is simply assumed by the vast majority of early Protestant thinkers.[3] It was an ecumenical and ubiquitous concept shared by Catholics and Protestants, Lutherans and Calvinists, Ramists and Aristotelians, theologians and jurists.

In the most general sense, early Reformed theologians associated natural law with what Heinrich Bullinger called certain "general *principia* of religion, justice, and goodness" which God graciously wrote upon human hearts and minds.[4] Calvin referred to natural law as the means by which human beings recognize the difference between what is good and evil, what is just and unjust.[5] In addition to Bullinger and Calvin, it is easy to find other prominent Protestant theologians who assumed the existence of something called *lex*

"The *Foedus Operum*: Some Factors Accounting for Its Development," *The Sixteenth Century Journal* 14:4 (Winter 1983): 457–67; Peter Lillback, "Ursinus' Development of the Covenant of Creation: A Debt to Melanchthon or Calvin?" *Westminster Theological Journal* 43 (1981), 247–88; and William Stoever, A *Faire and Easie Way to Heaven: Covenant Theology and Antinomianism in Early Massachusetts* (Middletown, CT: Wesleyan University Press, 1978); and more recently, the fourth part of Andrew Woolsey's *Unity and Continuity in Covenantal Thought: A Study in the Reformed Tradition to the Westminster Assembly* (Grand Rapids, MI: Reformation Heritage Books, 2012).

3   Susan Schreiner, *The Theater of His Glory: Nature and the Natural Order in the Thought of John Calvin* (Grand Rapids, MI: Eerdmans, 1995); Irena Backus, "Calvin's Concept of Natural and Roman Law," *Calvin Theological Journal* 38:1 (2003): 7–26; Paul Helm, "Equity, Natural Law, and Common Grace" in *John Calvin's Ideas* (Oxford: Oxford University Press, 2004); Stephen Grabill, *Rediscovering the Natural Law in Reformed Theological Ethics* (Grand Rapids, MI: Eerdmans Publishing, 2006).

4   Heinrich Bullinger, *Sermonum Decades Quinque* (Zurich, 1557), 36b; cf. the English edition provided by the Parker Society, *Decades* 2.1 [vol. 1] (Cambridge: Cambridge University Press, 1851), 194.

5   While the concept of natural pervades Calvin's theological and exegetically writings, one of the most thorough accounts is located in *Institutes of the Christian Religion* (1559) 2.2.12–17. Excellent commentary of Calvin's concept of natural law can be found in Schreiner's *The Theater of His Glory* and Jennifer Herdt's essay "Calvin's Legacy for Contemporary Reformed Natural Law," *Scottish Journal of Theology* 67:4 (November 2014), 414–45. David Van Drunen and Stephen Grabill also offer commentary on the topic, although they do not account for the normative concerns that Herdt raises in her essay. Herdt notes that Calvin's conception of

naturalis or *ius natural* – including Ulrich Zwingli, Peter Martyr Vermigli, Martin Bucer, Philipp Melanchthon, and even Martin Luther. In short, as Muller, Letham, Grabill, and other scholars have pointed out, it is more difficult to identify early Protestant theologians who do *not* refer to natural law than those who *do*.

Thanks to this recent historical scholarship, it now seems clear *that* the concept of natural law was embedded within the early Protestant tradition. However, it is another matter to determine what *function* natural law served in Protestant thought, and how it relates to other species of law in covenantal discourse.

One of the most systematic treatments of natural law in sixteenth-century Protestantism is contained within Girolamo Zanchi's treatise "On Law in General." His work was so profoundly influential on the early Reformed tradition in general and Althusius' political thought in particular that some scholars suggest that Althusius simply culled key definitions and phrases from Zanchi's treatise on law for his *Politica*.[6] Considering scholarly practices of the time, it would not be surprising if this were true.

Zanchi's treatise on law is part of a larger body of work that some scholars have described as a Protestant version of Aquinas's *Summa*. His discussion of law in general is placed alongside a series of other theological topics, including discussions of the nature of evil, original sin, and the Decalogue. His account of natural law in particular is embedded within a discussion of several other species of law: eternal, divine, and various forms of positive human law.

The foundation of Zanchi's account is the claim that God is the *summum bonum*, the highest good and the "most perfect embodiment of reason."[7] This supremely good and excellent God rules the world through his eternal law. This eternal law of God is in fact the source of all human reasoning and judgment. God "communicates" his eternal law to all human beings, "and by it we rule our own activities, and from it flow out our laws." Human beings therefore

natural law does not provide specific action-guiding moral knowledge, as later theories of natural law attempt to do. See Grabill, *Rediscovering*, 70–97; and David Van Drunen, *Natural Law and the Two Kingdoms: A Study in the Development of Reformed Social Thought* (Grand Rapids, MI: Eerdmans, 2009).

6   Frederick S. Carney, "Translator's Introduction," in *Politica Methodice Digesta*, trans. Frederick S. Carney (Indianapolis, IN: Liberty Fund, 1995).

7   Girolamo Zanchi, "De lege," thesis 4, in *Operum theologicorum*, book four (Geneva: S. Gamonetus, 1613), 187. This phrase is from Jeffrey Veenstra's translation in "On the Law in General," *Journal of Markets & Morality* 6:1 (Spring 2003): 317–98. The original Latin lacks the notion of "embodiment," simply stating that God is the *ratio iustissima*. In subsequent quotations of Zanchi, I will generally employ the Veenstra translation, but indicate my own alterations of significant phrases by referring to the original Latin in brackets.

participate in God's providential rule of creation through their own judgments about the good.[8] Natural law is a principle of divine reason written on the hearts of all human beings, directing us to pursue the good and avoid evil.

On these terms, Zanchi also describes natural law as a sort of instinct, or a secret impulse, that "pushes" us toward establishing right relations with God and neighbor.[9] In other words, natural law is a theological explanation of how it is that human creatures make judgments about good and evil in accordance with divine wisdom. Zanchi claims that after the human fall into sin, God rewrote this "principle of reason" onto all human hearts so that all persons are able "in general" to recognize what is "good and evil, what is just and unjust, upright and shameful."[10]

It is important to note here that the crucial words *in general* – or, alternately, according to genus – do not appear in the modern English translation. However, they are in Zanchi's original Latin. This is significant. Much of what follows in Zanchi's relatively brief discussion of natural law concerns the *inadequacy* of natural law to provide determinate content for particular moral or political judgments. Zanchi employs the concept of natural law to provide what we might call a theory of rationality – that is, an account of how rational human beings are able to make judgments about good and evil. It gives us what Zanchi calls "general or natural" *principia* that instruct or "propel" us toward goodness and justice.

However, our characteristically human inclination to desire the good does not ensure that we are able to recognize the *proper* good or to attain it by the *proper* means. Zanchi argues that natural law "has not been so effectively written on the hearts of all people that it alone is effective enough to protect people from evil or to push them to good."[11] After all, Zanchi suggests, if

---

[8] Zanchi, "De lege," thesis 4. Citing the authority of Augustine and Aquinas, Zanchi claims that it is through this most perfect reason of eternal law that "God rules the world and thus is the reason for all things that happen."

[9] Zanchi notes that before the fall, the law directed us to offer worship to God and to preserve an "upright and equitable relationship" with our neighbors. He argues that this law was almost entirely blotted out by the fall, but graciously re-inscribed by God afterward. Zanchi, "De lege," thesis 7, 188–90.

[10] Zanchi calls natural law the "divina recte agendorum ac vitandorum ratio atque regula, omnium hominum mentibus a Deo ipso immediate etiam post peccatum inscripta: qua generatim quid bonum et malum, equum et iniquum, honestum et turpe." Zanchi, "De lege," thesis 8, 190. The modern translation goes as follows: "Natural law is the will of God, and, consequently, the divine rule and principle for knowing what to do and what not to do. It is, namely, the knowledge of what is good or bad, fair or unfair, upright or shameful, that was inscribed upon the hearts of all people by God himself also after the Fall," "On the Law in General," 327.

[11] Zanchi, "De legibus humanis," in *Operum theologicorum*, 195.

natural law offered all human beings a set of universal and determinate *conclusions*, then everyone everywhere would make identical judgments about particular goods and particular evils. We know this is not true, first, because individuals make different judgments about the good all the time, and second, because our inclination toward the good and toward just relations with God and neighbor must now compete with what Zanchi calls a "law of sin and bodily desire."[12] What we take to be good and just is often only the semblance of goodness and justice. Zanchi emphasizes that this does not mean that the natural *principia* are altogether lost, but that our conclusions or judgments about the good are quite varied and often distorted by inordinate or misplaced desires.[13]

On these terms, Zanchi argues that we must account for both the contingency of social life and the mysterious movements of the Spirit of God.[14] While all persons participate to some degree in God's eternal law simply because they are rational beings, the conclusions or consequences that follow can look quite different across cultures and times. He writes, "It is manifest that the law of nature is one and the same in all nations with respect to *principia*, but not the same with respect to conclusions."[15] Likewise, when he later reflects on the application of punitive legal judgments, Zanchi argues that natural law only instructs us *that* wrongdoing "must be punished." Therefore, "wise individuals according to their own senses of justice and

---

[12] While Veenstra translates this as "the law of sin and separation," Zanchi's Latin refers to the *lex peccati et membrorum*. Scholastic theologians often associated the *lex membrorum* with concupiscence.

[13] "Human beings warped this instinctual natural law: Every living thing knows that it is right and good to protect itself, but that in order to do so, people now rush to any injustice or violence," Zanchi, "De lege," thesis 7. One of Zanchi's theological colleagues at Heidelberg, Franciscus Junius, makes similar comments in his 1602 treatise *De Politiae Mosis Observatione*. All human legislators must recognize the imperfections of their application of law, according to Junius. Whatever a person comes to understand (*sapit*) about human order (*humano ordine*) is obtained through reason (*per rationem*) – and this is only possible for a few people (*a paucis*) "over a long time and admixed with a great host of errors," *Opuscula Theologica Selecta*, ed. Abraham Kuyper (Amsterdam, 1882), 330. Cf. Aquinas, *Summa Theologiae*, I.I q1.a1.

[14] It is also important to note that Zanchi – like many of his contemporaries – believed that natural law is "more fully" written on the hearts of the elect, since God has graciously chosen to draw them more efficaciously toward the good. See Zanchi, "De lege," theses 8 and 9. In his chapter on Zanchi and Althusius, Grabill notes this passage from Zanchi, but does not reflect on its implications for the *purpose* of natural law in a theological or political system, *Rediscovering the Natural Law*, 142. Cf. the similar account in the Leiden Synopsis on the *principia* and *conclusiones* of natural law. *Synopsis purioris theologiae* (1625), disputatio XVIII, "Concerning the Law of God."

[15] Zanchi, "De lege," thesis 9, 193.

fairness apply and define what natural law teaches in general to the different forms of punishment according to the severity of the crime."[16]

What Zanchi says about the purpose of natural law is instructive for his conception of law in general. Unlike later generations of natural lawyers, Zanchi does not view natural law as sufficient to generate determinate moral judgments about the good. Rather, he suggests, "it is useful and necessary for the human race to have many different laws besides natural law." This is true because

> natural law, although it has been written on hearts, only remains in the aforementioned general principles, and not all people excel in ingenuity so that they might assemble [*colligere possint*] particular conclusions and laws from these principles [*principia*]. Therefore, there is a need that wise and prudent individuals [*sapientes et prudentes*] be stirred by God even within the nations themselves, who clearly explicate their laws from natural law for the wellbeing and protection of the republic.[17]

This final phrase is key, as it helps to summarize Zanchi's conception of law. For Zanchi, law in general exists so that members of a particular fellowship might be directed toward what is good and just. Natural law is a particular species of law that God gave to humanity in creation to incline us toward the good. In our common life together, however, natural law is not sufficient. For the flourishing of the political community, virtuous individuals must make particular judgments and enact certain laws that accord with this natural law. In other words, particular social arrangements, customs, and positive laws must accord with the general principle that, for the sake of human fellowship, justice ought to be pursued and injustice avoided.

Within this conception of law, Zanchi endorses the Augustinian and Thomistic maxim *lex iniusta non est lex* – an unjust law is not law. Law cannot obligate simply because it is promulgated by some established human authority. Stated positively, Zanchi argues that human law can obligate us when it accords with natural and divine law.[18] We might identify true (and therefore

---

[16] Zanchi, "De legibus humanis," thesis 2, 195. Zanchi even refers twice to the puzzling passage in 1 Corinthians chapter eleven where the Apostle Paul writes that it is contrary to nature for men to have long hair. Zanchi's equally puzzling rejoinder is that while this may be true for most nations, including Paul's ancient Greek audience, it is apparently not so for the Persians, for whom long hair is evidently *not* a transgression of the natural law. According to Zanchi, all people know the general principle that "good and proper behavior should be maintained. Still, for a man to grow out his hair, and for a woman to cut it, though it is not shameful for the Persians, for many other peoples—the Greeks most of all—it is." "De lege," thesis 9, 193.

[17] Zanchi, "De legibus humanis," 194.

[18] Zanchi, "De legibus humanis," thesis 3, 196.

binding) laws by noting whether they support or oppose the external worship of God, good customs, or the shared goods of the community.[19] On these terms, Zanchi states that just law 1) must issue from a proper authority; 2) must be directed at the common good – and not the private good or pleasure of the one who issues the directive; and 3) must not make "unfair demands that are beyond one's ability."[20]

In addition to these considerations of the common good in *political* life, Zanchi also addresses laws that are unjust because they oppose proper reverence for God and God's laws. Quoting Aquinas, Zanchi contends that some laws are unjust by "contradicting the divine good," as when tyrants compel their people to idolatry. When such unjust laws "force us to do something contrary to God's glory or that opposes his law, not only are we not required to obey them but *are forced to resist them.*"[21] After all, scripture affirms that "it is better to obey God than man."[22]

Further, Zanchi distinguishes between positive laws that aim at the common good in *political* society and those that pertain to right relations with God. He notes that we might recognize the injustice of certain positive laws by reference to the terms above without making the inference that it is *also* a violation of divine law. In other words, we can judge that a civil law that aims at a magistrate's private advantage is unjust, and we can do so apart from consideration of specific divine laws. However, divine law does introduce another normative standard by which Zanchi's readers – almost all of whom, presumably, were Christian – might recognize the justice or injustice of particular laws. In fact, specific divine laws may sometimes change or expand the terms of obligation to one's neighbor. For instance, Zanchi cites

[19] Zanchi writes: "neque cum cultu Dei, neque cum bonis moribus pugnent, neque saluti hominum bonumque publico adversentur," thesis 3, 196.

[20] Zanchi's Augustinian-Thomist definition of legitimate law finds parallels in other contemporaneous Reformed accounts. For instance, see Franciscus Junius' definition of law as "the ordering of reason to the common good established by one who has care of the community," *True Theology* I, thesis 5; and also Althusius' colleague Clemens Timpler, who defined civil laws along similar normative terms: Civil laws are those which the political magistrate makes for a given republic. They must be in accordance with divine law, natural law, right reason, and moral virtue. Civil laws should also be just, moral, useful, and necessary; relatively few in number; uncorrupted by glosses; possible to obey; and in conformity with the nature and customs of that given country (patria) where they apply. *Philosophiae practicae* vol. 3 (Hanau, 1611), IV.4.2. See also David Pareus on the nature of good law, *In divinam ad Romanos S. Pauli Apostoli Epistolam Commentarius* (Heidelberg, 1613), 1271–2.

[21] Emphasis added. Cf. Zanchi quotation of Aquinas' *Summa theologiae*, I.II q96.a4 (the English edition mistakenly cites article 5).

[22] Cf. his similar account in *De Religione Christiana Fides* (1601) chapter XXVI, "De magistratu."

Christ's instruction to his disciples, "If anyone forces you to go one mile, go also the second mile." It would seem that in the context of the political community, we would find this command unjust by reason of its supererogatory character. At the very least, we would be reluctant to impose a uniform obligation on citizens to return good for evil. Even so, Zanchi suggests that there are instances when we might rightly choose to obey commands that seem unjust – according to the terms of our political relationships – for the sake of some other rationale. So long as Christians do not forsake the love of their neighbor or commit a scandalous crime, Zanchi suggests, persons of good conscience will have to make case-by-case judgments in these complicated matters. The implication, although not spelled out by Zanchi, seems to be that the obligation to walk the second mile may not obtain to a citizen of the political community *qua* citizen. However, the obligation *may be just* in light of other considerations or relationships.[23] At the same time, Zanchi insists that a Christian must never obey a political command that entails impiety to God. This would violate the most fundamental terms of the Christian's obligation to God.

We must pay careful attention to the logic of Zanchi's conception of law at this point. *Both* human and divine law must be aimed at justice, namely, the establishment of right relations between members of a particular fellowship. On this principle, all species of law – whether natural, human, or divine – agree. Law is that which aims – or ought to aim – to protect the common good of the fellowship. Law may become unjust and therefore non-binding for a number of reasons: when it issues from a false authority, fails to protect the common good, or makes impossible demands. The fundamental difference between divine and human law for Zanchi is that the former issues from a perfectly good, loving, and excellent divine sovereign who is unable to command anything against his nature. By contrast, human law can and often does miss the mark. The vicious often hold seats of power. The idolatrous often oversee the local *cultus*. In cases where the vicious and idolatrous issue an unjust command – e.g. for private advantage or irreligious ends – this "law" fails to obligate the members of the community. Further, the members of the community may judge that they are *obligated* to resist. For Zanchi, this is principally true in cases of idolatry, but the radical implications of this principle will become even clearer in the work of the Reformed resistance theorists.

Zanchi's analysis of law's power to obligate takes another significant turn when he addresses the issue of social contingency. Set aside cases of explicit

---

[23]   Zanchi, "De legibus humanis," thesis 4, 196.

injustice, tyranny, or idolatry. What should a community do when faced with a situation in which obedience to the express letter of the law would result in harm to community itself? Zanchi answers that it is the *end* of the law – namely, protection of the common good – that ought to determine its power to obligate:

> If, then, it should happen that although one may want to adhere to the letter of the law, that law fails to the ruin of those people for whose sake it was enacted—consider the good of the society. There may be a time when the letter of the law should not be followed at all, but the purpose of the law and the spirit of the law-giver must be examined and followed.[24]

He explains that all positive laws must accord with natural law by aiming at "the common good and the welfare of human beings." It is "only for as long as they do so that they have the power to obligate." In fact, if it should happen that "by sticking to the letter of the law, we act against the welfare of human beings, we have acted more against the law than in accordance with it."[25] No true law could have injustice as its end. Rather, true law has as its purpose the preservation of the goodness and justice of an antecedent fellowship.

COVENANTAL LAW IN CREATION

Zanchi and his Reformed contemporaries had many theological reasons for making these claims about the nature of law. As we saw in some detail earlier with regard to Oecolampadius, Musculus, and other early Reformed theologians, the relationship between the divine sovereign and his creatures is paradigmatic of the perfect coordination of authority and obedience. God is the perfectly good Lawgiver who issues his directives for the wellbeing – or salvation[26] – of his people. The terms of this relationship find their *ratio* in the faithful love of the sovereign for his people, and their fulfillment in the recognition and reciprocating love of the people for their good ruler. In his doctrinal *locus* on the love of God, Zanchi expressly links the human recognition of what is good, just, and worth loving with God's own love for all that he created. God is by his very nature a loving sovereign who "has both willed and done good to all things that he has made." By loving his creation and his created subjects, "God infuses goodness into things." It is this faithful love directed toward the world that makes things good, and also what makes human

---

[24]   Zanchi, "De legibus humanis," thesis 5, 197.
[25]   Zanchi, "De legibus humanis," thesis 5, 198.
[26]   "Wellbeing" is translated from the Latin *salus*.

beings able to *recognize* that which is good.[27] We come to love what God loved first. Human fealty to God is an expression of this phenomenon.

These assumptions about the nature and relationship of authority, goodness, and faithful love are shared by many of Zanchi's contemporaries. For instance, Calvin wrote in similar terms that people render service to God because they have already enjoyed his favor and love as God's children: "No one, indeed, will voluntarily and willingly devote himself to the service of God unless he has previously tasted his paternal love, and been thereby allured to love and reverence him."[28] The recognition of God's goodness and favor prompts the faithful acts of human obedience and love.

This pattern carries through early Reformed treatments of the creation of humanity. At least as early as Bullinger's *De Testamento* (1534), we can identify a confluence of the theological concepts of creation, law, and covenant. Bullinger writes that in creating humanity, God offered a covenantal relationship to his people. This creational covenant is evidence of God's "ineffable mercy and divine grace," since his offer of a relationship proceeds "out of the sheer goodness which is God's nature," rather than on account of any human merit. "Whatever we are and whatever things have been created for our use and delight, we owe to divine goodness and mercy." Later in his third series of pastoral sermons, Bullinger argues that God created humanity in order to be in a particular sort of relationship with God. God bestowed "innumerable benefits" on humanity's first parents in paradise. In return, Adam and Eve were "to declare and show thankfulness and obedience to [their] good God and benefactor; which occasion he offered [them] by the making of the law."[29] Framed in this way, the law is what directed the first human persons to their proper end – fellowship with God.

Here, it is important to underscore that the law given in creation was for the good of humanity. The divine sovereign's law was issued as a gift: "God ordained not that law to be a stumbling-block in Adam's way, but rather to be a staff to stay him from falling." By this means, God provided a way for instruction in virtue, the end of which was perfect "felicity" and life.[30] For this

---

[27]   In context, Zanchi argues: "as we love things because they are good, so all good things have their nature because has loved and does love them. For God infuses goodness into things by loving them, and this truly is to love, just as we, by comparison, love things because they are good ... Therefore, it appears the love of God is more excellent then ours, because it is more effectual, and is the cause of goodness in every single thing. So it is clear that all things are beloved of God. For whatever he makes, he makes it good," Zanchi, *De Natura Dei* (Neustadt an der Weinstraße, 1598), 4.3 q2, 472–3.

[28]   Calvin, *Institutes*, I.5.3.

[29]   Bullinger, *Sermonum Decades Quinque*, 165b; cf. *Decades*, 3.10, 375.

[30]   Bullinger, *Sermonum Decades Quinque*, 166a; cf. *Decades*, 3.10, 377.

reason, God's command that Adam and Eve not eat from the Edenic tree was not an arbitrary law, but "a sacrament or sign" of the good provision of God.[31]

When describing the nature of political law, Bullinger makes analogous arguments. Laws are "the strongest sinews of the commonwealth," and that which give "life" to those who are appointed to rule over the political body. Drawing on the traditional maxim, Bullinger calls the civil magistrate the "living law" (*lex animata*), and law the "dumb magistrate." When a civil magistrate interprets and executes the law, "the law is made to live and speak." As such, law in general is that which directs individuals toward a proper end, and that which ought to restrain the whims of princes.[32]

We find similar conceptions of law among many other covenantal theologians in the late-sixteenth and early-seventeenth century. While Bullinger speaks in more general terms about the relationship between covenant and law, later theologians offer more detailed theorization of the ways in which law directs humanity toward right relations with God and neighbor. One of the earliest works to make an explicit connection between natural law, creation, and covenant comes from Zacharias Ursinus, who served as professor of theology at the University of Heidelberg until Zanchi inherited the position in 1568. Ursinus, the principle author of the Heidelberg Catechism, also wrote a minor catechism called the *Summa Theologiae*, which appeared in 1561 or 1562. In this text for the first time, Ursinus refers to a *foedus naturale* which was "made by God with humanity in creation" prior to humanity's fall into sin. He explains that the law of this covenant tells us something about "what kind of

---

[31] The sacramental character of the tree was a common trope among the early Reformed. E.g. John Calvin, *Commentary on Genesis* (1554), 3:22–24; Johannes Wollebius, *Compendium Theologiae Christianae* (1626), I.VIII; John Owen, *The Greater Catechism* (1645), chapter V, q5. Hermann Witsius later interacted with a similar statement from Zanchi; while he rejected Zanchi's idea that the tree of life was a sacrament *simpliciter*, he still held that it signified the "pleasures of divine love with which the happy man was one day to be fully regaled," *The Economy of the Covenants Between God and Man*, trans. William Crookshank (London, 1822), I.6.14. Cf. Mark Beach's useful bibliography in *Christ and the Covenant* (Gottingen: Vandenhoeck & Ruprecht, 2007), 119n120.

[32] Bullinger, *Sermonum Decades Quinque*, 65b–66b; cf. *Decades*, 2.7, 337–42. Bullinger argues that this conception of law and authority stands against one in which princes "suppose that they at their pleasure may command what they want and that all people must take it for law." This form of rule is "extreme tyranny." In fact, the prince is only properly called the living law insofar as he rules in accordance with the law. As in Zanchi's account, Bullinger argues that the general substance of laws pertaining to justice remain "inviolable." While not employing Zanchi's more sophisticated account of the species of law, Bullinger argues that law dictates certain general obligations, such as the prohibition of murder. Yet, these general precepts require prudent magistrates to rightly interpret the law and enforce it with varying measures of rigor, depending on circumstances and the parties involved, *Sermonum Decades Quinque*, 66a; *Decades*, 340.

human beings God created and for what purpose." Ursinus' later writings associate this covenantal law given in creation with the natural law that God "engraves" on all human hearts and minds.[33] As with Zanchi, Ursinus believes that this natural law directs us toward fellowship with God[34] and can be described as that which "agrees with the eternal and immutable wisdom and norms of justice in God."[35] For Ursinus, as for Zanchi, law "commands that which is upright and just, otherwise it is no law."[36]

Similar accounts of the relationship between the creational covenant and natural law populate many early Reformed covenantal writings. For instance, the Basel theologian Amandus Polanus wrote that the law of the covenant is – by definition – annexed to the promise of some good. The conditions and penalties of the covenantal law are given to protect the promised good. In the case of the creational covenant, the good is eternal life and communion with God.[37] We find analogous statements throughout early covenantal writings, on the continent and the British Isles as well.[38]

In short, the early Reformed believed that the creational good of fellowship with God was necessarily attended by certain commands or laws which directed humanity toward the right relationship with its creator. Covenantal law was not antithetical toward true fellowship. In fact, the most fundamental law of creation – to desire what is good and pursue justice – was given by God so that humanity might learn what is truly worthy of reverence and love. As

---

[33] See Lyle Bierma, "Law and Grace in Ursinus' Doctrine of the Natural Covenant: A Reappraisal," in *Protestant Scholasticism: Essays in Reassessment*, ed. Carl Trueman and R. Scott Clark (Carlisle: Paternoster, 1999). Bierma concludes with an excellent discussion of the gracious nature of the natural covenant.

[34] In his commentary on the Heidelberg Catechism, Ursinus writes that God created humanity so that "he might continually communicate [*perpetuo communicaret*] himself to humanity." Ursinus, *Commentary on the Heidelberg Catechism*, a translation by G. W. Williard (Columbus, OH, 1851) of *Corpus doctrinae christinae*, commentary on question 6.

[35] "Lex moralis est doctrina congruens cum aeterna et immota sapientia et regula iustitiae in Deo," Ursinus, *Corpus doctrinae christinae* (Heidelberg edition, 1616), 584.

[36] Ursinus, *Corpus doctrinae christinae*, 583. For a representative account from a later covenant theologian, see Hermann Witsius on the obligating force of law: "It is not the rigor of coercion that properly constitutes a law, but the obligatory virtue of what is enjoined, proceeding both from the power of the lawgiver, and from the equity of the thing commanded, which is here founded on the holiness of the divine nature, so far as imitable by man." *Economy*, 1.3.6.

[37] Amandus Polanus, *Syntagma theologiae christianae* (Hanoviae, 1609) VI.33, 2904. Polanus defines the divine covenant as a *pactum* "in which God promises to men some good and requires of them again that they perform those things which he commands."

[38] In addition to Polanus, Ursinus, and the theologians mentioned above, other representative accounts can be found in Caspar Olevianus, *De substantia foederis gratuiti inter Deum et electos* (Geneva, 1585), especially part one; Robert Rollock, "De Foedere Dei," *Analysis dialectica Roberti Rolloci Scoti* (1594); and John Ball, *A Treatise of the Covenant of Grace* (1645), especially chapter 2.

Richard Muller writes of the covenantal tradition as a whole, it is a profound mistake to assume that divine love and law are at odds with each other.[39] Contrary to the disciplinarian reading in contemporary scholarship, covenantal love assumes covenantal law, and vice versa. The natural law that directs us to pursue just relations with God and neighbor is "inseparable from the goodness and love of God."[40] Or, in the words of a later covenant theologian, love is not "rendered less voluntary by the command. For the law enjoins love to be every way perfect, and therefore to be most voluntary, not extorted by the *servile fear* of the threatening."[41] As with Zanchi's discussion of the love of God, we have in this instance a covenantal relationship – or what I have described as a covenantal *consociation* – in which it is the function of law to direct members of the community toward their true good. The law does not arbitrarily determine this good. Rather, law is the instrument of a wise and excellent authority who issues commands so that his subjects may continue to have rightly ordered fellowship with him and with each other. This is no "servile" state, but the essence of true fellowship.

COVENANTAL LAW IN A FALLEN WORLD

Within this conception of covenantal law, Zanchi, Ursinus, and their fellow Reformed theologians read the biblical account of humanity's fall into sin as an instance of covenantal infidelity. While God graciously provided all the gifts and provisions that humanity required to flourish in the world, the first humans chose to break covenant with God by disobeying his law.[42] In breaking God's covenantal law, humanity alienated itself from fellowship with God and neighbor. After this fall, human relations are characteristically marked by the conditions of sin: a propensity toward infidelity, and an inclination to call that which is evil *good*, and that which is injustice *justice*. In order to restore fellowship with God and neighbor, new covenants and new laws that accounted for human sin would be required.

It is possible to analyze these new covenants and new laws in two ways. On one side, theologians such as Zanchi and Ursinus argued that restoring *spiritual* fellowship between humanity and God requires the mediation of

---

[39]   Richard Muller, "The Covenant of Works and the Stability of Divine Law in Seventeenth-Century Reformed Orthodoxy: A Study in the Theology of Herman Witsius and Wilhelmus a Brakel." In *After Calvin: Studies in the Development of a Theological Tradition* (Oxford: Oxford University Press, 2003), 93–5.

[40]   Muller, "The Covenant of Works," 93.

[41]   Witsius, *Economy*, 1.3.6.

[42]   For example, Ursinus, *Commentary*, commentary on questions 6 and 7.

Christ, the Son of God whose life, sacrificial death, and resurrection makes reconciliation possible. Reformed theologians from Zwingli to Calvin to Alsted consistently maintained that fallen human beings cannot accomplish this reconciliation on their own, apart from the redemptive work of Christ. In mature covenant theology, the terms of this reconciliation are discussed by reference to what they called the redemptive covenant of grace.[43] On the other side, Reformed theologians and political thinkers also acknowledged that the conditions of the creational covenant and its natural law still apply to social and political life after the fall. Reformed theologians will explain this phenomenon in various ways. Zanchi argues that God graciously "re-inscribes" humanity's natural inclination toward goodness and justice after the fall.[44] Other theologians simply argue that the fall distorted but did not destroy humanity's inclination toward the good.[45] In any case, Reformed thinkers consistently acknowledged that God did not leave fallen humanity without aid. God continues to govern the world so that human beings are able to enjoy some measure of the goodness of creation and fellowship with each other.[46] While sin now distorts humanity's perception of justice and goodness, we still have an inclination toward fellowship with God and neighbor, although even the most basic forms of human fellowship are now shot through with sin and domination. As Zanchi phrased it, in our pursuit of what is good and just, human beings commonly "rush to any injustice or violence."[47]

In light of this consideration, two questions arise: How can law still serve to direct communities toward justice when the corruption of sin pervades human relations? And how might members of particular political communities come

[43] While a comprehensive treatment of the covenant of grace lies beyond the scope of my present work, it is important to note that law plays a multifaceted role in the Christian's spiritual fellowship with God. For these early Reformed theologians, the law has several uses. As Matthias Martinius notes, the law retains its normative use in the covenant of grace. Law does not merely condemn our failings, especially in the redeemed life of the believer, since "in certain respects law and gospel are concurrent," *De Gubernatione Mundi* (Bremen, 1613), 225.

[44] Zanchi, "De lege," thesis 8, 191.

[45] While language and emphasis vary, this is the formulation that remains fairly constant. Note for instance the Leiden Synopsis of 1625, which argues that the *principia* of natural law "remain unchanged" after the fall but the *conclusiones ex principiis* "stagger with wretched hesitation whenever one goes from general things to particular ones, and they deviate from the sound rule of equity, as is shown by the examples of the very unfair laws and overly corrupt customs that are found in the histories of the gentile peoples." *Synopsis Purioris Theologiae*, disputatio XVIII, "Concerning the Law of God."

[46] The surveys of Stephen Grabill and David Van Drunen are helpful on this topic. Grabill, *Rediscovering*; and Van Drunen, *Natural Law and the Two Kingdoms*.

[47] Zanchi, "De lege," thesis 7. Alsted likewise argues that the moral virtues which lead individuals to obey good laws are pleasing to God, even though they do not lead to salvation (*placet Deo, sed non ad salutem*), *Encyclopaedia septem tomis distincta* (Herborn, 1630), IV, 1246.

to recognize the difference between just laws that aim at the common good
and unjust laws that dominate and oppress?

While speaking with different emphases, Reformed theologians generally
agree that even after the fall, the purpose of law in political communities
remains the same: it exists to restrain evil and direct individuals toward a good
and just fellowship with neighbor. This is the testimony of theologians ranging
from Martin Bucer[48] to John Calvin[49] to Girolamo Zanchi[50] to Franciscus
Junius[51] to Matthias Martinius,[52] among many others.

Yet, while the purpose of law may not change, its efficacy does. For the early
Reformed, it is important to see that law, insofar as it is ordered toward the
good of fellowship with God and neighbor, is in itself a *good* thing. At the same
time, early Reformed theologians consistently attended to the radical and
systemic ways in which humanity misperceived or outright perverted the
goodness of natural, human, and divine laws for unjust ends. Both emphases –
the creational goodness of law directed at true fellowship on one side and
recognition of humanity's capacity to misuse and disorder law on the other –
work in tandem. In order to answer the question about how an imperfect

---

[48]   For instance, Bucer writes: "By nature and custom we are so minded that we wish every man to
       do us good, and no man to do us evil. If we used the same standard toward every other man,
       doing him good, we would put out life in that right order to which the Law and the Prophets
       point. Were we able to that, we would already be perfect and have fulfilled the whole Law."
       He subsequently argues that it is the nature of Christian to perfect this obedience to the Law,
       not out of self-interest, but for love of neighbor. *Instruction in Christian Love*, trans. Paul
       Traugott Fuhrmann (Eugene, OR: Wipf & Stock, 2008 [1523]), 29.

[49]   Calvin, *Institutes*, IV.20, especially section 9. See also Calvin's comments on the postlapsarian
       "gifts" of the Spirit. After the fall, Calvin argued, humanity is afflicted by the moral and
       intellectual corruptions of sin; even so, "however much fallen and perverted from its original
       integrity, [the human mind] is still adorned and invested with admirable gifts from its Creator.
       If we reflect that the Spirit of God is the only fountain of truth, we will be careful, as we would
       avoid offering insult to him, not to reject or condemn truth wherever it appears. In despising
       the gifts, we insult the Giver," *Institutes*, II.2.15.

[50]   Zanchi, *De Religione Christiana Fides*, X.7–10. In sum, Zanchi argues that in general "the law
       has still the same use" before and after the fall, for both Christian and non-Christian alike. He
       distinguishes among various uses of law in a traditional Reformed manner, noting that even
       though moral law "cannot justify us, yet it may always draw us nearer to Christ." Zanchi likely
       has in mind certain radical Lutheran or antinomian theologians, such as Johannes Agricola,
       who argued that law, as a general concept, is antithetical to the Christian gospel.

[51]   In *De Politiae Mosis*, Junius argues that the Mosaic law, in particular, is evidence of God's
       prudent, providential care for his people. Through the provision of this law, the people are
       given confirmation of "the covenant, the promises, and the truth, faithfulness, and constancy
       of that divine grace that would not wither away through the vice of human beings, and the
       authority of the law." Christ himself taught that "he did not come to abolish the law, but to
       fulfill it," *Opuscula*, 331.

[52]   Martinius, *De Gubernatione Mundi*, VI.16, 224.

human community might distinguish between just and unjust laws, we must account for both emphases in Reformed thought.

On this topic, two of Althusius' contemporaries at Herborn offer evocative theological accounts. Matthias Martinius, who served as professor of theology at Herborn from 1596 to 1607, is representative of many Reformed theologians at the turn of the seventeenth century, both in his assumption of covenantal language and in his view of the conditions of political life after the fall. In his sixth disputation on providence, entitled "On Human Governance in Covenants," Martinius writes that humanity's creational covenant with God entailed various obligations that aimed at proper reverence or obedience to God (*religio*) as well as human flourishing or blessedness (*hominis beatitudinem*).[53]

After providing a thorough and fairly standard Protestant account of humanity's fall into sin, Martinius argues that humanity may be tutored in two *scholae*: the school of nature or the school of grace. The latter professes the good news of the gospel and trains heavenly citizens in specific Christian virtues. It promises perfect fellowship with God and neighbor that will only be truly fulfilled in the next life. By comparison, the school of nature may be a "lesser" school, but it nevertheless equips individuals to order our life together rightly, profitably, and wisely.[54] Human knowledge, art, and wisdom remain as *insignia* of the created goodness of humanity, even though none of these remain free from sin's corruptions.[55] All forms of human consociation (*consociationes*)[56] bear the mark of sin and domination, throughout domestic, economic, and political contexts. In fact, it is quite striking that the latter half of Martinius' disputation is an expansive world history that chronicles the breakdown of various human relationships and modes of common life. Only the eschatological kingdom of Christ, the "second Adam," would accomplish the perfect restoration of humanity's covenantal relations with God and neighbor.[57] Still, Martinius notes that God, the good sovereign, graciously governs humanity through the preservation of various virtues, arts, and sciences. God remains present and faithful, bearing with his subjects' imperfections; otherwise, no good thing would last.[58]

---

[53] Martinius, *De Gubernatione Mundi*, VI.16, 224.
[54] Martinius, *De Gubernatione Mundi*, VI.73, 169.
[55] Martinius, *De Gubernatione Mundi*, VI.130, 287–8.
[56] Considering the publication date of this work (1613) and his close association with Althusius at Herborn and later in Emden, it is likely that Martinius adopted this term of art from Althusius' *Politica* (first edition 1603). Compare my discussion of the term in chapter five.
[57] Martinius closes his disputation on covenantal governance with an ode to the new covenant and the second Adam, whom Martinius argues is the perfection and fulfillment of all God's covenantal promises, *De Gubernatione Mundi*, VI.132.
[58] Martinius, *De Gubernatione Mundi*, VI.131.

Johann Heinrich Alsted, who studied under both Althusius and Martinius at Herborn, develops his conception of political life with many of the same theological commitments. Along with other early Reformed theologians, Alsted acknowledges that the radical corruption of sin affects all human relationships.[59] Like Zanchi, Alsted notes that natural law by itself is insufficient to direct human communities toward specific goods. He believes that in creation God wrote the natural law – which he calls the eternal norm of justice (*aeterna justitiae regula*) – on all human hearts.[60] This law contains only the "rudiments" or "first lessons" of the norms of justice. Individuals must come to acquire the virtues necessary to make right judgments that accord with justice. In order to acquire these virtues and make right judgments, further instruction is required.[61] This instruction comes through a variety of means. For Alsted and many of his contemporaries, the divine law contained in the Decalogue is one important source of instruction. It is, Alsted writes, an "outline" of the first lessons of justice that God gave to humanity in creation.[62] Divine law provides humanity with further general instructions about what it means to pursue the good and avoid harm: We are to recognize God for who he is, worship him, honor those who have care of us, avoid theft, libelous speech, unfaithfulness, and so on.[63]

Divine law, however, is not the sole source of instruction. Like his teacher Martinius, Alsted notes that various *scholae* of nature or grace are needed for this process of formation.[64] On this matter, Alsted has a great deal to say.[65] He

---

[59]   In particular, note his locus on sin and sin's penalty in *Encyclopedia* V.25.15. As Byung Soo Han points out, Alsted's rather standard Reformed orthodox account of sin is often underplayed in contemporary scholarship, "The Academization of Reformation Teaching in Johann Heinrich Alsted," in *Church and School in Early Modern Protestantism* (Leiden: Brill, 2013), 283–94.

[60]   From Alsted's locus, "De Lege," *Encyclopedia* V, 1599.

[61]   See his discussion of synderesis, education, and the cultivation of virtue in the chapter entitled "On the causes and effects of moral virtue," *Encyclopedia* IV, 1244–51.

[62]   Alsted writes: "Lex naturae in corde hominis est quoad rudimenta, in Decalogo quoad lineamenta," *Encyclopedia* IV, 1249. This discussion of natural law takes place within this expansive chapter on moral virtue.

[63]   *Encyclopedia* V, 1599–1605.

[64]   Alsted adopts the "school of nature" terminology in many places, particularly throughout his *Theologia naturalis* (Frankfurt, 1615). See Emidio Campi's helpful discussion of natural knowledge, natural theology, and the *liber naturae* in the Reformed context of early seventeenth-century Herborn, *Shifting Patterns of Reformed Tradition* (Gottingen: Vandenhoeck & Ruprecht, 2014), 270–6.

[65]   It is remarkable how little contemporary scholarship exists on Alsted, who was highly esteemed by many of his contemporaries and intellectual descendants. Howard Hotson is one of the few recent scholars to highlight the work of Alsted, as well as the profound impact he had on the thought of G. W. Leibniz. See *Johann Heinrich Alsted 1588–1638: Between Renaissance,*

believes that God governs the world in such a way that every form of human community characteristically aims to cultivate specific common goods and virtues. While spiritual communion with God is the highest and best good, all sorts of political or "natural" fellowships are able to identify their own shared goods, as well.[66] Even after the fall, these communities – whether political, ecclesial, scholastic, or domestic in nature – provide the context for what Alsted calls the *instauratio*, or renewal, of the image of God in human communities.[67]

In pursuit of this end, Alsted argues that every form of social relationship assumes some ordering of goods, services, and authority. This entails particular relations of command and obedience. Here, as Alsted argues in his encyclopedic chapter on moral theology, reflection on the human condition teaches us that our life together is characteristically organized by membership in various social orders (*ordines* or *status hierarchicus*). These relational orders must be constituted by the pursuit of certain shared goods. Alsted points out that members of various communities are able to enjoy these shared goods insofar as they cultivate the virtues necessary to pursue and protect them. Obligations (*officia*) arise in response to the recognition of the common goods and virtues of each relational order.[68]

For instance, in the domestic sphere, the relationship of command and obedience between parents and children is oriented toward the children's wellbeing, education, and ability "to recognize the gifts of God," among other things.[69] Likewise, in academic contexts, the relationship of professor and student should be ordered to intellectual excellence, pious living, and the

Reformation, and Universal Reform (Oxford: Clarendon Press, 2000); *Paradise Postponed: Johann Heinrich Alsted and the Birth of Calvinist Millenarianism* (Dordrecht: Springer, 2000); and Howard Hotson and Maria Rosa Antognazza. *Alsted and Leibniz: On God, the Magistrate and the Millennium* (Wiesbaden: Harrassowitz, 1999).

66   For instance, Soo Han notes that Alsted believes that scholastic communities pursue the renewal of the image of God through intellectual endeavor: "scholastic felicity" is "located in the union and communion of the minds of the good, and truly in the wisdom of living well," among several other qualities. "The Academization of Reformation Teaching in Johann Heinrich Alsted," 291.

67   The fourth volume of Alsted's *Encyclopedia* contains a systematic treatment of the particular goods, virtues, and duties that pertain to these various contexts. Further distinctions among various forms of human society are drawn in Alsted's locus on moral theology, V.7.9–12.

68   On the importance of relational orders in the early modern *politica* genre, see Robert Von Friedeburg, *Self-Defence and Religious Strife in Early Modern Europe* (Burlington, VT: Ashgate, 2002), 104–6. While von Friedeburg is very helpful on the matter of relational order in the service of an *ars conservandi*, he does not address the traditional sources of this view of political life, thereby making it seem as if the emphasis on relational orders was primarily an early modern response to religious strife.

69   See Alsted's locus "De Statu oeconomico," *Encyclopedia* V, 1688–9.

imitation of good and praiseworthy exemplars (*bono et laudabili vitae exemplo praelucere*).[70] So also, in political life, Christian magistrates and their subjects are joined together in pursuit of certain goods. Alsted explicitly frames this order or fellowship in covenantal terms. He writes that there ought to be a covenant between God and the members of the political community (*inter deum et rempublicam debet esse foedus*). This covenant should exist, he continues, so that the republic might be the people of God (*ut respublica sit populus Dei*) and fittingly arrange for faithful administration of its laws. It is this political covenant – one that we will analyze in more detail in subsequent chapters – that provides the basis for the obligations that obtain to Christian princes, magistrates, and their people. Just as rulers are obligated to administer justice (*jus et justitiam administrare*), so are the ruled to love, honor, revere, and support the magistrate, commending him to God.[71]

According to Alsted, the political community can and ought to reflect the paradigmatic covenantal relationship between God and his people. At the same time, as the heir to an Augustinian and Thomist tradition, he recognizes the temptations and imperfections of life in the earthly city. These two aspects of political life are perhaps best embodied in one of his most striking aphorisms: "the republic is an example and image (*documentum et imago*) of eternal life."[72] Alsted explains this aphorism by calling attention to the fact that the earthly commonwealth possesses many formal similarities to the future eschatological kingdom. For instance, it is the duty of citizens to obey the external demands of justice. However, he notes, we can see that our conformity to these normative standards is always imperfect in this life. Hitting an Augustinian note, Alsted suggests that "we were not made for this life, but to expect another" in which our adherence to the norms of justice will be perfect and complete. Our life in the earthly republic teaches us that "the justice of God requires . . . that those who earnestly seek after the common good in a perfect

---

[70] Alsted writes on the scholastic order in *Encyclopedia* V, 1689.

[71] "[Officia] . . . subditi Christiani est, magistratum suum amare, honorare, timere, alere, Deo commendare," *Encyclopedia* V, 1689–90. For another representative account of earthly *ordines* see the Heidelberg theologian David Pareus' commentary on chapter 13 of the Epistle to the Romans, Pareus, *In divinam ad Romanos* (Stephanus Gamonetus, 1609). Pareus, whose commentary was famously banned and publically burned at the order of King James I of England, held both to a strong doctrine of resistance to tyranny and to a broadly Aristotelian conception of the *ordo politicus*. Much like Alsted, Pareus defined this relational order as, properly, a just arrangement or relationship (*iusta dispositio*) between magistrates and subjects, 991. An *ordo*, as he defines it, is a relationship (*relatio*) or a reflection of a relationship oriented toward a particular end. See the discussion of "Non enim est potestas nisi a Deo," 992ff.

[72] Alsted, *Theologia naturalis*, 731.

political community [*perfecta politia*] receive some reward for their labors." However, it is often the case in this present life that the "reward" of those seeking justice and the common good is "insult, incarceration, and exile" (*maledicta, carceres, exilia*).[73] Vicious and licentious persons often pervert the norms of earthly justice. In such cases, the life of the republic is twisted toward injustice and disorder. Finally, Alsted writes that our political community serves as a true image of heavenly fellowship insofar as both are constituted by a rightly ordered relationship between a ruler and his subjects. In both sorts of community, Alsted states, it is the role of the ruler to defend the wellbeing of his people, while the people in turn receive the full rights of citizenship.

It is important to note the implications of Alsted's analogy of divine and human commonwealths. Alsted's aphorism should not be dismissed as an incidental piece of theological speculation. In many senses, it is a prism of early Reformed covenantal thought, a tradition which did not – and simply could not – conceive of political and spiritual fellowship as unrelated social orders. The former is, or ought to be, an example and image of the latter. The fellowship that God offers to his people, and the laws that he issues to protect that fellowship, provide the paradigmatic normative standard for social relations.

The interplay of creation and fall, goodness and corruption, perfection and imperfection, is emblematic of the Reformed theological and political tradition as a whole. Theologians such as Zanchi, Ursinus, Martinius, and Alsted do not attempt to underplay the perverted or fragmentary aspects of sin and domination any more than they doubt the faithfulness of God to preserve the social goods of human fellowship. The origin and ends of the covenant and its law do not undergo a fundamental change even after the fall, although the common goods of the covenant are no longer so easily enjoyed by its members. For all these reasons, the law of the covenant is something for which Alsted and others believe humanity has reason to be grateful. At the same time, they believe it is something that ought to strike fear into the hearts of the vicious and idolatrous who hold seats of power – as we will soon see. After all, the law of the covenant promises not only blessings for the just, but penalties for those who break the bonds of fellowship.

NORMATIVE IMPLICATIONS OF COVENANTAL LAW

Subsequent chapters will address several of the specific social and political applications of this conception of covenantal order. Even now, however, it is

---

[73] Alsted, *Theologia naturalis*, 731.

possible to see that the normative implications of this consociational view challenge several of the contemporary assumptions I laid out in the introduction. First, and most fundamentally, it is clear that Reformed theologians such as Zanchi, Ursinus, and Alsted did not conceive of covenantal law apart from the common good of fellowship. This runs directly contrary to the assumptions of the disciplinarian reading. Covenantal law finds its origin in the sovereign's expression of faithful love for his people. Law directs – or ought to direct – individuals toward the end of rightly ordered fellowship. This is true for all manner of covenantal relationships – domestic, ecclesial, political, and spiritual. The *officia* that attend these relational orders do not exist simply at the whim of a divine or human ruler. Rather, covenantal obligations arise within particular relationships for the sake of preserving some shared goods and in order to foster the moral or intellectual formation of the participating members. When historical narratives claim that early Protestant social thought abandoned traditional or "teleological" perspectives, they have evidently failed to pay attention to a host of prominent Protestant voices.[74] In the writings of theologians such as Bullinger, Zanchi, and Alsted, there is a clear and precise concern for the ways that law and obligation relate to the common goods of social relationships. Traditional conceptions of law and the common good were not abandoned, but claimed as an inheritance and then developed in innovative political arguments – to which we will turn next.

Similarly, aspects of the contractarian reading neglect the theological connection between covenantal discourse and a traditional, non-voluntarist, conception of the nature of authority and the purpose of law. Law, if it is true law, cannot be arbitrary or mere artifice wielded by the most powerful. It must have a proper source, means, and end. It must issue from a true, good, and just authority. It must account for the context and wellbeing of the community for which it was issued. And it must have as its aim the preservation or restoration of a just relationship in which persons are able to enjoy various rights and shared goods. This, at least, is the assumption of the theological texts we have addressed so far. It remains to be seen whether Kahn and others are right to

---

[74] None of the principle figures addressed in this chapter appear in *The Unintended Reformation*, nor do any of the principle political thinkers of the next chapter. Likewise, as Muller and others have pointed out, a great deal of mid-twentieth-century scholarship in historical theology has a very narrow scope, rarely venturing beyond the writings of Luther, Calvin, and a limited number of English and Scottish Puritans. Cf. Richard Muller, "Calvin and the 'Calvinists': Assessing Continuities and Discontinuities Between the Reformation and Orthodoxy," in *After Calvin* (Oxford: Oxford University Press, 2003), and "Not Scotist: Understandings of Being, Univocity, and Analogy in Early-Modern Reformed Thought," *Reformation and Renaissance Review* 14:2 (2012): 127–50; Woolsey, *Unity and Continuity in Covenantal Thought*, 80–158; Beach, *Christ and the Covenant*, 19–64.

assume that covenantal discourse is quick to shed its theological commitments, and embrace its latent voluntarism, once translated into political thought. This is the question for chapter three.

Lastly, the secular republican reading is one that must be addressed more fully in subsequent chapters. At present, it is simply important to note that concern over human flourishing and the common good is interwoven throughout early Reformed theological writings. From the side of the theologians, at least, there appears to be no clear dichotomy between divine and human covenantal orders, since the latter function as reflections of the former. It is the nature of both human and divine law to direct individuals toward participation in the common good. While particular divine laws may generate new relationships and new sets of normative judgments, as we saw in Zanchi's example of a supererogatory command, the end of law remains the same. That is to say, participating in fellowship with God may entail certain duties and sacrifices that participation in civil society does not. At the same time, both forms of life-sharing involve the pursuit of just relations by means of obedience to certain normative standards. As we turn to address specific political applications of this view, we will need to examine the manner in which these normative standards are employed to establish or contest the justice of specific social arrangements.

3

Breaking Covenant

Theological Reflection in Political Crisis

Buried deep within what some scholars consider the first modern encyclopedia, Johann Heinrich Alsted included this maxim on the nature of the commonwealth: "A covenant ought to exist so that the republic might be the people of God." As we have seen in previous chapters, covenantal language suffused Reformed theology at the end of the seventeenth century. What is relatively more novel is the application of this language to the *political* community.

Alsted's maxim, and the theological commitments that underwrote it, is key to understanding the political context of the time. As one of the most influential encyclopedists of the early modern age, Alsted would not have taken himself to be introducing a novel theological claim about the political order; he was merely summarizing a commonplace of his ecclesial and scholastic circles. This chapter will, in effect, unpack the context for Alsted's commonplace, revealing how theological ideas supported some of the most important developments of political thinking in the concluding centuries of the sixteenth century.

The concept of covenant was a ready-to-hand concept in early Reformed thought. It was employed to speak in political terms about theological relations and norms, as we have already seen, and to speak in theological terms about the political order. With this chapter, we turn our attention toward the latter application. However, in turning our focus from theological to political texts, it is important not to overstate the difference in genre. Theological and political texts occupied the same world – intellectually and socially. Theological conceptions of covenant and law were inextricably bound up with late-sixteenth-century Reformed political thought in the aftermath of the St. Bartholomew's Day Massacre and the first Dutch Revolt. In what follows, we will examine representatives of this strand of covenantal thought during a period of political crisis: Theodore Beza's *De jure magistratuum*, a series of often-anonymous treatises written in defense of the Dutch Revolt, and the influential work of Philippe de Mornay, the *Vindiciae contra tyrannos*. Each of these works reveals important aspects about the role that the concept of covenant came to play as continental Reformed theorists were pressed to defend resistance to institutions thought to be vitiated by absolute and arbitrary power. These late-sixteenth-century texts set critical terms for subsequent theoretical debates between Johannes Althusius and his absolutist rivals, which we will address in subsequent chapters.

By attending to the interrelation of theological and political concepts in these texts, I aim to include important voices and arguments that have often been marginalized as "religious," and therefore placed beyond the pale of modern (secular) political discourse. That said, I will not argue that theological and covenantal discourse offers the singular key to understanding early (or late) modern political thought. Rather, early modern thinkers, saturated in theological discourse and debates, drew on multiple authorities and traditions of thought to articulate a conception of authority and covenantal law oriented toward the common good. Covenant theology was such an authoritative discursive tradition. It held particular significance for Reformed thinkers – such as Beza, Mornay, and fellow theorists of political resistance – for whom the divine covenant with humanity was considered a historical reality that established a relationship and normative order of inestimable value.

A BRIEF WORD ABOUT CONCEPTUAL HISTORY

The conceptual relationship between covenant and law has a legal and political history that wends through late antique and medieval texts, treatises, and legal codes. Roman law, and the history of its reception in medieval canon and civil law, has garnered a great deal of scholarly attention in recent decades. Scholars such as Quentin Skinner, Anthony Black, Brian Tierney, Annabel Brett, and Daniel Lee have given us a deeper understanding of the Roman, republican, and conciliarist sources of early (and late) modern political thought. Skinner's early work – in the same vein as J. W. Allen – traced the connection between early covenantal political thought and late medieval scholasticism.[1] Black's seminal essay made a case for the central role that jurists played in tying together various strands of legal, commercial, and theological thought in the late medieval and early modern social contract.[2] Tierney has shown how several key concepts of modern political thought have

---

[1] In particular, parts two and three of *The Foundations of Modern Political Thought*, vol. 2 (Cambridge: Cambridge University Press, 1978).
[2] Anthony Black, "The Juristic Origins of Social Contract Theory," *History of Political Thought* 14 (1993): 57–76.

a premodern scholastic ancestry.[3] More recently, Brett and Lee have developed and amended the work of Skinner, among others, showing how Roman and Germanic jurisprudence was central to the development of early modern conceptions of law, right, and social contract.[4]

There is no need to duplicate this recent scholarship. The various jurisprudential sources are clearly relevant to the early modern concept of covenantal law, and I will reference them when they relate to the theological valence of covenant and covenantal law. In the subsequent chapters, several of these overlapping matters will become directly relevant to the disputes between covenantal resistance theorists such as Althusius and their absolutist detractors. At the same time, a fulsome understanding of the early modern concept of covenantal law requires recognition of the *theological* as well as the jurisprudential sources. And it is the theological voices that have regrettably dropped out of the historiographical conversation, even as the jurists have earned a great deal of attention in recent decades.

It is worth noting some of the rationales given for this prioritization of the political and jurisprudential over the theological. In his *Foundations*, Skinner identifies the development of theories of political resistance as part of the shift from premodern theological to modern secular political thought. While he acknowledges that many of these theorists were Reformed in their confessional commitments, he argues that it is "evident that there are virtually no elements in the theory which are specifically Calvinistic at all."[5] The theological

---

3   Brian Tierney, *The Idea of Natural Rights: Studies on Natural Rights, Natural Law and Church Law, 1150–1625* (Grand Rapids, MI: Eerdmans, 1997); *Religion, Law, and the Growth of Constitutional Thought 1150–1650* (Cambridge: Cambridge University Press, 1982). Jean Porter's work on scholastic natural law is also relevant on this matter, although she focuses on medieval canon theologians rather than lawyers, *Natural and Divine Law* (Grand Rapids, MI: Eerdmans, 1999).

4   Annabel Brett, *Liberty, Right, and Nature: Individual Rights in Later Scholastic Thought* (Cambridge: Cambridge University Press, 1997); *Changes of State: Nature and the Limits of the City in Early Modern Natural Law* (Princeton, NJ: Princeton University Press, 2011); Daniel Lee, "Private Law Models for Public Law Concepts: The Roman Law Theory of Dominium in the Monarchomach Doctrine of Popular Sovereignty," *The Review of Politics* 70:3 (June 2008): 370–99; "Roman Law, German Liberties, and the Constitution of the Holy Roman Empire," in Quentin Skinner and Martin van Gelderen, eds., *Freedom and the Construction of Europe*, vol. 1, eds. Quentin Skinner and Martin van Gelderen (Cambridge: Cambridge University Press, 2013), 256–73; *Popular Sovereignty in Early Modern Constitutional Thought* (Oxford: Oxford University Press, 2016).

5   Skinner, *The Foundations of Modern Political Thought*, vol. 2, 321. In this sentiment, Skinner echoes J. W. Allen's claim that "As political thinkers, [the Calvinist resistance theorists] were far nearer to William of Ockham than they were to Calvin." In fact, it was the tension between their Reformed confessional commitments and their late medieval political ideas that "necessarily produced a certain incoherence," *A History of Political Thought in the Sixteenth Century* (London: Methuen, 1928), 313.

context is accidental to the development of modern political doctrines. Black is less straightforward on this point, noting "it is true that Calvinism did to a considerable extent coincide with the diffusion of contractarian ideas of government among wider sections of the population." In fact, "aspects of Calvinist theology breathed new life into the language of 'covenant.'" At the same time, Black contends:

> there were significant differences between the type of covenant envisaged by theologians and believers as existing between God and the Christian, or again amongst congregations of believers, and the type — or rather the various types of agreement envisaged by those developing political contractarianism in that same cultural milieu.[6]

While Black's broader point is well taken – Reformed covenantal thought can hardly be identified as the *only* relevant source for early modern contractarian thought – it is striking that he spends no time engaging with the primary theological sources. The disjuncture between theological and political conceptions of covenant is simply asserted.[7]

So, we need to ask once again: How should we account for *both* the political *and* the theological valence of the concept of covenant? In an important coauthored essay, published the year after Quentin Skinner's *Foundations*, Harro Höpfl and Martyn Thompson offered a corrective to a common historiographical approach to this issue.[8] They noted that scholars all seem to recognize *that* contract or covenant was a central concept to early modern political thought, but no one agrees on *why* or *how*. In offering explanations, many historians make the mistake of looking for the essence of the concept of contract or covenant. In this way, many historians have erroneously assumed that early modern use of covenantal semantics must indicate the presence of a late modern secular concept *in nuce*.

Höpfl and Thompson reject this approach and instead advise that a history of the concept of contract or covenant should "be based on those political writings whose central contentions were made by recourse to one or another term from the family of contract-synonyms."[9] We have already encountered

---

[6] Black, "Juristic Origins," 58.

[7] Gerhard Oestreich, following earlier scholarship, also posits "an insurmountable contradiction" between the religious covenant between God and humanity and the political contract based on some notion of popular sovereignty. However, as with Black, Oestreich does not develop this claim. Gerhard Oestreich, *Neostoicism and the Early Modern State* (Cambridge: Cambridge University Press, 1982), 149.

[8] Harro Höpfl and Martyn Thompson, "The History of Contract as a Motif in Political Thought," *The American Historical Review* 84:4 (Oct. 1979): 927–8.

[9] Höpfl and Thompson, "History of Contract," 927.

the range of Latin terms to which Höpfl and Thompson refer in their essay (*foedus, pactum, contractus*), as well as a few others (*testamentum* and *consociatio*). The significance of these terms will be most adequately revealed in the way that the primary sources employ and relate them to other (theological or political) concepts.

Höpfl and Thompson acknowledge, as I noted in chapter one, that this linguistic bundle of covenant-contract terms pervaded early modern social, commercial, and legal contexts. However, it was only in the years of crisis following the massacre of French Huguenots on the feast day of St. Bartholomew in 1572 that the concept of covenant became a central paradigm in Protestant political thought.[10] A series of Reformed thinkers picked up the "merely casual references to covenants" of earlier political writings and analyzed the concept in new ways. For influential Reformed theologians and jurists, the concepts of covenant and covenantal law were not merely accidental to political life, but used to theorize about its very origin and ends.

Gerhard Oestreich once whimsically attributed this sudden rise of covenantal political thought to the "magical ring" that the notion of mutual covenants and obligations had in Reformed ears.[11] Accounting for the theological valence of covenantal thought may not provide us with an exhaustive explanation of this phenomenon. At the very least, however, it should go some ways toward making the so-called magic intelligible to us.

COVENANTAL LAW IN POLITICAL CRISIS

The strange, tragic, and still somewhat murky history of the St. Bartholomew's Day Massacre has been told many times.[12] Historians still debate how many thousands – or tens of thousands – of French Huguenots were killed in Paris and surrounding cities, how involved members of the French royal family were involved in orchestrating the mass murder, and the long-term impact that the

---

[10] Höpfl and Thompson, "History of Contract," 929. John Witte makes a similar point in *The Reformation of Rights: Law, Religion and Human Rights in Early Modern Calvinism* (Cambridge: Cambridge University Press, 2007), 81–7.

[11] Oestreich, *Neostoicism*, 142.

[12] Representative histories include Barbara Diefendorf, *Beneath the Cross: Catholics and Huguenots in Sixteenth-Century Paris* (Oxford: Oxford University. Press, 1991), 93–106; Robert Kingdon, *Myths about the St. Bartholomew's Day Massacres* (Cambridge, MA: Harvard University Press, 1988); N. M. Sutherland, *The Massacre of St. Bartholomew and the European Conflict, 1559–1572* (London: Macmillan, 1972); and Geoffrey Treasure's recent volume *The Huguenots* (New Haven, CT: Yale University Press, 2013), 167–75.

event had on political and ecclesial relations in western Europe. What is clear, however, is the effect the tragedy had on Protestant political thought.

Despite the intermittent civil wars leading up to the massacre in late August of 1572, French Huguenots had held on to some hope for royal recognition or at least toleration. Beyond France, in fact, the international Reformed community intervened regularly on behalf of the Huguenots. Writing in exile, Calvin famously dedicated the first edition of his *Institutes of the Christian Religion* to Francis I in the hopes of convincing "his own prince and lord" of the injustice committed against Calvin's French coreligionists.[13] His successor in Geneva, Theodore Beza, pled the Huguenots' case constantly from 1551 through the aftermath of the Massacre. In 1562, following a smaller-scale massacre near Champaign, Beza called for punitive justice on behalf of the aggrieved Huguenots before the French king, the queen mother, and other assembled royalty. He noted that although the Huguenots remained loyal to the crown, the egregious injustice committed against them must be addressed: "Sire, it belongs to the Church of God, in whose name I speak, to endure blows and not to inflict them. But it will also please your Majesty to remember that she is an anvil that has worn out many hammers."[14] After the events of August of 1572, this posture of strained, aggrieved passivity was no longer so easy to maintain. Höpfl observes that the Massacre "effectively meant the end of the project for an evangelical conversion of the whole of France: the issue now was survival."[15]

Protestants immediately decried the massacre as part of a wide-ranging Catholic plot, and the sense of betrayal and injury was compounded by the bald-facedness of the crown's complicity. This introduced a new challenge for Protestant political actors and theorists. Before the massacre, resistance to Catholic nobility could – however tenuously – be framed as resistance to something other than the crown itself. After the massacre, as Philip Benedict notes, "Protestant mobilization could no longer be justified simply as a matter of protecting royal authority against evil Catholic councillors, for the crown

[13] Calvin appeals to Francis: "Justice, then, most invincible Sovereign, entitles me to demand that you will undertake a thorough investigation of this cause, which has hitherto been tossed about in any kind of way, and handled in the most irregular manner, without any order of law, and with passionate heat rather than judicial gravity," from Henry Beveridge's translation of the "Prefatory Address."

[14] *Histoire ecclésiastique des églises réformées au royaume de France*, vol. 2 (originally published in 1580 and sometimes ascribed to Beza himself), reprinted and edited by G. Baum and E. Cunitz (Paris, 1884), 1–6.

[15] Harro Höpfl, "The Ideal of *Aristocratia Politiae Vicina* in the Calvinist Political Tradition," in Irena Backus and Philip Benedict, eds., *Calvin and His Influence, 1509–2009* (Oxford: Oxford University Press, 2011), 56.

openly assumed responsibility for the liquidation of many leading Protestant noblemen."[16] The new political circumstances intensified the Protestants' understanding of their own besieged status not just in France, but also across Europe. Particularly in Dutch and northern German counties, Reformed communities under Catholic rule came to identify with the plight of the Huguenots.

In the Netherlands, the conflict between the Dutch Protestants and their Catholic rulers broiled over several decades, parallel to the situation in France. As Robert von Friedeburg points out, local counts under the influence of William I of Orange "considered themselves participants in the struggle across their borders," an attitude entrenched after the 1572 massacre. Rulers of Reformed counties such as Nassau and Sayn-Wittgenstein (Althusius' birth-place) corresponded with many of the Reformed theologians in Heidelberg, asking them about theoretical grounds for resistance to tyranny and possible military intervention in France on behalf of the Huguenots.[17]

The situation in the Netherlands became even more heated in 1580 when the Spanish king Phillip II declared William, the de facto political leader of the Dutch Protestants, an outlaw. In response, William enlisted several Huguenot theologians to write his response. Loyseleur de Villiers, the princi-ple author, consulted with Philippe de Mornay and Mornay's mentor Hubert Languet, and penned William's *Apologie* in 1581.[18] The tract was published in four languages and spread quickly through western Europe. Famous not only for its qualified defense of religious toleration, the *Apologie* also helped to spread salacious rumors about Philip's adulterous and murderous proclivities. In addition, William reported a story about how the kings of France and Spain

[16]   Philip Benedict, *Christ's Churches Purely Reformed: A Social History of Calvinism* (New Haven, CT: Yale University Press, 2002), 146.

[17]   Gerhard Menk, *Die Hohe Schule Herborn in ihrer Frühzeit (1584–1660)* (Wiesbaden: Selbstverlag der Historischen Kommission für Nassau, 1981), 260–2; Robert von Friedeburg, *Self-Defence and Religious Strife in Early Modern Europe. England and Germany, 1530–1680* (Burlington, VT: Ashgate, 2002), 109. See also Pierre Mesnard on the relationship between French Huguenot and Dutch resistance, *L'essor de la philosophie politique au XVIe siecle* (Paris: Boivin, 1936).

[18]   The House of Orange's connection to French Reformed theologians extended to later gen-erations. The orthodox Reformed theologian Andre Rivet served as William II's tutor and wrote a mirror-of-princes volume on the princely virtues, *Instruction du prince chrestien* (Leiden, 1642). See G. O. van de Klashorst, H. W. Blom, and E. O. G. Haitsma Mulier, eds., *Bibliography of 17th Century Dutch Political Thought: An Annotated Inventory, 1581–1710* (Amsterdam: Holland University Press, 1986), 40. Later, Frederic Rivet – Andre's son – had a hand in the education of William III. There is little material on these relationships, although Brita Lang has addressed the ways in which the connection between the Rivets and the House of Orange may have directly influenced John Locke, "An Unidentified Source of John Locke's *Some Thoughts Concerning Education*," *Pedagogy, Culture & Society* 9:2 (2001): 249–78.

had concocted a plan to exterminate all suspected Protestants "in France, and in this country, and throughout Christendom."[19] Similar charges appeared throughout the Protestant community. Beza, for instance, considered the various Catholic aggressions as a coordinated campaign of the papacy itself, perhaps even "a plot worked out at the Council of Trent."[20]

Rumors like these only confirmed the worst fears of Protestant leaders across Europe. Philip's sins and transgressions multiplied in the Protestant imagination just as the reported number of Huguenot dead in the streets of Paris in August of 1572 doubled with every retelling.[21] Catholic authorities, in response, accused the Protestants of slander and impious rebellion to divinely-ordained authority – both royal and ecclesial. In Philip's sanctioned response to the *Apologie*, he argued that William had "demanded articles more grievous, impertinent, hurtful, offensive, and full of impiety against God and us, their sovereign Lord and natural Prince."[22] It was clear that William had gone "against his covenants and promises sworn."[23]

Broken covenants, impiety, vicious behavior, deceit, and disorder were key charges on both sides of the conflict. While polemical treatises like William's *Apologie* and Philip's *Proclamation* deploy equally excessive rhetoric and scandalous accusations, it is nevertheless possible to identify substantive disagreements. Various parties conceived of the purpose of law and the relationship between law and regal power in a number of different ways. Various parties had implicit – and often explicit – conceptions of covenantal law and political authority.

Within this turbulent context, leading Protestant political figures such as William looked to theologians for counsel, and drew on theological concepts and arguments in a time of crisis. In fact, many Protestant leaders and theorists of this period had trained in theology or served as ministers themselves.

By the 1570s, as we have already seen, the concept of covenant was deeply embedded in Reformed discourse. It had acquired a strong theological resonance, evoking the nature and ends of God's relationship with his people. The concepts of covenants and covenantal law, already theorized by theologians with respect to the social obligations that obtained between God and God's

---

[19]   From the English edition of William I's *The Apologie of Prince William of Orange Against the Proclamation of the King of Spaine*, edited by H. Wansink (Leiden: Brill, 1969 [1581]), 61.

[20]   Beza's letter to Christopher Hardesheim, Sept. 4, 1572, in Alastair Duke, Gillian Lewis, and Andrew Pettegree, eds., *Calvinism in Europe 1540–1610: A Collection of Documents* (Manchester: Manchester University Press, 1992), 113.

[21]   Robert Kingdon's volume on the propaganda surrounding the Massacre remains a standard: *Myths about the St. Bartholomew's Day Massacres.*

[22]   *A Proclamation and an Edict in form of a Proscription*, in Wansink, *Apologie*, 163.

[23]   *Proclamation*, in Wansink, *Apologie*, 157.

people, would become resonant terms within Reformed political thought. We will return to the explicit theories of resistance to idolatry and tyranny contained in these treatises in a later chapter. At present, we will focus on the manner in which these treatises of resistance applied the concepts of covenant and law to sustain their arguments against unjust rule.

LAWS, COVENANTS, AND ANTECEDENT NORMS

Beza's De Jure Magistratuum

Even before he was designated as Calvin's successor in Geneva, Theodore Beza served as a key spokesman for the Huguenots – those exiled in Geneva and those still besieged in France. He spent decades of his life laboring for the Huguenot cause, traveling with Gaspard II de Coligny and Henri de Bourbon, speaking in colloquies, arguing before the royal court, and writing numerous petitions to other Protestant leaders who were in a position to provide crucial material support.[24] At the same time, after Calvin's death in 1564, Beza served as moderator of the Company of Pastors and on the theological faculty of the academy in Geneva.[25]

Beza wrote *De jure magistratuum* in 1573, likely the summer after the St. Bartholomew's Day Massacre. He submitted a Latin manuscript for publication in Geneva in 1573, was rejected for fear of the political backlash, and eventually published the work anonymously in French in Heidelberg the following year.[26]

The first and foundational question for Beza's treatise concerns the binding nature of a command or law. Is there an eternal and immutable normative standard that demands our obedience without exception? Certainly there is, according to Beza: The will of God is the *iustitiae regula* that ought to order

---

[24] See Emidio Campi, "Theodore Beza and Heinrich Bullinger in Light of Their Correspondence," in *Shifting Patterns of Reformed Tradition* (Gottingen: Vanderhoeck & Ruprecht, 2014), 169–83; and also John Southworth, *Theodore Beza, Covenantalism, and Resistance to Political Authority in the Sixteenth Century* (PhD diss., Westminster Theological Seminary, 2003), esp. 165–97.

[25] See Robert Kingdon, *Geneva and the Consolidation of the French Protestant Movement, 1564–1572* (Madison, WI: University of Wisconsin Press, 1967); Gillian Lewis, "The Geneva Academy," in Andrew Pettegree, Alastair Duke, and Gillian Lewis, eds., *Calvinism in Europe: 1540–1620* (Cambridge: Cambridge University Press, 1996), 35–63; and Scott Manetsch, *Calvin's Company of Pastors: Pastoral Care and the Emerging Reformed Church, 1536–1609* (Oxford: Oxford University Press, 2012).

[26] See Julian Franklin's editorial note on *De Jure* in Franklin, ed., *Constitutionalism and Resistance in the Sixteenth Century* (New York, NY: Pegasus, 1969), 98–9.

our obligations.[27] This identification of the *voluntas Dei* with the norm of justice is not surprising; similar statements occur throughout early Reformed theological writings, as we have seen. However, for Beza, as for Zanchi and the theologians discussed in earlier chapters, the will of God is authoritative precisely because the God who directs us toward certain ends is himself good, just, and excellent by his very nature. While *De jure* does not theorize about the relationship between the divine nature and *voluntas Dei*, we have records of several of the theological disputations that took place under Beza's oversight in the Genevan academy, several of which address this point. The theological arguments follow a familiar course: God's power is infinite, yet the will of God "is bound" such that "God cannot do any of these things which either are repugnant unto his personal properties . . . or are contrary unto his essence." Therefore, God cannot have defects or weakness "as to die, to lie, to sin, etc."[28] Even more precisely, "God is most good, so his will is most upright, and the rule of all justice, so as it cannot command anything that is evil."[29]

The relevance of this theological context to the first *quaestio* of *De jure* becomes apparent within just a few sentences. Beza writes that insofar as the *voluntas Dei* provides us with a normative standard for relationship of command and obedience, any political command must accord with divine justice. Our obligation to obey civil rulers, Beza acknowledges, would obtain at all times "if they perpetually commanded from the voice of God" (*si ex Dei ore perpetuo imperarent*). It is quite clear, however, that this is not always the case. Therefore, two crucial exceptions apply to our political obedience. Impious or irreligious commands (*impia mandata . . . sive irreligiosa*) are those that direct us toward ends that violate our duties to God – summarized in the first table of the Decalogue. Iniquitous commands (*iniqua praecepta*) are those that prevent us from rendering what is due to our neighbor out of love. What is owed depends on our particular social role, whether public or private.[30]

In this question and throughout his treatise, Beza provides support for his claims by reference to alternating series of rational arguments and *exempla* – a practice that would elicit criticism from rival theorists, as we will see in the next chapter. According to Beza, we can reasonably reject the absolute,

---

[27] *De jure magistratuum* (Lyon: Jean Mareschall, 1576), 3. The Latin edition was published as a translation "e Gallico in Latinum," although Franklin notes that the records of the Geneva council imply that the Latin manuscript was the original.

[28] *Propositions and principles of diuinitie*, sixth principle, "The Omnipotency of God" (Robert Waldegraue: Edinburgh, 1591), 12.

[29] *Propositions*, eighth principle, "Concerning the Goodness, Favor, Love, and Mercy of God," 16.

[30] Beza, *De jure*, 3–4.

exception-less account of political obligation on account of its implicit conception of authority. If political commands acquired the power to obligate solely based on human will (*ex solo hominum arbitrio*), this would imply that human authority and dignity is equal to that of God's own self. This cannot be true, Beza, argues, because there is a sort of glory and dignity that belongs only to God. In support of this point, Beza provides a string of examples of just disobedience to unjust precepts, primarily from the Hebrew Bible: the midwives' refusal of Pharaoh's unjust commands to kill innocent children, the faithful response of Daniel's companions to Nebuchadnezzar's impiety, and the Maccabees' revolt against Antiochus. In summary, Beza "infers that the authority of all magistrates, however great their power and rule, is bounded by two things by God himself, piety and charity."[31]

The subsequent *quaestiones* develop these latter themes. For Beza, piety and charity are virtues that direct us to render what is due to God and neighbor, respectively.[32] In general, he acknowledges, our social life and obligations are such that political subjects assume the justice of magisterial commands. In fact, Beza denies that a magistrate is ordinarily bound to justify all his commands to all people (*quaestio* 2): it is just or equitable (*aequum*) that there are many civil judgments that virtuous subjects ought to leave to the discretion of political rulers. At the same time, he contends, there will be occasions when circumstances disquiet the consciences of private persons. In such cases, it is proper to inquire about the "reason and justice" of political commands. If a command is determined to be contrary to piety or charity, as in the first question, some form of disobedience is legitimate.

We will return to Beza's mechanisms for resistance in a later chapter, and the ways in which the virtues of piety and prudence condition a just response

---

[31] Beza, *De jure*, 5–6. Interestingly, in the section on *Politica* in his *Encyclopedia*, Alsted quotes the entirety of Beza's first *quaestio* (without citation) following his discussion of the *ius* of sovereignty, IV.XXIII.III.XLVIII, 1404.

[32] Beza leaves this distinction undeveloped in the *De jure*. Many of Beza's contemporaries and successors make a somewhat analogous distinction between piety (directed toward God) and civil righteousness or justice (directed toward neighbor). Althusius employs this distinction in his *Politica*. Analysis of the different moral taxonomies lies beyond the scope of this chapter. However, it is worth noting that Beza's distinction between piety and charity is rather idiosyncratic. For instance, Althusius' colleague Clemens Timpler has a more sophisticated analysis of moral and theological virtues in which he clarifies that piety may be considered both as a species of moral virtue (within the discipline of ethics) and as a specifically Christian virtue (within the discipline of theology) that is formed by the Holy Spirit through a series of intermediary practices (such as prayer and meditation), *Philosophiae practicae*, pars prima (Hanoviae, 1612), 22. Considering the circumstances under which the *De jure* was written, it is perhaps understandable why Beza's analysis would lack the rigor of later accounts.

to tyranny. What remains necessary now, however, is to relate Beza's conception of law in general to his references to covenant and natural law.

By comparison to some of his Reformed contemporaries, Beza's political use of the concept of covenant is relatively limited.[33] In a similar vein as Calvin's occasional references to mutual obligation,[34] Beza considers the notion of covenant as one possible way to describe the relationship of command and obedience between rulers and the ruled.[35] Notably, his brief discussion of political covenants is directly related to his conception of natural law.[36]

Beza's analysis of this relationship appears in the middle of his response to the sixth *quaestio*: "Do subjects have any remedy against a legitimate sovereign who has become a degenerate tyrant?"[37] Embedded within an extensive series

[33] In Beza's theological writings, by contrast, the concept is widespread. His treatments of the sacraments, marriage, the unity of the old and new testaments are all suffused with the sort of covenantal language that we have already seen in Reformed theological writings in chapter one. Interestingly, until Andrew Woolsey's recent work, the covenantal aspect of Beza's theology was almost entirely overlooked. Woolsey quite reasonably supposes that this oversight is explained by several misbegotten presumptions in mid-twentieth-century historical theology (e.g. the alleged dichotomy between predestinarian Calvinism and covenantal theology), Woolsey, *Unity and Continuity in Covenantal Thought* (Grand Rapids, MI: Reformation Heritage Books, 2012), 344–95.

[34] Contrary to some earlier scholarship, Höpfl notes that Calvin's references to *mutua obligatio* should not be pressed in the mold of a proto-contractarian theory of political association. Rather, Calvin used the concept of mutual obligation, connected as it was to that of covenant, as one way to describe the relationship of accountability between God, king, and subjects. See Harro Höpfl, *The Christian Polity of John Calvin* (Cambridge: Cambridge University Press, 1982), 172–206, esp. 278n66. While avoiding the political ramifications, Woolsey's summary of Calvin's views on covenantal obligations is useful, *Unity and Continuity*, 306–17. Similar occasional references to covenantal obligations can be traced through the early Scottish and English reformation as well, cf. George Buchanan's *De Jure Regni Apud Scotus* (Edinburgh, 1579), LIII.

[35] Höpfl and Thompson note that at this time jurists such as Francois Hotman did not make paradigmatic use of the concept of covenant. Beza and Calvin employ the concept with increasing frequency, but it is not until the work of Mornay and subsequent thinkers that covenant is used as a fundamental paradigm for political life, "History of Contract," 930.

[36] As I indicate below, Beza's reference to political covenants are primarily related to his relatively brief discussion of natural law. This should amend John Witte's claim that Beza has a fully fledged theory of a "three-party covenant" among God, the ruler, and the ruled. This more extensive covenantal conception of political life applies more accurately to Mornay and Althusius, as we shall see. See Witte, *Reformation of Rights*, 124.

[37] It is notable that Beza rarely discusses natural law at any length. Witte makes a contrary claim in *Reformation of Rights*, 127, including footnote 129. It is important to note, however, the Bezan sources that he cites are not primarily about natural law, but the Mosaic law. For Beza and his contemporaries, the two species of law are certainly related, insofar as theologians held that the divine law given to the Hebrew people was in some way a written elaboration of natural law. However, the difference between the two species of law (one written, one unwritten) is equally important to grasp, as I argued in the previous chapter. Conflating the two can lead to a misreading of Beza and his contemporaries.

of *exempla* from biblical, ancient, and medieval history, Beza introduces the concept of natural law with particular regard to its relevance for political covenants (*pacta*).[38] For Beza, natural law is a synonym for justice or equity (*aequitas*). Equity or natural law, he claims, is that upon which all human relationships depend (*a quo uno pendet totius humanae societatis conservatio*).[39] Any contracted arrangement or social order must accord with this normative standard. But what is this equity or natural law?

One possible reading of Beza assumes that this "natural law" is a set of timeless and universal conclusions, many of which are relevant to contractual agreements and political obligations. This natural law is the "universal rule of justice," as rendered by the Julian Franklin translation, and is "so definite and firm that nothing clearly contrary and repugnant to it should be found proper and valid among men."[40] On these terms, for instance, John Witte has argued that Beza's *De jure* provides us with a systematic theory of subjective natural rights, one of which is the intrinsic right of individuals to enter voluntarily into a political community.[41] Likewise, David Van Drunen claims that for Beza and fellow resistance theorists, natural law "is no bare or minimalist moral standard, but declares a vast and even detailed morality."[42]

However, this reading makes two critical misjudgments. First, Beza does not conceive of natural law as a free-standing set of individual rights or conclusions about moral or political order. In fact, he does not even refer to natural law as a "universal" moral code, per se, but as the "general norm of law and justice, sustained by the common principles [*principiis*] of nature." This general norm of law and justice remains fixed in humanity even after the fall, Beza continues, so that "nothing that is manifestly opposed and repugnant to them [that is, the *principia*

---

[38] Skinner states that Beza's shift to "rational" argument marks a shift away from theological argument toward a more secular and radical conception of popular sovereignty. This claim overlooks a critical feature of Beza's work. Throughout the treatise, Beza shifts back and forth, not between theological and rational argument, but between arguments from *exempla* and *ratio*. In fact, his arguments from reason are as informed by theological and scriptural commitments as are his arguments from biblical history. Cf. Skinner, *Foundations*, vol. 2, 326.

[39] Beza, *De jure*, 80.

[40] Franklin, *Constitutionalism*, 125.

[41] Witte, *Reformation of Rights*, 134–41.

[42] "The Use of Natural Law in Early Calvinist Resistance Theory," *Journal of Law and Religion* 21:1 (2005/2006): 156. It is not clear whether Van Drunen still holds to this interpretation, since he has modified his own account of natural law, which he now explicitly calls a "minimalist ethic," *Divine Covenants and Moral Order: A Biblical Theology of Natural Law* (Grand Rapids, MI: Eerdmans, 2014).

of human nature] should be considered as just and defensible among human persons."[43]

The implications of this reading become clearer when we consider the context of the sixth *quaestio*. Beza introduces the concept of natural law while analyzing the status of *pacta* between rulers and subjects that are ostensibly consensual, yet oppressive in nature. What should we make of political covenants or arrangements in which "a people knowingly and voluntarily" (*scienter et sponte*) consent to something "manifestly irreligious and contrary to natural law"? It is important to note that Beza does not refer here to the norm of justice and natural law in order to uncover a set of determinate, self-evident conclusions about moral acts or social relations. These are absent from his analysis. Rather, his claim is actually quite simple: Beza holds that individuals desire that which they consider to be good or just. Conversely, it would be specious to think that rational agents would desire something that is contrary to the *principia* that make human creatures the sort of beings we are.

Crucially, this conditions the role that so-called "consent" plays in legitimizing specific political arrangements. A people might ostensibly agree to a range of political relationships that are actually judged to be contrary to justice and goodness. The relevant question then becomes: Why would they do so? Why would an individual or community consent to enter a covenant of arbitrary command and servile obedience when this particular relational order – by definition – is an injustice contrary to the *principia* of human nature? In such cases, Beza writes, we must entertain the possibility that there are other relevant factors at play.

For Beza, analysis of this sort involves proper recognition of the conditions that surround the political command. He refers to the contract between Minos and the people of Athens. While the old tales record that the Athenians consented to the annual sacrifice of their sons and daughters to Minos' beast, Beza writes, this is not an adequate description of the relationship between the parties. Rather, it is more accurate to describe the arrangement as one of enforced "submission" to Minos' "lust and tyranny."[44] By introducing these moral terms, Beza has characterized the relationship as patently objectionable.[45]

---

[43] "Haec enim generalis iuris et aequi regula communibus, naturae principiis subnixa (quae adhuc post lapsum in homine, quantumvis corrupto resident) tam certa firmaque est, ut nihil quod illis aperte adversetur et repugnet, pro iusto et rato inter homines sit habendum," Beza, *De jure*, 81–2. My rendition is closer to Gonin's English translation of the 1595 Latin edition (which Franklin acknowledges to be more literal than his own, *Constitutionalism*, 99).

[44] Beza, *De jure*, 82.

[45] Even worse for Beza, we should note, are cases in which rulers impose their will in ways that require impiety of their subjects – endangering not only the body but also the soul.

Amending the reading of Witte and Van Drunen, therefore, Beza does not conceive of natural law as something that provides a vast and determinate set of moral conclusions. Rather, natural law is the general norm of justice and equity. As such, rational agents must learn to make prudent determinations of general norms in light of particular circumstances. This in fact explains why Beza interweaves so many *exempla* from biblical and secular history, ancient philosophy and mythology, and "arguments from reason." It is by attending to these virtuous and vicious examples that Beza thinks we will be better equipped to distinguish between justice and injustice. Right judgment is needed in order to tell the difference between legitimate political rule and the libidinous domination of a tyrant like Minos. In superficial terms, both forms of rule involve varying degrees of rule, command, even coercion; distinguishing between the two requires the proper application of moral terms. While one might call this a "natural law ethic," Beza would likely just call it practical wisdom – the prudent application of the norm of justice.

Beza presses this line of argument beyond instances of immediate (and manifest) contractual domination, including cases in which "some nation which either from imprudence or as a result of false flatteries" or loyalty to some dynastic line "submitted itself without any express condition." Once this contract or oath of loyalty is made, "should we therefore say that all things that he may wish will be permissible to that ruler?" Clearly not, he thinks. We must recognize and protect those things that by their very nature are holy and legitimate (*ea que natura sua sancta et legitima*). Even in the absence of express contractual safeguards, the norm of justice must be recognized and applied. Otherwise, princes have license to act arbitrarily (*pro arbitrio*).

Throughout his argument, Beza has in mind unnamed antagonists whom he believes remove this antecedent standard of justice from consideration, such that the ruler stands in a relationship of accountability only to God. These theorists "so far exalt the authority of kings and supreme rulers as to dare maintain that they have no other judge but God alone to whom they have to render account (*rationem reddere*) of their deeds." In response, Beza challenges proponents of absolute political power to "furnish proof that there has been any nation anywhere which has consciously and without intimidation or compulsion of some kind submitted itself to the arbitrary rule of some supreme ruler without adding an express or tacit intuition of the condition that it be justly and fairly ruled and guided by him."[46]

There are two implications of this reading of Beza's *De jure*. First, while not theorized as clearly as in Zanchi's account, Beza does not conceive of natural

---

[46] Beza, *De jure*, 80–1.

law as a free-standing set of moral conclusions, let alone something from which an individual right to voluntary political association might be deduced. After all, it is precisely this notion of consent and volition that Beza complicates in his account of just political order. For Beza, the crucial task of moral and political analysis is to recognize the (just or unjust) conditions of a relationship for what they truly are. While a tyrant might describe his relationship with his subjects as one based on consent, Beza claims that there is an antecedent standard that holds the tyrant to account. According to this standard, the relationship is not legitimatized by "consent," per se, but properly described as unjust, as it conforms only to the tyrant's *arbitrium*.

Second, in Beza's conception of law and covenant, we do not have a broadly theoretical account of covenantal relationships as constitutive of political life. However, insofar as Beza adheres to a traditional account of law and right order, we can see how such a covenantal, or consociational, conception of politics might fit into such an account. Where Beza stressed the need for a normative standard that is antecedent to the ruler's *arbitrium*, subsequent Reformed thinkers would turn to the covenantal relationship itself.

Treatises of the Dutch Revolt

We can find analogous arguments about law, covenants, and their relation to an antecedent norm of justice in Dutch treatises appearing soon after Beza's *De jure*. In 1567, Philip replaced his half-sister, Margaret of Parma, with Fernando Alvarez de Toledo, the duke of Alba, as governor of the Netherlands. Relations between Catholics and Protestants under Margaret's stewardship had hardly been stable – thanks to Protestant iconoclastic uprisings and Philip's support of a brutal decades-long inquisition – but the situation immediately deteriorated under Alba. Prior to his arrival, several of the leading nobles fled, including William. Others stayed, including many of the moderate Catholic nobles who opposed the inquisition even as they remained supportive of Philip's reign. When Alba arrived, he had many of these nobles – Protestant and Catholic alike – arrested on charges of heresy. Public executions followed soon after.[47] Ernst Kossmann and A. F. Mellink describe Alba's rule in these terms:

---

[47] See Parker's narrative of the first revolt in *The Dutch Revolt* (New York, NY: Penguin, 1984), 68–117; E. H. Kossmann and A. F. Mellink, eds., *Texts Concerning the Revolt of the Netherlands* (Cambridge: Cambridge University Press, 1974), 1–51; Martin van Gelderen, *The Political Thought of the Dutch Revolt 1555–1590* (Cambridge: Cambridge University Press, 2002); Jonathan Israel, *The Dutch Republic* (Oxford: Oxford University Press, 1995),

He ruled the Netherlands arbitrarily. His principles were simple. Catholic orthodoxy and obedience to the natural sovereign constituted for him self-evident necessities, to depart from which amounted to rebellion. A rebellion having taken place, the sovereign who so far had heeded the privileges of his subjects, now disregarded them in his rightful anger. Of course, he was justified in doing so; privileges after all are not contracts between sovereign and people but gifts generously granted that may be withdrawn should the subjects' behaviour make that advisable.[48]

While Dutch Protestants and many Catholics opposed Alba's political administration, creating a durable coalition proved difficult. Entrenched regional, religious, and economic differences stood in the way. Throughout William's campaigns against Alba, and eventually the crown itself, he wrote (or commissioned) treatises summoning the provinces to a unity centered on the "old traditional freedom" enjoyed by generations of free Dutch persons. In his 1568 tract, "Warning to the Inhabitants and Subjects of the Netherlands," William argued—with a customary amount of historical embellishment— that the Dutch provinces "have always been ruled and reigned over by their princes and overlords with all gentleness, right and reason and wholly in accordance with their freedoms, rights, customs, traditions and privileges, which have always been observed."[49] In response, princes "always had to commit themselves by a formal contract and to swear a solemn oath that they would maintain these rights and realize them." The subjects' obligation to obey obtains insofar as these liberties are protected. When these liberties, "together with the religion of God are lying there oppressed and destroyed," it becomes clear that the people have been brought into a condition of "unbearable slavery."[50]

Various treaties, contracts, leagues, and covenants were proposed over the course of the revolt. Following a bloody uprising of Spanish mutineers in 1576, the Dutch leaders in the States General brokered a provisional peace – the Pacification of Ghent – between the Dutch rebels and the new representative of Spanish rule, Philip's half-brother, Don Juan of Austria. Among the terms of

---

155–230; and Graham Darby, ed., *The Origins and Development of the Dutch Revolt* (New York, NY: Routledge, 2001).

[48] Kossmann and Mellink, *Texts*, 13.

[49] van Gelderen's analysis of the relevance of the Joyous Entry of Brabant (1356) to the Dutch pamphleteers is useful, *Political Thought*, 27–30, 110–15, 131–3.

[50] *The Prince of Orange's Warning to the Inhabitants and Subjects of the Netherlands* (1568), in Kossmann and Mellink, *Texts*, 86. See van Gelderen's helpful account of this stage of William's campaign in *Political Thought*, 120–6.

this treaty, Spanish troops would leave the Netherlands and suppression of Protestantism would cease.

The peace was tenuous at best. With relations between Catholics and Protestants fraying, a series of Dutch pamphlets appeared, calling for unity across the provinces. The 1579 treatise, *A Discourse Containing a True Understanding of the Pacification of Ghent*, argued in support of the treaty and its policy of religious toleration. Strikingly, the author defends the arrangement by reference to the nature and end of contracts: "It is in the nature of contracts that at their conclusion the aim is always to appease the parties in such a way that no discord will arise between them and that they will remain friends forever." The end of friendship remains constant precisely because this fellowship is what a contract or covenant seeks to protect. When particular problems arise and threaten to undermine the friendship, "the contract must be renewed and reworded immediately and steps be taken to resolve these problems so that the general aim of remaining friends forever be not diverted or lost."[51]

One of the central issues causing divisions in the provinces was the matter of free religious practice. The author of the *Discourse* argues that certain sacrifices are required on both sides: "at present we can see that to preserve the state we must concede their freedom to adherents of the reformed religion as has been done in Holland and Zeeland; otherwise we shall endanger the whole country." Correspondingly, it is required that the "adherents of the reformed religion in other provinces should not give offence to the Catholics of their towns or disturb them in their practice." Similar sentiments are present throughout the writings of other Dutch and Huguenot leaders during these years of peace, including one noteworthy tract written by Mornay himself. He argues that for the sake of "harmony and unity" religious difference must be protected:

> We ruin ourselves by war and internal discord. As lovers of ourselves and of what concerns us, let us demand peace and union. The Church ruins itself when war makes us, instead of Christians, people who despise all religion. Let us stop debating and fighting and in tears turn back to God, beseeching Him to re-establish religion among us to His glory.[52]

In response to the tenuous peace, many expressed concern over what might happen if Philip coerced the Dutch into a revised treaty. One of William's

---

[51] *A Discourse Containing a True Understanding of the Pacification of Ghent*, in Kossmann and Mellink, *Texts*, 175.

[52] Mornay, *A Discourse Upon the Permission of Freedom* (1579), in Kossmann and Mellink, *Texts*, 163–5.

counselors, Philips of Marnix – who studied theology under Calvin and Beza in Geneva – insinuated that any new treaty proposed by the Spanish king would merely be a cover for exacting revenge on the rebellious provinces. In particular, he suggested that Philip's own conception of authority gave him motivation to dominate the Dutch provinces. A ruler such as Philip, who manifestly considers "himself a powerful king, victorious, and extremely angry," would desire "to maintain the Roman Catholic religion to the utmost of his power and to destroy the other completely." In fact, he would be "spurred on by the pope, who has absolute power to force him to it and to absolve him of all oaths and contractual obligations, however solemn they may be." Marnix concluded that the revised peace terms would encourage the Spanish "to restore the edicts and the inquisition in their full severity every-where, to re-erect the scaffolds, gallows and wheels, to relight the fires, to prepare new graves, and to do all that the cruelty of the ecclesiastical order ever devised to maintain its domination."[53]

After years of resistance to Philip's representatives, the Dutch States General issued its Act of Abjuration in 1581, formally renouncing the Spanish crown. The following year, one of the most ardent defenses of the Abjuration, *Political Education*, was printed anonymously in Mechelen. Scholarly attention, so far, has largely concentrated on the republican and jurisprudential aspects of the treatise. For instance, while van Gelderen notes that *Political Education* appeals to biblical and theological authorities, his analysis is fixed on the republican sources.[54] Likewise, John Coffey argues that the treatise lacks "any reference to the godly kings of Judah extirpating false religion," and other material that is "uniquely Calvinist."[55] Both these readings, however, overlook important theological and covenantal aspects of the treatise. In fact, as the argument of *Political Education* unfolds, it becomes increasingly apparent that Reformed theological commitments are quite central to its conception of authority, law, and covenant.

In defense of the Abjuration, *Political Education* argues that the bonds of fellowship in the Dutch provinces must be strengthened by a common oath (*eedt*). The content of the proposed oath itself is fairly straightforward – calling citizens to renounce Philip publically and to remain loyal to the provinces. More significant, however, is the way in which the treatise theorizes about the nature and ends of covenantal oaths in relationship to political authority.

[53]   Kossmann and Mellink, *Texts*, 266–7.
[54]   van Gelderen, *Political Thought*, 157–65; cf. his introduction to *The Dutch Revolt*, xxiv-xxvi.
[55]   John Coffey, "The Language of Liberty in Calvinist Political Thought," in Skinner and van Gelderen, *Freedom*, vol. 1, 308.

The author writes that the political circumstances surrounding the Abjuration make the oath "honest, profitable, righteous, lawful, proper, possible, feasible and . . . necessary." These criteria, corresponding to traditional criteria for just law, show that the oath is the proper means to unite the Dutch people. Appealing to Cicero, the author argues that "maintenance of friendship" is a defense against "eternal slavery."[56] The oath serves to "commit and bind us all" to the common good of the country.[57]

After an extended defense of the necessity of the oath by appeal to authorities as diverse as Aristotle, Cicero, Livy, and the apostle John, the treatise provides a theoretical account of the nature and ends of political life. The discussion begins with the commonplace statement that God himself ordains the nature and end of political governance. In reference to its nature, political governance ought to be distinguished from what it is not: tyranny. Despite formal similarities, therefore, an aristocracy is qualitatively different than oligarchy, a democracy from anarchy. Likewise, in reference to its proper end, we can recognize true political governance through a process of negation. Good governance does not convert the common good into its own property. It does not "misuse the power which is rendered to it, for intemperate and unreasonable desires." It does not "change right into wrong" or "govern at will, as the King of Spain does, when he writes 'for so it pleases us.'"

Citing Augustine's *City of God*, the author goes on to distinguish this conception of arbitrary power, characterized by "lust for dominance," with a conception of authority in which *imperatores* care for the welfare of their subjects. Rightly ordered, the relationship of political command and obedience would produce a mutual benefit. Paraphrasing Seneca, he recalls a golden age in which prudence "nourished" the judgments of wise rulers, "fortitude stemmed adversity, and clemency multiplied and glorified the subjects." In this way, "to rule was an office, not an empire," for political rule "is nothing but to counsel divinely and with justice, and that the sole end of the government consists in the welfare and prosperity of its community and subjects."[58]

For the author, the paradigmatic example of this just political rule is God's own relationship with his people. Before the time of kings and stadholders, he argues, "God's people knew no other king but God." After the establishment of

---

[56] *Political Education* (*Politicq Onderwijs*, Mechelen, 1582), in *The Dutch Revolt*, ed. and trans. Martin van Gelderen (Cambridge: Cambridge University Press, 1993), 172. I rely on van Gelderen's translation of the Dutch text.

[57] *Political Education*, 177.

[58] *Political Education*, 184. Interestingly, Seneca himself indicates that this idealized view of social relations is no longer feasible.

the kingly office, however, the nature of political rule still relates to divine authority. While God has use of "his own jurisdiction, the kings have it from God." At length, the author argues for this point by reference to a series of psalms, proverbs, and narratives from the Hebrew Bible. Against virtuous exemplars such as Solomon, he depicts sundry "Machiavellians" as "courtiers or toadies" who aim to "support kings in their tyranny" by saying that "God has rendered all his power to the kings, retaining heaven for himself."

It is this Machiavellian claim that prompts the author's discussion of a twofold oath – one that has striking parallels with Mornay's discussion of a twofold covenant in the recently published *Vindiciae,* as we will see. All kings "are bound by oath in two respects, first to God and then to the people." Numerous biblical narratives show that all forms of human political rule – whether monarchical or not – rely on this antecedent relationship with God.

What then of broken oaths and covenants? On this matter, the author makes two significant theological arguments. The first relates to the author's distinction between divine and human power, and the second to his conception of natural law and covenantal oaths.

Following an extended discussion of the effects of the inquisition, which the author uses to demonstrate the "miserable slavery" of the Dutch people under Philip's rule, he turns, like Beza, from stories and examples to rational argument. For the reader who is "so blinded by his evil passions" that he is not yet persuaded of the vicious injustice of Spanish rule, the author underscores the most egregious aspect of Philip's tyranny: The inquisition, he claims, revealed Philip's intention to tyrannize not only the external goods of his subjects, but even worse – their very conscience and soul. Violation of bodily goods is a serious injustice, but domination of the rational soul is a violation of an even greater degree. Whenever a king "exploits" his subjects "for slavery, tyranny, or any other form of irrationality," he destroys the very terms of his rule. He violates that which makes individuals human. We can see from scripture, the author continues, that God out of "great mercy and liberality" instituted external relations of command and obedience for our good, but he reserved jurisdiction of the soul for himself. Political governance "has no has command" over this part of the human person. No piece of the soul may be justly rendered to Caesar.[59]

---

[59] *Political Education,* 207–8. Later in this discussion the author makes reference to Spanish tyranny in the Americas. Likely in reference to Bartholome de Las Casas' histories, the author writes that he wishes Dutch proponents of Spanish rule "would reread them often." The accounts of Spanish conquest and tyranny "testify in such a way that even someone with a permanent heart of stone could not read them, without being moved by compassion and pity," 209.

The normative significance of the good and just rule of God becomes even clearer in the author's discussion of the contrast between divine and human justice. Citing Peter Lombard, the author claims that God is the sort of ruler whose judgments are "veracious and just." None of his retributive punishments are issued "without reason." "God himself is bound to fulfill his promises."[60] In contrast to this non-voluntarist paradigm of divine justice, the author turns to a series of examples from sacred and secular history of rulers who assumed that the royal prerogative placed them above the constraining power of their own people. Philip, Pharaoh, Nebuchadnezzar, and Alexander the Great all serve as types of this oath-breaking species of rule. The incongruity is neatly drawn: The reader is prompted to compare these oath-breaking, finite, human sovereigns with the divine sovereign of infinite power who freely chooses to bind himself to his people in covenantal oaths.

In the later sections of *Political Education*, the contrasting examples of divine and human authority relate directly to the concept of natural law and covenantal oaths. Returning to his immediate political concern, the author echoes his earlier claim that the oath of loyalty is both necessary and legitimate, insofar as it satisfies the criteria of just laws: it is "enacted and effectuated for the sake of fairness and utility," it issues from an authoritative agent, and it is both just and in accord with the written laws of God and the unwritten law of nature.[61]

The reference to natural law is worth underscoring, particularly since it occurs at the outset of the concluding section on the relationship between justice and law. According to the author, these latter concepts must be distinguished, even as they are fundamentally related. "One cannot exist without the other. For he who abolishes justice, abolishes the law as well. And where there is no law, justice cannot be found."[62] The precise distinction between the concepts is equally important. For the author, justice regards our obligations in general terms. "Everywhere there is only one justice, namely to live virtuously without hurting the other and to render to everyone what is his." Justice is, quite simply, the first precept of natural law: "to do good, to avoid evil." Law, by comparison, concerns particular judgments made about this norm of justice in particular circumstances. This is why, as the author explains, civil laws vary among various nations. Further, particular applications of the norm of justice require attention to the status of the relevant parties.

---

[60]   *Political Education*, 207.
[61]   *Political Education*, 216.
[62]   *Political Education*, 216.

For instance, the author argues, when considering the legal application of the norm of justice we must recognize when individuals are not in a position to defend themselves against unjust aggressors. This point is quite relevant to his immediate political concerns: The Dutch people at present are not equipped to guard against injustice on their own. One possible solution would be to seek out the protection of another strong prince (several foreign sovereigns were petitioned by the States General, in fact). However, the author suggests that a better solution lies in the oath itself – or rather, in the fellowship the oath is intended to strengthen. In the very writing of the treatise, he aims to "induce the community to the other remedy, namely the animation and creation of unity."[63] Drawing an analogy to a marital oath, the author points out that the establishment of a formal public covenant serves not only as a firm "bond" between parties, but also "causes them greatly to love each other even more."

This theme of covenantal love pervades the concluding pages of *Political Education*. Recalling biblical covenants such as the one made between Abraham and his former rival Abimelech, the author notes "God's people often swear under the kings, when they make a covenant with God to uphold their religion in all purity and piety." This covenantal relationship between God and God's people conditions any authority that kings might claim to hold over their subjects. Not only does God stand as guarantor of the covenant with his people, it is through this covenant that the people themselves acquire standing in their relationship with the king. The covenantal oath offers protection against the threats of kings:

> If God himself, our father Abraham and others, God's people, Paul and other Christians have not objected to taking an oath and to confirming matters by oath, which they intended to complete and uphold, then why should we be ashamed to take an oath of fidelity and to forsake our enemy with it? Unless in our minds we are convinced that we would rather come to be slaves than fight against the king, our mortal enemy.[64]

Even worse, the account continues, those who fail to take the oath betray a lack of love and fidelity, since it is through participating in the covenantal relationship that citizens will be able to manifest these virtuous attitudes toward their neighbors.[65]

---

[63] *Political Education*, 217.

[64] *Political Education*, 218.

[65] In van Gelderen's analysis of this discussion in *Political Education*, he refers to sources and influences such as Roman law, French and Spanish political theorists, and Italian humanists and republicans. However, he does not address the pervasive and explicit theological content

Finally, by creating a community in which love and fidelity may find expression, the oath creates a bond among diverse parties – a theme that Althusius would theorize two decades later: "Just as a man consists of many parts and members, so the community consists of many people and subjects." Within the covenanted community the individuals who would otherwise suffer injustice from the powerful can now band together for mutual support, in order "to defend and stand up for each other in trial and tribulation." Using sacramental language, the author writes that an oath is "an indubitable external sign" of what the heart wants, loves, and intends to preserve – in this instance, the wellbeing of the Dutch people.[66] Only by publically entering into this relationship, as did the people of Israel under King Josiah, will there be

> a lovely resonance in the common good. With all misunderstanding taken away and all pettiness averted, each will serve his office and duty properly. The government will order godly, rightly and lawfully, and the subjects will obey what is honest, profitable and agreeable, to the inexpressible delight of all inhabitants, insofar as after a good war a constant and permanent peace can be expected.[67]

Otherwise, the inevitable result would be "eternal slavery."[68]

---

and connotations of the covenantal themes and concepts in the treatise. van Gelderen, *Political Thought*, 162–4.

[66] *Political Education*, 221.

[67] *Political Education*, 222.

[68] *Political Education*, 223. While the conceptual and chronological scope of Jonathan Israel's history of the Dutch Republic outstretches my present concerns, my reading of *Political Education* and related texts reveal two specific points of overlap and difference between his account and mine. First, Israel assumes that there were two dichotomous motivations for the Dutch Revolt. The orthodox Reformed saw it as a "struggle about religion, for the 'true faith.'" By contrast, for the Dutch nobles, it "was a struggle for freedom from oppression and tyranny." *Dutch Republic*, 369. As I have argued, this dichotomy is overdrawn. Leading Dutch nobles, such as William, consulted with orthodox Reformed theologians in order to articulate the grounds for resistance, and many of the most influential political treatises employed deeply theological language in their discussions of freedom, domination, and covenantal right order. Second, it is notable that Israel almost completely omits reference to the significance of covenant or the development of covenant theology (although he does attend to other doctrinal *loci*, such as predestination). Covenant theology makes a brief appearance in Israel's discussion of late-seventeenth-century confessionalization. He claims that later disputes over covenant pertained were confined "to the theological sphere" (666). This interpretation is representative of Israel's inclination to bracket theological matters. On matters related to the present chapter, Israel makes one brief reference to Mornay (as a counselor to William) and the *Vindiciae*, but makes no mention of the central theological concepts or arguments of the treatise, 210–11. Loyseleur de Villiers is not mentioned at all. He does not indicate that Marnix studied theology in Geneva. Nor does he mention the theological arguments in *Political*

It is important to notice that for the anonymous author of *Political Education* the nature and ends of a covenantal oath had clear and immediate political connotations. Just as in the mutual pacts made by Hebrew patriarchs, judges, kings, and subjects, Dutch citizens were prompted to recognize the great good that would result from a formal covenantal relationship. Insofar as this unity and fellowship among Dutch citizens was perceived to be under threat, the fledging people should agree to particular covenantal bonds, terms, laws, or conditions to ensure that all would continue to participate in the common good.

This conception of covenant and covenantal laws reveals many influences – theological, biblical, and jurisprudential. It also quite clearly displays the contingent nature of the political crisis facing the provinces after the Abjuration. The covenantal language that pervades the treatise, particularly toward the conclusion, reflects the ways in which the concept of covenant was recognized as a useful paradigm for theorizing about the nature of political life and law in general. In even more fundamental terms, this aspect of Reformed political thought is evident in the influential treatise of another counselor of William of Orange, the Huguenot theologian and political polemicist Philippe de Mornay.

Vindiciae Contra Tyrannos

Unlike several of the theological and political treatises discussed so far, Mornay's[69] *Vindiciae contra tyrannos* has elicited a fair amount of recent

---

Education. While Israel's history of the Revolt remains one of the best and most comprehensive recent accounts, oversights such as these indicate that the neat dichotomy between theology and politics must be revised. Coffey makes a similar point in "The Language of Liberty in Calvinist Political Thought."

[69] The authorship of the *Vindiciae* is a matter of centuries-long scholarly debate. At present, most scholars identify Mornay as the primary or exclusive author. However, opinion has varied ever since the treatise was published. In addition to Mornay, other associates of William of Orange have been considered possible candidates, including Johan Junius de Jonghe or Mornay's mentor, Hubert Languet. Mornay's wife, Charlotte Duplessis-Mornay, seems to indicate that Mornay wrote the treatise during a stay in Jametz in 1574, *A Huguenot Family in the XVI Century: The Memoirs of Philippe de Mornay, Written by His Wife,* trans. Lucy Crump (London: Routledge, 1926), 139. More recently, some scholars have suggested that Mornay and Languet worked in concert, a hypothesis that seems quite plausible, since both were likely traveling with William at the time. This hypothesis is preferred by George Garnett, *Vindiciae Contra Tyrannos,* ed. and trans. George Garnett (Cambridge: Cambridge University Press, 2003), lxxvi. While acknowledging that Mornay's mentor may have had some role in penning the treatise, I will follow the consensus opinion and refer to Mornay as the author throughout. See Beatrice Nicollier De Weck's analysis of Languet's possible involvement, *Hubert Languet* (Geneva: Librairie Droz, 1995) 465–87.

attention from a variety of sources. Scholars of early modern English prose and poetry have noted its significance,[70] while others have written about the ways in which the *Vindiciae* reflects the influence of an international community of Protestant humanists, including Philip and Mary Sydney, Charlotte Duplessis-Mornay, Hubert Languet, Bullinger, Ursinus, and Beza.[71] Interestingly, historical theologians have paid less attention to the treatise, despite its extensive use of theological concepts and biblical references.[72]

For historians of political thought, the *Vindiciae* has played a prominent role in the development of modern secular political theory – albeit a confounding one. Political historians often identify two particular conceptual tensions in the treatise. The first tension, associated with the secular republican interpretation of Skinner and others, concerns the alleged secularizing nature of covenantal law. The second tension, associated with the contractarian interpretation, concerns the fictional nature of the original covenant or contract. Before turning to the *Vindiciae* itself, I need to provide some context for these conceptual tensions.

Near the end of his *Foundations*, Skinner suggests that Mornay and other Huguenot theorists mark a turning point in early modern political thought. While earlier Reformed thinkers had advanced *theological* views of authority and resistance, the political crises in France and the Netherlands pressed Beza, Mornay, and other Protestants to turn to "scholastic and Roman law traditions of radical constitutionalism." This move entailed a rejection of

> the characteristically Protestant tendency to suppose that God places all men in a condition of political subjection as a remedy for their sins. Instead they began to argue that the original and fundamental condition of the people must be one of natural liberty. This in turn enabled them to abandon the orthodox Pauline contention that all the powers that be must be seen as directly ordained by God. Instead they inferred that any legitimate political society must originate in an act of free consent on the part of the whole populace.[73]

---

[70] Robert Stillman, *Philip Sidney and the Poetics of Renaissance Cosmopolitanism* (Burlington, VT: Ashgate, 2008).

[71] See De Weck on the *Vindiciae*, 465–87; also the index of correspondence, 489–614. *The Correspondence of Philip Sidney and Hubert Languet*, William A. Bradley, ed. (Boston: Merrymount Press, 1912); Tracey Sedinger, "Sidney's 'New Arcadia' and the Decay of Protestant Republicanism," *Studies in English Literature 1500–1900* 47:1 (Winter 2007): 57–77; and Elizabeth Pentland, "Philippe Mornay, Mary Sidney, and the Politics of Translation," *Early Modern Studies Journal* 6 (2014): 66–98.

[72] Southworth's unpublished dissertation is an exception that proves the rule.

[73] Skinner, *Foundations*, vol. 2, 320.

Still, Skinner acknowledges that some theological commitments lingered within Huguenot political writings even after the St. Bartholomew's Day Massacre. In particular, he points to Mornay's *Vindiciae* as a paradigmatic example of a Protestant political theory which tried to patch together "two quite different views of the nature of the covenant," one theological and one political. In reality, Skinner argues, the two views of covenant were "barely compatible." The political conception of covenant was tied up with a conception of authority that arises from the consent of the people. The theological conception of covenant, by contrast, was grounded in a conception of authority that arises from a relationship among God, the king, and the people.[74] Skinner characterizes this conceptual tension as the difference between a secular contract (*pactum*) and a religious covenant (*foedus*).[75] While the tension destabilizes Mornay's political theory, the development of the secular conception of contract and authority was itself an

> epoch-making move from a purely religious theory of resistance, depending on the idea of a covenant to uphold the laws of God, to a genuinely political theory of revolution, based on the idea of a contract which gives rise to a moral right (and not merely a religious duty) to resist any ruler who fails in his corresponding obligation to pursue the welfare of the people in all his public acts.[76]

Despite the counter-criticisms offered by scholars such as Carlos Eire[77] and Anne McLaren,[78] this particular reading of early Protestant political thought

---

[74]   Skinner, *Foundations*, vol. 2, 325.

[75]   Skinner, *Foundations*, vol. 2, 331.

[76]   Skinner, *Foundations*, vol. 2, 335.

[77]   Carlos Eire, *War Against the Idols: The Reformation of Worship from Erasmus to Calvin* (Cambridge: Cambridge University Press, 1989), 305–10. Eire counters Skinner's claim that there was nothing particularly Calvinistic about resistance theory by focusing on the importance of idolatry to the treatises. The preoccupation with idolatry, Eire argues, was clearly associated with typically Reformed theological concerns. I am arguing that the centrality of covenantal theological language offers a parallel corrective to Skinner.

[78]   Anne McLaren, "Rethinking Republicanism: *Vindiciae Contra Tyrannos* in Context," *The Historical Journal* 49:1 (March 2006): 23–52. McLaren argues that Skinner habitually glosses over the biblical citations and allusions in the *Vindiciae* while underscoring classical Roman and medieval jurisprudential sources, even when they seem peripheral to the argument. McLaren does not have much to say about the implications of the biblical material, or the treatise's relationship to the Reformed theological context. As Garnett's response has indicated, she also overstates her case when she argues for "the relative and absolute insignificance" of jurisprudential sources by comparison to the "absolute dominance" of scriptural references (32–3). Garnett argues that McLaren's methodology is flawed, both in the way that she chose to measure legal and biblical citations, and in her peculiar choice to focus on the reception history of the treatise in seventeenth-century England. George Garnett, "Law in the *Vindiciae, Contra Tyrannos*: A Vindication," *The Historical Journal* 49:3 (September 2006):

has remained in circulation. For instance, van Gelderen cites Skinner's claim while suggesting that the epoch-making turn toward secular theory was made by *both* French and Dutch Protestants.[79] Likewise, von Friedeburg applies Skinner's *pactum/foedus* dichotomy to Althusius' consociational view of political life (a misinterpretation I will address in chapter five).[80]

The second conceptual difficulty identified in the *Vindiciae* concerns the seemingly fictive nature of a founding social contract. The quandary is one that has occupied exegetes of the *Vindiciae* for many decades. In his chapter on monarchomach resistance theories, John Neville Figgis provided a blistering critique of the notion of a founding covenant or contract: "it is unhistorical, abstract and self-contradictory." It posits a legal fiction as the grounds for all political life and authority and contravenes "all our notions of political organisms and public utility." How could we say all government arises from a covenant or contract, Figgis asks, when there is no sovereign or antecedent authority in existence to make the covenant binding in the first place? The very notion of a founding covenant introduces a circular argument.[81] Even worse, the incoherence of the concept provides cover for all manner of political tyranny, since "a prince might easily keep his contract and yet be a tyrant, e.g., Philip II in Spain."[82]

877–91. At the same time, neither Garnett nor McLaren attend to the nuances of Reformed covenantal thought on the continent at the time the *Vindiciae* was written. If McLaren had analyzed the original theological context for the *Vindiciae*, and the importance of covenantal thought to Reformed intellectual life in Mornay's world, she might not have left herself open to several of Garnett's criticisms. This is unfortunate, since her overall point against Skinner and Garnett's reflexive secular republican interpretation remains viable, as I indicate below. Cf. the criticisms of Harro Höpfl and Annabel Brett, who have each objected to Skinner's use of the terms "scholastic" and "scholasticism," his account of the development of a state-of-nature doctrine, the lack of attention to political prudence (Höpfl), and the tendency to dichotomize Thomist Aristotelianism and civic republicanism (Brett). Annabel Brett, "Scholastic Political Thought and the Modern Concept of the State," and Harro Höpfl, "Scholasticism in Quentin Skinner's Foundations," in Annabel Brett and James Tully, eds., *Rethinking the Foundations of Modern Political Thought* (Cambridge: Cambridge University Press, 2007) Specifically on the matter of Skinner's secularist readings, see John Coffey, "Quentin Skinner and the Religious Dimension of Early Modern Political Thought," in Alister Chapman, John Coffey, and Brad Gregory, eds., *Seeing Things Their Way: Intellectual History and the Return of Religion* (Notre Dame, IN: University of Notre Dame Press, 2009).

[79] Van Gelderen, *Political Thought*, 275–6.

[80] Friedeburg, *Self-Defence*, 112.

[81] The question of circularity later applies to strains of social contractarian theory, and is perhaps most importantly figured in the mythical Lawgiver of Rousseau's *Social Contract*. See Martin Loughlin's helpful analysis in *The Foundations of Public Law* (Oxford: Oxford University Press, 2010), 112–17.

[82] John Neville Figgis, *Studies of Political Thought from Gerson to Grotius, 1414–1625* (Cambridge: Cambridge University Press, 1907), 148.

Along similar lines, Skinner's predecessor J. W. Allen argued that the covenant in the *Vindiciae* is a conceptual façade. It would seem to imply some constitutive and "deliberate act of will," since a *pactum* ordinarily arises from the consent of the parties involved. However, the covenantal relationship always already exists for the individuals involved. "There is, really, nothing voluntary about it." The political covenant is not the product of human willing; it "expresses nothing but the immutable will of God." According to Allen, then, it is "not very clear" why Mornay employed covenantal language. Since there was no real historical covenant between human parties, why call it a covenant in the first place?[83]

In sum, there is a perception that the *Vindiciae* suffers from a fundamental incoherence, or at least conceptual instability, in its theorization of covenant and covenantal law. First, it employs contradictory accounts of authority. Second, under the auspices of a fictional original *pactum*, it feigns at providing an account of popular consent, but in reality resorts to a theocratic and hierarchical view of political order. It should be noted that both of these readings argue that the *Vindiciae* fails to hold together on account of residual theological commitments. Skinner, Allen, and other political historians have set out to disentangle the theological and political threads, perhaps hoping to recover the secular kernel from the theological shell. In what follows, I will not follow suit, principally on the grounds that Mornay himself saw no need to, and likely would have regarded such an effort as useless – and no doubt impious.

Even if Mornay had not studied at Heidelberg – one of the intellectual hubs of covenant theology in the late-sixteenth century – it should not be surprising that a Reformed Protestant in the late-sixteenth century employed covenantal language in a treatise about (unnamed) rulers who had broken faith with their subjects. Mornay and his mentor Languet, as we have seen, were at the center of Protestant political thought and action, both in France and the Netherlands. Mornay was himself a survivor of the St. Bartholomew's Day Massacre, and subsequently served as an ambassador for the Huguenot cause in England and with William of Orange. It was in this context that the *Vindiciae* was written.[84]

---

[83]   Allen, *A History of Political Thought*, 319. As we have already seen in some detail, Victoria Kahn relies on a similar reading of the nature vs. fictive nature of political covenants in *Wayward Contracts*.

[84]   In addition to the *Vindiciae*, scholars attribute a handful of anonymous treatises on religious toleration to Mornay. He was also well known among his contemporaries for his theological writings on ecclesiology (Traicté de l'église [Geneva 1577]), the "iniquitous" history of the

Mornay's account of covenant and law in the *Vindiciae* follows many of the patterns we have seen among Reformed theologians and political thinkers. Like Beza, Mornay's first *quaestio* concerns the relationship between divine and human law: "Whether subjects be bound, or ought, to obey princes if they command anything against the law of God." Mornay's response echoes that of his coreligionists: Only the will of God is perpetually just, while the human will often fails to accord with this norm of justice. Therefore, only the command of the God whose will accords with justice should be obeyed without exception. Those princes who "arrogate to themselves immense power which is not derived from God" lack authority to demand obedience.[85] When princes unjustly demand such obedience, individuals ought to imitate the examples of Christ and the Christian martyrs, who were called traitors to the commonwealth despite the justice of their cause.

Like Beza and other Reformed theologians, Mornay posits that while God's jurisdiction and power (*potentia*) are infinite, the same cannot be true of human rulers. God's authority accords with his own creation of, and care for, the world and its inhabitants. Human authority, by contrast, is constrained by certain boundaries, insofar as earthly rulers are simply stewards who must render account (*rationem reddere*, as in Beza) to the true proprietor of creation.[86]

Drawing on language that is found in the earliest Reformed writings of Oecolampadius, Musculus, and others, Mornay makes the claim that the *populus* itself is the eternal inheritance of God (*populus ipse, Dei populus et hereditas perpetuo dicitur*). Correspondingly, the king is rightly described as the administrator of God's inheritance. Mornay here introduces the concept of covenant to describe the relationship between the divine sovereign and the "pious" royal administrators. This political covenant arises from an antecedent relationship between God and the people: "When this covenant is confirmed (*sancitur foedus*) between God and king, it is confirmed on the condition that the people should be and perpetually remain the people of God."[87]

As other scholars have noted, the covenants described in the *Vindiciae* invoke a familiar feudal relationship:[88] The king functions as a vassal of the

papacy (Mornay's Latin title does not lack for spiritedness: *Mysterium iniquitatis, seu Historia papatus* [Saumur 1611]), and natural theology (*De la verité de la religion chrestienne* [French edition 1581; Latin 1583]), all of which – unlike the *Vindiciae* and the treatises on toleration – were published under his own name.

85 *Vindiciae contra tyrannos* (Edinburgh 1579), 2. Cf. George Garnett, ed. and trans., *Vindiciae Contra Tyrannos* (Cambridge: Cambridge University Press, 1994), 14. I reference the 1579 Latin edition published in Edinburgh, as does Garnett's translation.

86 *Vindiciae*, 6 (Garnett, 17).

87 *Vindiciae*, 7–8 (Garnett, 18).

88 Oestreich, *Neostoicism*, 138–40, 144–8.

divine sovereign. If he violates the terms of his oath or covenant with his lord, the king may lose his right to the kingdom.[89] In addition to these feudal terms, Mornay makes dozens of biblical and theological references, most prominently, to narratives of the kings and prophets of Israel and Judah.

It is one of these biblical narratives that Mornay uses to introduce the twofold political covenant for which the *Vindiciae* is best known. The sequence of this twofold covenant is significant. The first part consists in the covenantal relationship and obligations that obtain among God, the king, and God's people. Prior to the establishment of any particular social order or political administration, all human parties participate in this fellowship with God; the terms of the relationship are such that the people are obligated to render due worship and honor to their divine sovereign. The second part of the twofold covenant arises from the first and concerns the arrangement of relationship between the king and God's people. Here, Mornay cites 2 Kings 23, arguing that the king and people of Israel covenanted together with God to preserve the purity of divine worship. In this manner, the covenant, and the sworn oath that attended it, served to maintain the law of God.[90]

Like earlier covenant theologians, Mornay acknowledges that the external forms (*forma*) of covenantal relations described in the Hebrew Bible and New Testament change over time. However, the nature and ends of the covenantal relationship remain constant. Theologians such as Calvin, Bullinger, and Olevianus described this in terms of *substantia* versus *accidens*: The substance of the covenant remained constant even as particular elements and arrangements shifted over time.[91] The *ratio* or *finis* of the covenant – fellowship with God – would not and could not change, since God was its guarantor. On these same lines, Mornay argues that Christian kings (and heathen kings to some degree) are bound to the same terms as kings of ancient Israel.[92] After all, he argues, all earthly rulers receive their *potentia* from the divine sovereign, even if there is no official anointing.

Mornay's brief mention of heathen kings and their covenantal status is underdeveloped. He does not explain precisely the nature of the relationship between God and pagan rulers who had never heard the name of the God of

---

[89]   *Vindiciae*, 11 (Garnett, 20–1).

[90]   *Vindiciae*, 12 (Garnett, 22).

[91]   For example, see Calvin's commentary on Galatians 4:1; Heinrich Bullinger, *De Testamento Seu Foedere Dei Unico et Aeterno* (Zurich, 1534), 28; Caspar Olevianus, *De Substantia Foederis Gratuiti inter Deum et Electos* (Geneva, 1585).

[92]   *Vindiciae*, 18 (Garnett, 25).

the covenants, let alone sworn an oath of fealty to him.[93] As we will see later, Althusius' discussion of sacred and secular covenants attempts to provide a more coherent solution to this problem. At present, however, Mornay's discussion of heathen kings is notable insofar as it introduces his theological anthropology. Similar to the account in *Political Education*, Mornay writes that human persons are "made up of body and soul." Since God formed the body and "infused the soul," only he has the highest right over them.[94] Kings are granted the authority over the bodies and goods of their subjects only for their preservation. While their use is permitted to this end, their abuse – by definition – is not (*usum non abusum concedi*).[95]

Mornay's account of justice and covenantal law continues in the third *quaestio* when he inquires into the purpose or end (*finis*) of kings. He notes, "something is only considered just and good when it achieves that end for which it is instituted."[96] On this account, the royal office must have been instituted for the sake of some "great advantage." After all, since persons are free by nature (*homines natura liberi*), they would not have chosen to submit themselves to the rule of kings unless it was in pursuit of some other good end.

By theorizing political life on these terms, Mornay also characterizes the nature of a political command in a normative manner. Paraphrasing Augustine, Mornay writes that good rulers do not command out of desire for domination. In fact, a command is nothing other than to show concern or provide counsel.

Notably, the passage from Augustine concerns the ways in which God's eternal law providentially orders all manner of human relations.[97] Mornay's account follows Augustine's, pivoting from his description of political command to a more general account of law itself. Most fundamentally, he argues, law is "a sort of instrument (*organum*), divinely given, by which human societies are best directed and ordered to a blessed end."[98] As with Zanchi and other Reformed theologians,

---

[93] Setting aside the question of authorship, a fuller analysis of this point would likely need to account for Mornay's natural theology, as presented in *De la vérité de la religion chrestienne*.

[94] The Latin is "utroque ergo optimo iure uti solus poterat." Garnett translates *optimo iure* as "absolute right," which is somewhat misleading, as *optimum* is the superlative of *bonum*. In Roman law, full citizenship was associated with *civis optimo iure*, a status distinct from citizenship that did not permit enjoyment of certain goods or rights. Cf. George Mousourakis, *Roman Law and the Origins of the Civil Law Tradition* (New York, NY: Springer, 2015), 101–2.

[95] *Vindiciae*, 20 (Garnett, 27).

[96] *Vindiciae*, 107 (Garnett, 92).

[97] Garnett argues that Mornay distorts Augustine's meaning, 93n165. Relying on R. A. Markus' reading of Augustine, he claims that the passage from Augustine concerns a conception of "natural authority" that no longer holds true of human orders after the fall. It should simply be noted that this is a contested interpretation of Augustine.

[98] *Vindiciae*, 114–15 (Garnett, 97).

Mornay's account of law doubles as an account of human rationality. He writes: Law might be defined as "the reason and wisdom of many prudent men gathered together as one." It is the means by which humanity participates in God's judgments and providential rule: It is "is a mind, or rather, a congregated multitude of minds. For the mind is a particle of the divine breath, and he who submits to the law is considered to submit to God and, after a certain manner, to make God his judge."[99]

The reference to a "particle of divine breath" derives from one of Horace's satires, although it was also a commonplace that many early modern theologians used to describe the gift of human rationality. Martin Bucer employed it in his 1536 commentary on Romans, adding that the human mind is a "continual *actus* depending on God as a day on the sun, a river on the spring."[100] Erasmus had strikingly described God's creation of Adam as involving the bestowal of reason: "First Adam was formed from clay, his mind endowed with divine breath."[101] Intriguingly, the phrase appeared in a March 1578 letter from Philip Sidney to Hubert Languet.[102] Later Reformed covenant theologians used it as well.[103]

For Mornay, describing law in these terms serves a particular purpose. Right human action is that which accords with the law that participates in God's rule over the world. On this account, he argues, placing "the law over the commonwealth" is tantamount to setting "God over the commonwealth." By contrast, as Mornay cites Aristotle, when individuals chose to "obey the king rather than the law" they act against the rational principles of human nature, preferring "the command of a beast to that of a god." Placing the king above

---

[99]   *Vindiciae*, 116 (Garnett, 98).

[100] Martin Bucer, *Metaphrases et Enarrationes Perpetuae Epistolarum D. Pauli Apostoli* (1536), 85. See Brian Lugioyo, *Martin Bucer's Doctrine of Justification* (Oxford: Oxford University Press, 2010), 55–9. Cf. Stephen Gardiner's "Answer to Bucer," in P. Janelle, ed., *Obedience in Church and State: Three Political Tracts* (Cambridge: Cambridge University Press, 1930), 199.

[101] From Erasmus' *Paraphrase* of 1 Corinthians 11:8.

[102] An excerpt: "For to what purpose should our thoughts be directed to various kinds of knowledge, unless room be afforded for putting it into practice, so that public advantage may be the result, which in a corrupt age we cannot hope for? Who would learn music except for the sake of giving pleasure or architecture except with a view to building? But the mind itself you will say that particle of the divine mind is cultivated in this manner. This indeed if we allow it to be the case is a very great advantage but let us see whether we are not giving a beautiful but false appearance to our splendid errors," *Correspondence of Sir Philip Sidney and Hubert Languet*, 143. To my knowledge, no other scholarly work has drawn attention to the appearance of this phrase in Languet's correspondence.

[103] Cf. Francis Turretin's allusion, which appears in his *quaestio* on pagan virtue, *Institutio Theologiae Elencticae* (Geneva, 1688), I.10.q5; also see Herman Witsius' suspicion of the phrase as used by unnamed heretics who confused divine and human essences, *The Economy of the Covenants Between God and Man* (1677), III.14.15.

the commonwealth is in effect rejecting the divine gift of rationality and law in favor of bestial nature.[104] Worse still are the "impious conceits (*impia nugamenta*) of court flatterers" who argue that the king "makes something just or unjust by commanding thus or otherwise, as if he were God, who cannot sin in any way."[105] Certainly, Mornay adds, whatever God wills is just, inasmuch as God wills it.[106] As he adds later, God "never deviates from justice in anything."[107] This hardly holds true for human kings, however, who habitually deviate from the perfect and perpetual norm of divine justice.

The account of authority and law offered by Mornay echoes many of the statements and assumptions of his fellow Reformed theologians and political thinkers. However, his use of the concept of covenant to theorize the nature and end of political life seems to introduce a subtle shift in the traditional discourse about the topic. On this matter, Höpfl and Thompson write that, in comparison to earlier Reformed political thinkers, Mornay "used an idiosyncratic explanation of the scriptural covenant as a model of right order."[108] While Höpfl and Thompson aptly relate the concept of covenant to a normative standard of right order, it is not so clear that Mornay was being idiosyncratic. After all, if we place Mornay among his fellow Reformed theologians, the structure of his account should by now appear rather familiar: He asserts that the eternally good and just divine ruler holds sovereign right (*summum ius*) over his inheritance – his creation and creatures. In order that his creatures might enjoy fellowship with him, this divine sovereign freely entered into covenant with them. Further, so that his covenanted people might better understand how to act justly toward God and neighbor, God gave his law, specifying how they might attain their true and blessed end. This law accords with the norm of justice. By implication, as we have seen, those earthly rulers who command against this norm of justice are in fact issuing non-binding commands. Quite directly, the second part of Mornay's twofold

[104]   *Vindiciae*, 116–17 (Garnett, 98).
[105]   *Vindiciae*, 118 (Garnett, 99).
[106]   The Latin is: "Certe iustum est, quicquid Deus vult, eo tantum, quia vult." Garnett's translation implies a voluntarist conception of divine willing: "Certainly, whatever God wishes is just, is so simply because He wishes it." While it is possible that Mornay adopts voluntarist language here while explicitly rejecting it elsewhere, it seems better to correct Garnett's translation. The phrase *eo tantum* does not provide sufficient support for a causal relationship between the divine will and justice. Rather, Mornay seems to be employing a tautology, as my translation conveys. In effect, Mornay's reader should assume that whatever God wills is just precisely because it is in God's nature to will that which is just. As Mornay stresses throughout, the divine sovereign does not command arbitrarily, unlike many earthly princes.
[107]   *Vindiciae*, 214 (Garnett, 171).
[108]   Höpfl and Thompson, "History of Contract," 930.

covenant applies the terms and structure of covenant theology to the political relationship that (he believes) was initiated by God between the *populus* and its kings.

Within this framework, covenantal language provided Mornay and many of his contemporaries a set of terms adequate to explain what had gone wrong during a period of profound political crisis. Earthly rulers had broken faith with their people. The people could recognize the reality of this broken relationship by reference to the antecedent covenantal relationship they enjoyed with God himself. As it was conceived, therefore, covenant resonated with core Reformed theological commitments about the goodness and fidelity of the divine sovereign, as well as the nature and purported ends of political community – the prospects for unity, fulfilled obligations, and the proper coordination of command and obedience.

All of this bears on the charges of conceptual incoherence introduced by the secular republican and contractarian readings. The secular republican reading of the *Vindiciae*, and of early modern Protestant political thought in general, fails to account for the manifold resonance of covenant. In particular, Skinner's introduction of a dichotomy between a religious *foedus* (between God and the people) and a political *pactum* (between the people and the king) lacks textual support. First, and most simply, Mornay uses the terms themselves interchangeably throughout the treatise; as with covenant theologians, *foedus* and *pactum* operate as synonyms. Second, on a more conceptual level, it appears that Mornay's account of the twofold nature of the covenant evades Skinner's more fundamental criticism. While Skinner argues that the religious and secular covenants are each grounded on corresponding religious and secular sources of authority – namely, divine will or human consent – he fails to account for Mornay's more nuanced conception of political agency. As Garnett quite rightly points out, the first covenant between God and the people is what grants the *populus* the "authority and capacity" to promise and fulfill the terms of the subsequent covenant. That is to say, the *populus* acquires political agency through its participation in, and recognition of, the antecedent relationship with God. The terms of this relationship are fulfilled through obedience to the perfect law of God. Further, the *populus* acquires the right to hold the king accountable to the terms of covenantal law (and vice versa, of course). As Mornay argues: "God would surely not have confirmed a covenant with one who had no right to promise or fulfill what had been promised." The people do not have the status of slaves, after all.[109]

---

[109]   *Vindiciae*, 40 (Garnett, 41).

This aspect of the *Vindiciae* also addresses the charge that Mornay's political covenant provides only a pretense of agency to the *populus*, and instead reverts to a theocratic and hierarchical conception of authority based on divine authority and power. This charge is accurate on one point: the authority of a perfectly just God is intrinsically related to Mornay's account of popular consent in the political order. Mornay, like Beza and other Reformed theologians, does not advance a doctrine of popular consent that is abstracted from broader concerns about justice, which is itself related to his conception of the nature and authority of God.[110]

But there is more to say; facile charges of theocracy do not do justice to Mornay's account. Most importantly, Mornay claims that all members of the community, rulers and subjects, acquire political agency and authority through the antecedent covenantal relationship with God. The whole *populus*, after all, is God's inheritance. It belongs to him and it comes to recognize what is good and just through the revelation of God's law in the covenantal relationship. The purpose of the second part of the twofold covenant, Mornay holds, is to establish mutual accountability among the various parties to the covenant. Using striking terms, he states that the covenant among God, the king, and the people helps to spread the risk among unreliable debtors. In this way "the two parties – the king and Israel [which, according to Mornay, is the *populus* in the Old Covenant] ... are equally bound for the whole matter" (*aequaliter in solidum obligantur*). The co-debtors in the covenantal relationship bear responsibility to bring action against their faithless partner; otherwise judgment would fall on all alike.[111]

---

[110] This aspect of Mornay's account offers an important response to Daniel Lee's argument that monarchomach theories of law and sovereignty are "positively dangerous," since they "remove the concept of the political entirely from concepts of the state and sovereignty" and attribute "to the state a totalizing power that can be just as despotic in the hands of the people as it is in the hands of kings." A subsequent chapter will address this matter in the more sophisticated account offered by Althusius. However, contra Lee, even in the *Vindiciae* it is clear that the power of the *populus* is not arbitrary or unmoored from broader conceptions of justice and right order. Further, Lee's claim that monarchomach theories such as Mornay's de-politicize the concept of law and sovereignty can only stand insofar as the covenantal relationships and theological commitments are ignored. The antecedent fellowship with God conditions the terms of political agency and authority. See Daniel Lee, "Private Law Models for Public Law Concepts: The Roman Law Theory of Dominium in the Monarchomach Doctrine of Popular Sovereignty," *The Review of Politics* 70:3 (Summer 2008): 370–99.

[111] *Vindiciae*, 37–8 (Garnett, 39–40).

CONCLUSION: THEOLOGICAL COMMITMENTS AND
POLITICAL CONCEPTIONS

The implications of this reading extend beyond the *Vindiciae* to the various conceptions of covenant and covenantal law examined throughout this chapter. According to Mornay, Beza, and others, neither popular consent nor a founding social contract is sufficient to judge the rightness of particular arrangements of political life. Rather, we can recognize a good political order by whether it accords with the terms of an antecedent covenantal relationship. For Mornay and other covenant theologians, this antecedent relationship is constituted by the express desire of the divine sovereign to make his creatures his beloved people, and to provide them with rational principles and laws that direct them toward a good and blessed end. Earthly rulers and subjects ought to imitate this example of loving command and obedience, as ordered to the norm of justice.

On these terms, it is evident that the theological commitments of these early Reformed theorists were not ancillary to their political conceptions of covenant, law, justice, right order, or any number of related terms. In fact, the entire covenantal argument for right order depends on the fact that theological and political commitments were integral to one another. It was entirely possible for the early Reformed to conceive of one's relationship to divine and human sovereigns as pertaining to distinct interests, communities, and common goods – some eternal and some temporal. Clearly, what one owes to God will differ from what one owes to one's king, let alone to one's friend, neighbor, stranger, or enemy. At the same time, these various spiritual and temporal relationships and obligations rely on analogous sets of concepts and arguments about what constitutes true justice and right order. As we have seen repeatedly, Reformed theologians and political thinkers believed that human relationships ought to be the *imago et documentum* of eternal life. The fact that the divine sovereign chose to bind himself in covenants to his people only strengthens this belief. The Reformed make an *a fortiori* argument: If the divine sovereign chose to "follow human custom" (as Bullinger wrote) by covenanting with his people, how much more ought earthly sovereigns to follow suit. In this way, the *populus Dei* has a perfect exemplar of loving, virtuous rule. By reference to the faithful love and commands of the divine sovereign, citizens of the heavenly commonwealth have reasons to denounce the impiety and domination intrinsic to so many earthly commonwealths.

All of this complicates several of our received notions about the development of modern secular political thought. While much recent Anglophone scholarship has operated on the assumption that the theological and secular strands of early modern political thought can – and ought to be – disentangled, the concept of covenant complicates that project. For early Reformed theorists, theological language and arguments could be applied to a variety of political concepts. At the same time, these theologians and polemicists deployed classical republican language about liberty, *ius*, and the *bonum commune* in service of describing the legal and covenantal relationship between God and God's people, God and the ruler, and the ruler and God's people. At the very least, we must doubt whether the concept's secular kernel can simply shed its theological shell with little loss of meaning.

By recognizing early modern theological discourse as an important source of political thought, we are better equipped – even at the distance of several centuries – to understand why the concept of covenant had such a magical ring to certain ears. As we will see in the following chapters, the covenantal arguments deployed by Mornay and others became touchstones for subsequent Protestant political thought. For some thinkers, such as Althusius, the covenant would become a central feature of a comprehensive consociational account of political life. For others, the conception of covenant advanced by Mornay, Althusius, and others would represent one of the basest and most dangerous forms of political impiety.

4

The Unaccountable Sovereign

Rival Theological Accounts of Law and Political Agency

Away with those mousetraps of yours, unless they catch blind shrew-mice. Has anyone ever been so impious or impudent, if he held to any religion, who thought a people so bound and tied to kings that it is obligated to let kings carry it off to strange gods . . . ? There is no sane man that does not proclaim that the people can and ought to make good its promises and fulfill all the obligations of the covenant with God. But in this matter there is no need at all for the people to have power and jurisdiction over the prince; it was not comprehended in the covenant, nor does God exact it — that the people by force and arms lead back into the way a king who hunts after devious paths and insane errors.

William Barclay, *De regno et regali potestate* (1600)

In the final decades of the sixteenth century, Reformed political writings are emblematic of the ways that early modern thinkers could apply theological concepts to political norms and relations. As we have seen, Reformed thinkers adapted the concept of covenant – familiar to theologians and jurists alike – to reflect on the nature of law, authority, and the common good in political life. By the end of the century, this strand of covenantal discourse began to encounter direct challenges. Early modern critics linked Philippe de Mornay's *Vindiciae contra tyrannos* and Theodore Beza's *De jure magistratuum* to other seditious works, sometimes called monarchomach – or king-fighter – treatises. Theorists such as Alberico Gentili, William Barclay, and Henning Arnisaeus argued that the conception of law embedded in the monarchomach treatises was impious – with respect to God as well as the royal office. Further, critics condemned the notion of a double covenant between God and the people, on one side, and God, the king, and the people, on the other. The double covenant, they argued, entailed a dangerous conception of the norms and relations of political life. The covenant, as a political doctrine, was heretical.

The dispute between the monarchomachs and their critics gives rise to a series of conceptual complications. In what follows, I will show how rival absolutist conceptions of covenant and law rely on theological commitments about the relationship between command and obedience, and between divine and human authority. Both sides in the dispute had determinate conceptions of political piety, and what pious political acts ought to look like. Both sides took themselves to be applying theological norms to political relations in a way that justified a specific social order. We will see how the theological commitments and assumptions of these rival views are key to understanding the political debate. Further, by analyzing the theological terms of disagreement between the monarchomachs and their rivals, we will better understand the context for the consociational theory of Johannes Althusius, to which we turn next.

A RIVAL ACCOUNT: THEOLOGICAL AND REGAL VOLUNTARISM

When William Barclay coined the term "monarchomach" in 1600, he compacted a range of legal and theological criticisms of resistance treatises to a single point. All the arguments over constitutional order and the authority of lesser magistrates, as well as the idea of a double covenant between God, the king, and people, lead back to the fundamental question: Who can lay a hand on the Lord's anointed? For Barclay and others who followed in his stead, "monarchomach" was a synecdoche employed to underscore the ultimate, disastrous result of theories of political resistance.

As Daniel Lee has noted, the normative evaluation of this label has shifted radically over several centuries. When Barclay and others employed the term, they could expect their readers to share certain attitudes about the dignity or sacredness of the royal person and office. We do not share these attitudes, for many reasons. In modern historiography, Lee points out, progressive "Whig historicism" began valorizing monarchomach doctrines in the late-eighteenth and early-nineteenth centuries.[1] No longer considered seditious radicals, the monarchomachs acquired new titles and honors as the forerunners of modern liberalism, religious freedom, constitutional order, and even human rights.

---

[1] Daniel Lee, "Private Law Models for Public Law Concepts: The Roman Law Theory of Dominium in the Monarchomach Doctrine of Popular Sovereignty," *The Review of Politics* (Summer 2008): 370–1. We might trace this line back to earlier pro-monarchomach sources, such as John Milton, Algernon Sidney, and George Lawson, who are not so easily lumped in with the Whig historians. Cf. John Sanderson, *"But the People's Creatures": The Philosophical Basis of the English Civil War* (Manchester: Manchester University Press, 1989); Jonathan Scott, *Algernon Sidney and the English Republic 1623–1677* (Cambridge: Cambridge University Press, 2005); Conal Condren, *George Lawson's* Politica *and the English Revolution* (Cambridge: Cambridge University Press, 2002).

The honorifics would not last forever, though. Over the past several decades, scholars have complicated and challenged the older Whig narrative, noting that the development of modern doctrines of liberty and constitutionalism was more complicated, and compromised, than earlier generations of historians let on. There was no straightforward path "from Constance to 1688," as an earlier historian once put it.[2]

All this serves as a reminder that neither the monarchomachs nor the so-called absolutists fall neatly into latter-day political categories. Beza and Mornay, as we have already seen, were hardly democrats or secular liberals as we use the terms today. At the same time, these early modern theorists were arguing over competing conceptual definitions that do in fact matter beyond the narrow scope of the first two decades of the seventeenth century: What counts as "law"? Who counts as a "king" or "ruler-to-be-obeyed"? And who has authority to make judgments about these normative descriptions?

The answers to these questions determine what and who should be obeyed. Further, these answers determine the bounds of covenantal obligation and the agency of the parties involved. As such, these are the sorts of conceptual questions that matter for our understanding of the development of early modern political thought.

Scholars have noted the spate of absolutist treatises that appeared in the first decade of the seventeenth century, often penned in explicit condemnation of monarchomach writings.[3] There is some debate in contemporary scholarship over what counts as "absolutism," since the moniker itself was not invented until the early-nineteenth century.[4] I use the term advisedly as a retrospective category. For my purposes, an "absolutist" political theory satisfies three

---

[2] Compare, for example, the classic works by Otto Gierke, *Natural Law and the Theory of Society*, ed. and trans. Ernest Barker, 2 vols. (Cambridge: Cambridge University Press, 1934); *The Development of Political Theory*, trans. Bernard Freyd (New York: W.W. Norton, 1939); and Harold Laski, "Political Theory in the Later Middle Ages," in *The Cambridge Medieval History*, vol. 8 (Cambridge: Cambridge University Press, 1911–36) with the treatment of monarchomach theories in recent works by Lee, "Private Law Models"; Quentin Skinner, "From the State of Princes to the Person of the State," in *Visions of Politics*, vol. 2 (Cambridge: Cambridge University Press, 2002): 308–413; Robert von Friedeburg, *Self-Defence and Religious Strife in Early Modern Europe. England and Germany, 1530–1680* (Burlington, VT: Ashgate, 2002); and Kinch Hoekstra, "Early Modern Absolutism and Constitutionalism," *Cardozo Law Review* 34 (2013): 1079–98.

[3] Merio Scattola, "Von der Maiestas zur Symbiosis," in Emilio Bonfatti, Guiseppe Duso, and Merio Scattola, eds., *Politische Begriffe und historisches Umfeld in der Politica methodice digesta des Johannes Althusius* (Wiesbaden: Harrassowitz Verlag, 2002), 248.

[4] Robert von Friedeburg, Michael Seidler, and (as credited by von Friedeburg and Seidler) Horst Dreitzel, "The Holy Roman Empire of the German Nation," in Howell A. Lloyd, Glenn Burgess, Simon Hodson, eds., *European Political Thought, 1450–1700* (New Haven, CT: Yale University Press, 2007), 129.

primary criteria: First, the supreme ruler of the political community is obligated to obey only God and the natural and divine laws promulgated by God; second, if the supreme ruler breaks the law of God or nature, only God may exact a penalty; third, the will (*arbitrium* or *voluntas*) of the ruler is the final normative standard for civil justice and political relations. Consequent to this final criterion is the belief that when the ruler chooses to grant certain privileges or agency to the people, he or she may choose to revoke those privileges at any time without providing a reason.

The roots of modern absolutist thought extend back to medieval and ancient sources. As Ernst Kantorowicz, Michael Stolleis, and others have noted, late medieval and early modern jurists were able to draw "upon a repertoire of absolutist formulae from the classical world," in particular, the Ulpianic maxims, "the prince is above the law" (*princeps legibus solutus*) and "what pleases the prince has the force of law" (*quod principi placuit, legis habet vigorem*). Amid shifting territorial allegiances, and redistribution of feudal power, modern absolutism emerged over the course of the sixteenth and seventeenth centuries, although scholars differ over the exact origin and chronology.[5] Figures such as Jean Bodin, Adam Blackwood, Peter Gregoire, William Barclay, James VI of Scotland (later James I of Great Britain), Alberico Gentili, and Henning Arnisaeus often stand as early representatives of this strain of early modern thought.

A thorough analysis of absolutist theory lies beyond the scope of my present concerns. However, with respect to my earlier analysis of Reformed conceptions of covenant and law, two particular features require attention. In response to monarchomach writings, absolutists often advanced a pair of complementary critiques. The first regards the nature of law, and entails a commitment to theological and regal voluntarism. The second regards the covenantal relationship between ruler and the ruled, and assumes a paternalist understanding of political authority and agency. I will use Gentili and Barclay, respectively, to voice these two critiques.

Alberico Gentili, an Italian Protestant who served as the Regius Chair in civil law at Oxford, is best known today for his revisionary theories of just war and international law. Alongside Bodin and other contemporaries, he marks

---

[5] For instance, compare Julian Franklin, *Jean Bodin and the Rise of Absolutist Theory* (Cambridge: Cambridge University Press, 1973); Johann P. Sommerville, "English and European Political Ideas in the Early Seventeenth Century: Revisionism and the Case of Absolutism," *Journal of British Studies* 35:2 (April 1996): 168–94; J. H. M. Salmon, "The Legacy of Jean Bodin: Absolutist, Populism or Constitutionalism?" in *History of Political Thought* 17:4 (1996): 500–22; Nicholas Henshall, *The Myth of Absolutism: Change & Continuity in Early Modern European Monarchy* (New York, NY: Routledge, 2013 [1992]).

an important period of transition in Western jurisprudence, particularly in regard to the discipline's standing vis-à-vis ecclesial and theological authorities.[6] The relationship between lawyers and theologians was fraught throughout the late middle ages. Daniel Lee observes that theologians often viewed civil lawyers with suspicion, as "bad Christians" who disregarded certain traditional liberties and theological norms.[7] The tension persisted through the sixteenth and seventeenth centuries.[8] Perhaps most illustrative of this rivalry is Gentili's own famous exclamation, "Silence, theologians, in matters outside your domain" (*silete theologi in munere alieno*), which he directed against scholastic theologians who objected to his more permissive view toward preemptive war. Setting his rhetoric aside, however, Noel Malcolm and others note that Gentili's exasperation should not distract from the fact that he owed much to Protestant and Catholic scholastic theologians – even if he often repaid his debts by way of polemic engagement.[9]

Gentili famously opens his *De jure belli* (1598) with a warning about the limits of political and moral philosophy. Neither the political philosopher nor the moralist is properly equipped to write a book on the laws of war, he argues, because they focus on the formation of virtuous individuals and limit their purview to the *civitas* rather than the "lofty structures" of international law. Even the lawyers of previous generations – including Bodin – failed in this respect. Among other charges, Gentili believes that earlier jurists went astray by trying to analyze the validity of law through the use of historical and moral examples, rather than by direct appeal to nature. This resulted in countless contradictory examples that could not supply a system of law "which is regarded as natural and definite" (*naturale ac certum*). Gentili, unlike several of the theologians I analyzed in earlier chapters, is straightforward about his concern to rebut skepticism. Law extracted from nature must be clear enough to even the most foolish (*hebetes*) and vicious (*improbi*).

---

[6] See the helpful accounts in Diego Panizza, "Political Theory and Jurisprudence in Gentili's *De Iure Belli*: The Great Debate Between 'Theological' and 'Humanist' Perspectives from Vitoria to Grotius" in *The Roots of International Law* (Leiden: Brill, 2014), 211–47; Anthony Pagden, "'Making Barbarians into Gentle Peoples': Alberico Gentili on the Legitimacy of Empire," in *Burdens of Empire* (Cambridge: Cambridge University Press, 2015).

[7] Daniel Lee, "Roman Law, German Liberties and the Constitution of the Holy Roman Empire," in Quentin Skinner and Martin van Gelderen, eds., *Freedom and the Construction of Europe*, vol. 1 (Cambridge: Cambridge University Press, 2013), 257.

[8] Wim Decock's *Theologians and Contract Law: The Moral Transformation of the Ius Commune (ca. 1500–1650)* (Leiden: Brill, 2012).

[9] See Noel Malcolm, "Alberico Gentili and the Ottomans," in Benedict Kingsbury and Benjamin Straumann, eds., *The Roman Foundations of the Law of Nations* (Cambridge: Cambridge University Press, 2010), 127–45.

Others have written at length about Gentili's influence on the emergence of modern theories of natural law.[10] However, the conception of law Gentili advanced in *De jure* finds particular application not only in his treatment of war and the *ius gentium*, but his lesser-known treatise on royal power, *De potestate regis absoluta* (1605). Published soon after James unified the crowns of Scotland and England, Gentili's treatise employs the full range of absolutist maxims. Defending the proposition, "That which pleases the prince has the force of law," he argues that supreme rulers do not "acknowledge any one above them but God." Further, drawing on a late medieval theological distinction,[11] Gentili states that royal power falls into two categories, ordinary and extraordinary. Under the former description, royal power is nominally bound by established legal structures and norms. Under the latter, the ruler "may take away the right of anyone, even a great person, and without cause."[12] On these terms, the ruler has a plenitude of power, and when the ruler acts in this way, he acts "not by way of justice, but because it so pleased the ruler, and no one could say to him, Why do you do this?"[13] In this way, the will of the ruler comes before, or stands in the place of, the giving of reasons (*scilicet sit tum voluntas pro ratione*).

Gentili recognizes that this proposition leaves him vulnerable to the charge that he makes the earthly ruler "equal to God." In fact, several years earlier, James, prior to his assumption of the English crown, had asserted quite directly – while citing the authority of the Psalms – "kings are called Gods." They sit on God's earthly throne. Like James, Gentili affirms that the ruler is God on earth (*Princeps est Deus in terris*). At the same time, he entertains the

[10]   Scattola's essay provides an excellent comparison of traditional and modern uses of natural law, "Models in History of Natural Law," in: *Ius commune, Zeitschrift für Europäische Rechtsgeschichte* 28 (2001), 91–159. On Gentili, see *De jure belli* I.1, in which he emphasizes the givenness of nature, and – notably – appeals to the authority of theologians such as Tertullian; cf. Panizza, "Political Theory and Jurisprudence"; Annabel Brett, *Changes of State: Nature and the Limits of the City in Early Modern Natural Law* (Princeton, NJ: Princeton University Press, 2011), esp. 83; Peter Haggenmacher, "Grotius and Gentili: A Reassessment of Thomas E. Holland's Inaugural Lecture," in Hedley Bull, Benedict Kingsbury, Adam Roberts, eds., *Hugo Grotius and International Relations* (Oxford: Clarendon Press, 1990), 133–76.

[11]   It is notable here that the ordinary/extraordinary distinction of the late medieval nominalists was generally not picked up by covenantal theologians and political thinkers, as some earlier historians hypothesized, but by their absolutist opponents. In my first chapter, I addressed some of the attempts in twentieth-century scholarship to connect this medieval distinction with Reformed covenantal thought.

[12]   "Atque absolutatem definiunt, secundum quam potest ille tollere ius alienum, etiam magnum, etiam sine causa," *De potestate regis absolutam*, in Alberico Gentili, *Regales Disputationes Tres* (London, 1605), 10.

[13]   Gentili, *De potestate*, 11.

objection that it would seem that God's absolute power is an attribute "not communicable to any other."[14] In response, Gentili affirms theological voluntarism, simpliciter, and a qualified regal voluntarism. Rulers may act as God on earth, he claims, but this does not make them equal to God. That is to say, God is not bound by anything – the laws of nature, nations, or even God's own law. The supreme ruler is not absolute in this particular sense, Gentili claims, since – at least in theory – he remains bound to God and God's laws (*sub Deo et legibus Dei tenetur*).

Two elements of this qualified regal absolutism will become directly relevant to our analysis of Althusius' conception of covenant and law. First, the qualifications introduced by Gentili supply no actual legal or political mechanism for holding the ruler to account for any transgression of the laws he is ordinarily bound to uphold.[15] As Glenn Burgess points out, in de facto terms, Gentili offers "no limit to royal authority save the king's own conception of what constituted justice." Second, Gentili's regal voluntarism relates explicitly to his theological voluntarism. The temporal relationship between the ruler and the ruled is analogous to the relationship between the divine sovereign and his creatures. God and the ruler do not stand *sub lege* in the same manner as their subjects. Both the divine and earthly ruler retain the right to act outside the law in extraordinary circumstances. This is essential to the definition of divine and human sovereignty.[16] In this way, the precedent established in God's own power to act outside his laws provides normative grounds to justify the extraordinary and lawless actions of the earthly ruler. Arguing against the Reformed jurist Francois Hotman, Gentili declares that the legal validity of royal decrees does not depend in any way on the monarch's moral virtue or the judgments of the philosophers. He finds this opinion *ridiculum*.[17]

This absolutist conception of law, and its endorsement of qualified regal voluntarism, has direct application to absolutist critiques of the monarchomachs' use of covenant, even though Gentili's treatise does not deal directly with the concept. To address this particular challenge, we can turn to the work of the exiled Scottish jurist William Barclay.

---

[14] Gentili, *De potestate*, 16–17.

[15] Glenn Burgess, *Absolute Monarchy and the Stuart Constitution* (New Haven, CT: Yale University Press, 1996), 77. Cf. Gentili, *De potestate*, 27.

[16] Without employing Bodin's French term, Gentili adopts his definition of "absolute and perpetual power, which the Latins call *maiestas*," *De potestate*, 9.

[17] Gentili, *De potestate*, 23. See Benjamin Straumann, "The *Corpus iuris* as a Source of Law Between Sovereigns in Alberico Gentili's Thought" in Benedict Kingsbury and Benjamin Straumann, eds., *The Roman Foundations of the Law of Nations: Alberico Gentili and the Justice of Empire* (Oxford: Oxford University Press, 2011), 101–23.

A RIVAL ACCOUNT: COVENANTAL PATERNALISM

Raised as a Catholic in Aberdeenshire, Barclay emigrated to France to study law in Paris and Bourges several years after Queen Mary I of Scotland was deposed in 1567. Later, he joined the faculty at the new university in Pont-à-Mousson, alongside Peter Gregoire.[18] His *De regno et regali potestate* was published in Paris in 1600, and immediately attracted the attention of other absolutist theorists, including James VI of Scotland. When James VI became James I of Great Britain in 1603, Barclay briefly returned to England, where James offered him a post under the condition that he convert to Protestantism. Barclay refused, and spent the rest of his life and legal career in France.

Although published five years before Gentili's treatise, Barclay's critique of the monarchomachs was not the first to appear. It was, however, the most extensive and certainly one of the most influential.[19] *De regno* addresses the work of three theorists: the Scottish humanist George Buchanan, the French Catholic theologian Jean Boucher, and Mornay, whom Barclay addresses by his chosen pseudonym, Stephanus Junius Brutus. Barclay's two chapters on Mornay, which comprise the longest section of the book, present his most sustained polemic against the radical political use of covenant.

Like Gentili, Barclay argues that the implications of the monarchomach conception of law are both politically dangerous and theologically dubious. The latter point requires careful attention. Throughout *De regno*, Barclay interprets many of the biblical *loci classici* of the resistance theorists, while converting them to absolutist texts and adding his own theological gloss on the nature of royal power.

Kings rule at the "gift and grant of God," Barclay argues, and in a manner that befits God's own providential reign over creation. Just as God has absolute

---

[18] See the analysis of the Pont-à-Mousson theorists and its Scottish exiles in Skinner, "From the State of Princes to the Person of the State," 396–8; J. H. Burns, *The True Law of Kingship: Concepts of Monarchy in Early-Modern Scotland* (Oxford: Clarendon Press, 1996), 222–54; Claude Collot, *L'école doctrinale de droit public de Pont-a-Mousson* (Paris: Librairie générale de droit et de jurisprudence, 1965).

[19] For instance, compare Barclay's analysis with James VI's selective treatment of the idea of a mutual covenant in his 1598 treatise *True Law of Free Monarchies*. Scholars have speculated that James' principle target was his former tutor, George Buchanan, who had written briefly about the idea of a mutual compact between the king and people in his 1579 work *Dialogus de jure regni apud Scotos*. Buchanan's remarks on the mutual compact are similar to claims made by John Calvin, Theodore Beza, and others. However, as Höpfl and Thompson note, the concept is not theorized to the same degree as in the *Vindiciae*, let alone Althusius' *Politica*. See Harro Höpfl and Martyn Thompson, "The History of Contract as a Motif in Political Thought," *The American Historical Review* 84:4 (Oct. 1979): 930–2. Cf. Anthony Black, "The Juristic Origins of Social Contract Theory," *History of Political Thought* 14 (1993): 72–6.

right to confer dignity and power on the royal office, so the king has the right to dispose of this power as he wills. God may choose to confer this power by direct divine "inspiration" (*instinctum*) or through the "authorization" of the people. Regarding this latter act, in response to the monarchomachs, he concedes that the people may sometimes serve an "instrumental" role in constituting or electing the king. However, this sort of political agency expires once a king is lawfully inaugurated.[20]

This fact, Barclay continues, explains why it sometimes seems that the people constitute and sustain the royal office, as the monarchomachs claim. However, while the monarchomachs assert that the people are antecedent to the royal office, and that the support of the people is necessary for the royal person to maintain office, Barclay rebuts this claim by distinguishing between two ways of conceiving of the efficient cause of royal power. The first sort of efficient cause has to do with the production of a thing, as when an architect or builder is said to be the cause of some residence. When the architect dies, the residence does not pass away with him. So also, when the people elect a person as king, it does not matter whether they continue to support him: The election is accomplished and the power is immutably conferred. The second sort of efficient cause has to do with the conservation of a thing over time. In this sense, only God is rightly called the efficient cause of the king, and only God may withdraw the royal prerogative.[21]

In this way, the power that resides in the royal office, although sometimes conferred by the election of the people, stands independent of the people. God may use the people as an instrument, but they are accidental to the power itself. For Barclay, the political implications of this view are clear: Even if a rebellious people were to coerce a king into surrendering his right to rule, "he would still retain the dominion."[22] Although it sometimes seems that the people have the power to grant kings their *regnum*, the royal office is better described as the "remarkable artifice" of divine power: God can make kings "with no intermediary," and without any antecedent recognition of the people if he so chooses. That is to say, the divine creation of the royal office and person could be described as a work *ex nihilo*. Citing the authority of Gregory of Nyssa, Irenaeus, Tertullian, among other theologians, Barclay claims that kings are clearly born to the royal office, and that God willed that the world be ordered in this way.[23]

[20]   William Barclay, *De Regno et Regali Potestate* (Paris, 1600), III.2, 111–13.
[21]   Cf. Henning Arnisaeus on the same point, *De Jure Majestatis* (Strasbourg, 1673 [1610]), I.6.1–2, 83a–84a.
[22]   Barclay, *De Regno*, III.2, 114.
[23]   Barclay, *De Regno*, III.2, 110–11.

Barclay supports these claims through a series of biblical, theological, and legal sources. After framing his position in broad terms, he supports his argument through examples from the Hebrew Bible, the teachings of Jesus (*De Regno*, III.8), the apostles (III.9), Paul (III.10), the early church (III.11), and the later catholic church (III.12), before arriving at the testimony of the jurists in III.14. Throughout, Barclay interweaves appeals to these diverse authorities. In support of the Ulpianic precept, *quod principi placuit, legis habet vigorem*,[24] he appeals to the narrative of Joseph's vice-regency under Pharaoh in the time of Egypt's great famine (Genesis 47). The author of Genesis, Barclay argues, demonstrated that Pharaoh ruled at his own discretion, and had the supreme power to appoint anyone or decree anything he wished. The consent of the people was no matter to Pharaoh. Joseph ruled at the will of Pharaoh, and in Pharaoh's name could requisition the goods and services of those he ruled. Barclay draws on similar examples from the Deuteronomic prophecy of Israel's future monarchy and Gideon's assumption of "regal power" during the time of judges. While this feature of Barclay's work has received relatively little scholarly attention, *De regno* is as replete with biblical and theological allusions and appeals as the *Vindiciae*, even as it uses these authorities to argue for an opposing account of regal power and covenantal obligation.

As John Locke would later note, Barclay offers a paradigmatic account of paternalist political order. The king is *paterfamilias*. He "rules over his own with such power that not even the whole family has right and power over him."[25] Quoting from Origen's sermons on Leviticus: "We are under obligation not to contradict the father and mother in any way, no matter what they may say or do." Applied to the relationship between king and people, Barclay's paternalism entails that subjects may not "assault [kings] with evil words, nor coerce them with force and arms." No matter the gravity of the king's error, the people may not undermine their royal father.

Like Gentili and other absolutists, Barclay acknowledges that kings may indeed sin against God and the people, just as fathers may abuse members of their household. This seems an obvious truth to him. The real issue at stake regards the matter of political agency and accountability. Certainly, Barclay

---

[24] Peter Stein, *Roman Law in European History* (Cambridge: Cambridge University Press, 1999), 59–61. Charles Howard McIlwain also noted that the "practical absolutism" of Ulpian (deployed often by Barclay) stands in contrast to the gloss of Henry de Bracton, *Constitutionalism: Ancient and Modern* (Ithaca, NY: Cornell University Press, 1940), 72–3. For Bracton, the prince's will has the force of lex "in accordance with a *lex regia* which had been made."

[25] "Atqui Pater familias tali suis cum imperio praesidet, ut ne toti quidem familiae ius, ac potestas in eum sit," Barclay, *De Regno*, III.4, 130.

admits, the king's power should be limited in some way. Penalties ought to exist for a king who is too severe against his own subjects, just as a penalty ought to be inflicted on a paterfamilias who wrongfully kills any of his family. "But by whom?" Barclay asks. Should the family exact the penalty? Certainly not, he answers, since this would be an affront to God himself. In fact, we should not tolerate the idea that God would be "so neglectful that in punishing the prince and even the supreme head of the very realm, that he would want to overturn and pervert the customary and settled order of nature."[26] Citing the commentaries of Jerome and Ambrose, Barclay notes the biblical example of David's confession of adultery and murder. David, he claims, confessed his sin to God and God alone ("against you, and you only have I sinned," Psalms 51). For all these reasons, "the king is not subject to any judgment except God's."[27]

At this point in his argument, Barclay provides a summary of regal voluntarism that mirrors Gentili's account above, as he rehearses a series of juristic maxims. The king is "perpetually free of the laws." He enjoys the plenitude of power in civil matters, as the pope does in ecclesial matters. He may "change or mitigate the sentence of law at will" whenever he wishes. No one may say to him, "Why are you doing this?" After all, he "is the cause of causes, inquiry must not be made about his power, since there is no cause of the first cause." In fact, it is tantamount to sacrilege to dispute the power of the supreme ruler.[28]

It is this account of regal voluntarism that provides Barclay with the grounds for his critique of Mornay's conception of covenant, which occupies much of book IV of the *De regno.*

The entire basis of Mornay's argument is faulty, Barclay believes, because the *Vindiciae* conflates two matters: first, obedience to magisterial *commands* that are contrary to God's law; and second, obedience to *magistrates* who have commanded against God's law.[29] The first point is not under dispute, he claims. Mornay has made a superfluous argument: "Why remind Christian princes of an uncontroversial maxim: obey God rather than men?" Every Christian already believes the Petrine principle recorded in the fifth chapter of the book of Acts. As for the atheists, why tell them about this maxim "when they could not care less." "Do you think," he asks with a quick twist of the rhetorical knife, "that atheists ... will believe you or your Calvin, even if he should return from Erebus, about anything pertaining to God?"[30]

[26] "ita negligere, ut in Principe summo, atque adeo ipsius regni capite plectendo, consuetum hunc, ratumque naturae ordinem inverti, ac perverti velit?" Barclay, *De Regno,* III.4, 130.
[27] Barclay, *De Regno,* III.5, 139.
[28] Barclay, *De Regno,* III.14, 193–4.
[29] Barclay, *De Regno,* IV.2, 219–20.
[30] Barclay, *De Regno,* IV.2, 221.

Barclay continues, redoubling his affirmation to the Petrine principle: While Mornay calls kings vassals of God, this title – if anything – is too lofty. In light of God's ineffable sovereignty (*Majestas ineffabilis*) kings are "worms and dust which the wind hurls about." Clearly, we should obey God before mortals such as these. Even so – and here Barclay pivots – this tells us nothing about the nature of royal power, once granted by God. If the king neglects God or divine law, or "violates the law of nature or of nations," Barclay argues, "the regal dignity remains integral and intact."[31]

In support of this claim, Barclay turns to Mornay's lord-and-vassal analogy. George Garnett and others have noted the ways in which Barclay attacks – and often overstates his case against – Mornay's use of legal categories, and the matter of feudal obligations in particular.[32] What has received less scholarly attention, however, is the theological argument that Barclay employs at this point.

Mornay's feudal analogy claims that the king, acting as God's vassal, may continue in his office so long as he abides by the terms of the covenant. God, acting as lord over his *dominium*, will remain faithful to this covenantal promise. Barclay contests Mornay's understanding of how feudal obligations work in earlier sections of book IV. However, in a crucial passage in a later section he grants Mornay's feudal analogy for the sake of argument: Assume that God acts as a feudal lord with respect to the king and the people, Barclay writes. What does this entail? He answers Mornay:

> For you err egregiously in that you compare God to a lord, and the king to a vassal, in every way insofar as it pertains to the loss of fief and realm. As if in truth that infinite power and immense goodness of divine sovereignty would imitate or maintain those feudal customs, unknown to many nations . . . Do you not know that the benefices of which you speak, although they could be revoked at the whim of the lord at the beginning, as if from temporary and precarious possessors, yet by this right (*ius*) that you bring forth . . . the lord would be unable, no matter how much he desired, to take them away? Can it truly be that you establish the same thing concerning God, that what he gave he would not be able to take away, or to continue the benefice at the pleasure of his will? Can it be that you are ignorant that it was comprehended by

---

[31] Barclay, *De Regno*, IV.2, 222.

[32] See George Garnett's introductory commentary in *Vindiciae contra tyrannos* (Cambridge: Cambridge University Press, 1994), xxiv–xxv. Garnett has keenly noted that at key moments Barclay overlooks the fact that the first part of Mornay's double covenant is more relevant at this point, insofar as the terms of the king's vassalage are determined after God has entered into covenant with the people as a whole. As we noted in the last chapter, the first part of the covenant has already established the political standing and agency of the people; this is why the king's role as God's vassal is contingent upon the king's adherence to the covenantal terms.

feudal statutes that the lord would commit a crime or felony against a vassal on account of which he could be deprived of the dominion of the fief; because no one unless extraordinarily will attribute blasphemy to God.[33]

Barclay's theological argument is both forceful and quite revealing: Once Mornay has described the relationship between God and the earthly ruler in terms of the human custom of covenanting, he has subjected God to covenantal obligations. For Barclay, this is objectionable not only because it imputes certain terms of human relationality to God, but also because the terms themselves may entail blasphemy. After all, how could God bind himself to a covenantal relationship that – even hypothetically – makes God's ownership of the realm contingent upon his faithfulness? It seems an affront to divine sovereignty to apply covenantal conditions in any such form.

Barclay's critique underscores two significant assumptions of the doctrine of political covenant. First, Barclay understands that for Mornay and other Reformed thinkers, the terms of the covenant entail that God *does* in fact bind himself to the relationship and to provide for his people – his inheritance. God cannot simply choose to discontinue his "benefice" whenever he wishes. He makes promises that he must keep. This is true because, according to the Reformed theologians, God in his own nature is just and good, and cannot deviate from norms that are proper to himself.

Second, Barclay recognizes the political implications of this doctrine of God. Notice a key claim in the quote above. Barclay is not only concerned about preserving God's freedom to take away what he originally offered; Barclay is also concerned about circumstances in which God will be obligated to *discontinue* the benefice when a vassal has broken the terms of the covenant. If this is true, then we must ask: What sorts of royal sins give God reasons to remove his benefice? And who is licensed to exact this penalty? Barclay readily acknowledges that many kings commit the sort of felonies against God that, according to Mornay, warrant loss of the realm. Yet, Barclay writes, God "bestows many things on the unworthy," and "condones" and "benignly permits" that murderers and the greedy retain their "fortunes, honors, and power."[34] This introduces a tension that Barclay solves by wedding his voluntarism to his paternalism.

Before analyzing Barclay's paternalist solution, however, it is important to underscore his analogous conceptions of divine and human power. For Barclay, the absolute power of divine and human sovereigns is not conditioned by the sovereign's goodness or by the antecedent relationship that the

---

[33] Barclay, *De Regno*, IV.2, 225.
[34] Barclay, *De Regno*, IV.2, 226.

sovereign shares with his people. Sovereign power must be inviolable and free of covenantal conditions. According to Mornay, of course, this view runs directly contrary to the biblical histories of God's covenantal relationship with the king and people of Israel, and later the Christian church. In response, Barclay argues that these historical covenants offered "no condition threatening the freedom of the king," let alone God. Covenants, on Barclay's account, do not entail new normative obligations for the sovereign. Such conditions and relationships would, by definition, undermine the free nature of divine and royal power. The people may not ask God or the king for an account. Consequently, if God chooses to give the realm to the unworthy and to preserve the wicked in their power, no one can ask him, "Why are you doing this?" No one may appeal to an antecedent fellowship or common goods to hold the sovereign to account. In fact, if a people finds fault with the sovereign, and "proceeds to avenge itself by its own hand," it is "perverting divine and human judgments."[35]

Here we return to Barclay's fundamental distinction between obedience to the unjust *commands* of magistrates and obedience to the commands of unjust *magistrates*. On the terms of his theological and regal voluntarism, it is possible to identify circumstances in which subjects may choose not to obey an unjust command of the king. In such cases, a subject might choose flee the country, or – more likely – await the punishment that would attend her disobedience. She might pray for deliverance, in the hopes that God would punish the tyrant. In all this, the substance of Barclay's position is not very far off from some earlier Protestant theologians, including Calvin – assuming that we disregard the possibility of lesser magistrates intervening in the matter.

On the other hand, for Barclay there are no circumstances in which a private or public person – or the people as a whole – may legitimately rebel against a king *on the grounds that* the king has committed injustice or broken covenant with God, let alone the people. Recall once again that Barclay does not deny that kings may be so thoroughly perverse that they are rightly called unjust, immoral, or even tyrannical. Rather, he argues that no punitive agency is granted to the people. The people have no jurisdiction to intervene in this way, and if they did try to correct the king, they would be illicitly assuming the divine prerogative: "But who are you to resist the ordinance of God? Is it lawful for God to do with his own what he wants?"[36]

Here, it is important to underscore the perhaps surprising fact that Barclay acknowledges the legitimacy of a certain form of political covenant, albeit one

---

[35] Barclay, *De Regno*, IV.2, 226.
[36] Barclay, *De Regno*, IV.2, 229.

with decidedly different terms than Mornay's. Barclay's modified political covenant entails two relationships: one between God and the king, and another between God and the people. Crucially, the two covenantal relationships stand independent of each other. There is no mutual responsibility, no common surety in case of covenantal infidelity. In Barclay's words, there are not "two debtors of the promising, but different debtors of differing deeds."[37] If the king breaks covenant with God, the people are neither implicated nor licensed to intervene. Correspondingly, the covenant between God and the people obligates the people to offer pure worship to God, but it hardly grants political subjects any power over the prince.

According to Barclay, therefore, Mornay's fundamental error was to interrelate these two distinct covenantal relationships. The critical innovation of Mornay's double covenant – which Barclay recognizes as both ingenious and highly dangerous – was its three-party structure. The idea of a two-party covenant between the king and the people was hardly radical in itself. After all, Barclay, Arnisaeus, and other absolutist theorists are quite willing to admit the possibility of some contract between the ruler and the ruled.[38] Rather, the radicalism of Mornay's doctrine involved, first, describing the covenant as obtaining to God, the king, *and* the people, and second, relating this three-party political covenant to the antecedent relationship between God and God's people. In these two steps, Mornay makes the ruler and the ruled mutually accountable to God and the normative standards that emerge from the preexisting covenantal fellowship.

For Barclay, this muddles the nature of covenantal obligations and distorts the agency of the parties involved. In particular, he argues that Mornay is mistaken to think that if one of the codebtors – viz. the king – fails to fulfill his obligations, the other party – viz. the people – is held responsible.[39] Both Roman law and biblical history stand as witnesses against this assumption, according to Barclay. As stated in the epigraph above, Barclay believes that Mornay's political covenant is a smokescreen, or in his words, a mousetrap, designed to ensnare the people in a dangerously misguided conception of political agency. Properly understood, the covenant provides no grounds for such impiety. As he notes earlier, the idea that a people ought to rebel against the king because he broke covenant with God is akin to a slave drawing the sword against his master for the murder of a fellow slave, or a son against his father for the murder of a fellow brother.[40] In such cases, slaves, sons, and

---

[37] Barclay, *De Regno*, IV.8, 323–4.
[38] See Arnisaeus, *De Jure Majestatis*, I.6.3–12, 84b–94b.
[39] Barclay, *De Regno*, IV.8, 324.
[40] Barclay, *De Regno*, III.4, 131.

subjects have no standing or responsibility to act against the paterfamilias. It was not their covenant that was broken.

Rather than falling into this impious trap, Barclay argues that the people must remember their own obligations to the king, which stand independent of their covenant with God, or any mutual participation in the common good of the political relationship. Against Mornay's interpretation of the biblical covenant between God, King Asa, and the people of Israel, Barclay argues that the point of the text is not that the king is an equal party to the relationship, but that he is the one holding the people to account: "he is like to a paterfamilias if he should speak in that way to his family: 'If anyone this day goes out from the home, he will give him an excessive beating, from the least to the greatest.'" The king simply adopts the manner of the divine sovereign:

> The Father who subjected all things to Christ certainly excepted himself. Therefore, concerning the delinquent king who is judged by his subjects, not one word on this matter, and nothing of consequence can be collected from this covenant, no more than from other sanctions of other laws . . . unless we mock and misrepresent the words and senses of the scriptures.

On these terms, Mornay's covenantal doctrine is not merely the egregious error of an amateur jurist – although Barclay certainly thinks this is true. Mornay's covenant is much worse than that, insofar as it implicates him in both political and theological heresy.

CONCLUSION: TERMS OF DISAGREEMENT

Barclay's absolutist critique of Mornay's covenant requires us to attend to the ways in which he interweaves theological and political claims about the nature of divine and human power, law, and covenantal obligations. Alongside other theorists, Barclay and Gentili offer a two-pronged challenge to the emergent covenantal theories of resistance: The absolutist critique advances a voluntarist account of divine and human law. This account, in turn, supports a paternalist conception of political order that admits no impious form of mutual covenantal accountability. In effect, the absolutists shield the freedom of the divine and human sovereign from the threats entailed by the covenant. They do this not only for the sake of royal power, but the good of the people – who might otherwise be ensnared by the impious delusions of covenantal political agency.

The charge of impiety echoed beyond the treatises of Gentili and Barclay. Henning Arnisaeus, the Lutheran absolutist and the figure whom Horst Dreitzel names as Althusius' primary rival, repeatedly cast the monarchomachs as proponents of vice, disorder, and licentiousness. Every rebelling subject, he claimed, had on his lips the common proverb: "Faithful lord, faithful subject."[41] Yet what sort of principle is this? Mornay and others may say, "that which is commanded well is well-obeyed," but human experience informs us that there is "no prince so perfect or happy that he will not provoke some offense with his subjects." Better to recognize the inevitability of magisterial imperfection and to acknowledge that God himself has promised to exact punishment. "If a king is not dissuaded by these, why would he be deterred by the threat of breaking his oath to the people?" And "if a prince is already bound to protect the people and true religion by virtue of his office, what work is left for an oath?"[42]

When absolutist theorists leveled these charges against the monarcho-machs, it is critical to note two things. First, the absolutists and monarcho-machs disagreed over what *counts* as an act of political piety, not whether subjects are in fact obligated to perform such acts. Second, the absolutists and monarchomachs regarded piety to divine and human rulers as interrelated in some meaningful way. The difference between absolutist and monarchomach accounts regarded the manner in which they were related, and who was authorized to correct impious action.

In application, the rival conceptions of covenant and law center on the correlation – or lack thereof – between covenant and popular political agency. According to Gentili, Barclay, and others, political subjects have no standing – covenantal or otherwise – to penalize the impiety of the ruler, while the ruler *does* have authority to correct popular impiety directed toward God or the royal office. By contrast, the first generation of monarchomachs claimed that the people did have political agency in some meaningful sense. They did so by drawing on traditional conceptions of right-order and the common good and arguing that the people's antecedent relationship with God provided a normative standard for the relationship between the ruler and the ruled. However, what the first generation of monarchomachs lacked was a comprehensive account of the means by which the people come to *recognize* and *communicate* particular forms of power, right, and delegated authority. It was the second-generation Reformed monarchomach, Johannes Althusius, who would provide a more sophisticated account along these lines of the origins and ends of the covenantal political order. Or, as he would describe it, the consociation.

---

[41] Arnisaeus, *De Jure Majestatis*, I.6.1, 83b.
[42] Arnisaeus, *De Jure Majestatis*, I.6.6, 87b.

5

Consociational Politics

Althusius' Theological Account of Law and Covenant

Covenantal accounts of political life have provoked challenges not only from early modern detractors, but late modern ones as well. While the former often employed explicitly theological terms in their polemics, as we saw in the previous chapter, many late modern theorists have expressed puzzlement over the persistence of theological language in early modern covenantal thought. Early-modern political doctrines of consent, social contract, and popular sovereignty were supposed to silence the theologians. Late modern political historians have also continued to puzzle over the place of theological commitments in early modern politics. Was the silencing of the theologians (Gentili's infamous *silete theologi*) actually effective? And if not, why not?

Perhaps no text is more emblematic of this scholarly bafflement than Johannes Althusius' *Politica methodice digesta* (1603, 1610, and 1614). Althusius has until this point loomed at the periphery of my analysis of early covenantal discourse. Despite long periods of scholarly neglect, he has recently gained recognition as one of the most prominent and sophisticated political thinkers at the beginning of the seventeenth century. Harro Höpfl argues that Althusius' *Politica* provided a "vastly more sophisticated account" of political life than earlier Protestant thinkers such as Beza and Calvin.[1] Robert von Friedeburg, Michael Seidler, and Horst Dreitzel write that Althusius "was undoubtedly the most prominent Reformed political thinker" in his milieu,[2] while Daniel Lee states that he was "perhaps the most important political thinker on the Continent at the beginning of the seventeenth

---

[1] Harro Höpfl, "The Ideal of *Aristocratia Politiae Vicina* in the Calvinist Political Tradition," in Irena Backus and Philip Benedict, eds., *Calvin and His Influence, 1509–2009* (Oxford: Oxford University Press, 2011), 58.

[2] Robert von Friedeburg and Michael Seidler, "The Holy Roman Empire of the German Nation," in Howell Lloyd, Glenn Burgess, and Simon Hodson, eds., *European Political Thought 1450–1700* (New Haven, CT: Yale University Press, 2007), 134.

century."[3] His work drew the critical attention of many subsequent thinkers in the Western political canon: Hugo Grotius, Samuel Rutherford, George Lawson, Ulrik Huber, and Jean-Jacques Rousseau, among others. What many scholarly accounts have overlooked, however, is the fact that Althusius is a direct heir to the tradition of Reformed covenantal thought.

We might characterize Althusius' prominence in early Reformed political thought in two ways: first, in the sense that his work was given a quasi-canonical status by many of his immediate heirs and critics;[4] and second, insofar as his work was a crystallization and even culmination of the thought of many of his contemporaries. While recent scholarship has recognized these two facets of Althusius' significance, questions about his relationship with Reformed covenantal thought persist.

In past chapters, I have argued that covenantal and theological arguments are deeply embedded not only in the thought of monarchomach theorists such as Theodore Beza and Philippe de Mornay, but also in contemporaneous absolutist accounts. This chapter turns to the theological commitments manifest in the *Politica*, which are fundamental to understanding the scope and importance of Althusius' conception of the consociation, vis-à-vis rival absolutist accounts of covenant and law. By attending to this context, we will be able to recognize that Althusius' theory of political life employs many of the paradigmatic norms and relations of Reformed covenant theology. In particular, Althusius draws on this theological discourse in both his non-voluntarist conception of divine and human law, and his covenantal account of popular political agency.

[3]   Daniel Lee, "Private Law Models for Public Law Concepts: The Roman Law Theory of Dominium in the Monarchomach Doctrine of Popular Sovereignty," *The Review of Politics* 70:3 (June 2008), 398.

[4]   Bibliographic analysis of seventeenth-century writings provides insight into the authoritative significance of Althusius. For instance, the bibliography of Dutch political treatises, compiled by Gert Onne van de Klashorst and others, reveals several notable trends. Althusius is one of the most cited of the early modern authors, alongside thinkers such as Justus Lipsius, Jean Bodin, Henning Arnisaeus, and later Hugo Grotius and Christoph Besold. Treatises penned by orthodox ("Voetian") Reformed theorists tend to cite Althusius more favorably, while also emphasizing the trope of virtue and political prudence. Over the middle decades of the century, there is a discernable shift away from attention to virtue and just authority and toward juridical focus on sovereignty. Later Dutch political thought presents an interesting contrast, represented in the anti-Hobbesian and pro-Althusian accounts of Gisbert Cocq (1668 and 1680) and Ulrik Huber's defense of a form of absolutism – explicitly rejecting Althusius, Buchanan, and Mornay in the process (1683). See G. O. van de Klashorst et al., eds., *Bibliography of Dutch Seventeenth Century Political Thought, An Annotated Inventory, 1581–1710* (Amsterdam: Holland University Press, 1986). There is much more material to be mined here, which gives indications that canonical figures such as Hobbes and Descartes were responding to a more complicated and diverse political and theological milieu than we sometimes imagine.

ALTHUSIUS IN CONTEMPORARY SCHOLARSHIP

Like Mornay's *Vindiciae contra tyrannos*, Althusius' extensive use of theological and biblical sources has posed a challenge for those who are inclined to view the *Politica* as a seminal work of secular political theory. Historians and political theorists have attempted to resolve this tension in various ways. For some scholars, the theological elements of Althusius' political thought are seen as accidental to the secular elements. For others, Althusius' reliance on theological arguments and biblical exegesis reveal Althusius as a theocrat operating beyond the pale of modern political thought – and therefore of little use to contemporary theory.

These conflicting readings populate both German and Anglophone scholarship. In his classic work, *The Development of Political Theory*, Otto von Gierke claimed Althusius as the first genuine theorist of the social contract. "In spite of its stern Calvinistic spirit," he argued, the *Politica* shakes off "the whole theocratic conception of the State."[5] Writing several decades later, Gerhard Oestreich recognized the influence of Reformed thought on Althusius, but still posited that there was an "insurmountable contradiction" between the Reformed theological conception of covenant and political doctrines such as popular sovereignty.[6] After Oestreich, German scholarship tended to minimize the theological resonances of Althusius' work even further. Echoing the thesis of much mid-twentieth-century historical theology, Dreitzel has claimed that there was an "immense tension" between covenantal thought and orthodox (by which he meant, predestinarian) Reformed theology.[7] Heinz Schilling introduces a different sort of distinction between monarchomach theories, which he identifies as deeply theological and "eschatological" in character, and civic

---

[5] Otto von Gierke, *The Development of Political Theory*, trans. Bernard Freyd (New York, NY: Howard Fertig, 1966), 71.

[6] Gerhard Oestreich, *Neostoicism and the Early Modern State* (Cambridge: Cambridge University Press, 1982), 149. On this point, Oestreich endorses the earlier claim of Ernst Reibstein. While groundbreaking and insightful in many respects, Oestreich's volume suffers from some mid-twentieth-century historiographical misunderstandings. In terms of covenantal thought, he mistakenly claims that theologians such as Althusius' colleague Wilhelm Zepper borrowed the concept of covenant from Mornay's *Vindiciae* ("The theologian adopts the slogan of the politician," 143n21), ignoring the extensive prehistory of covenant theology in mid- and late-sixteenth-century Reformed thought.

[7] Horst Dreitzel, "Althusius in der Geschichte des Föderalismus," in Emilio Bonfatti, Guiseppe Duso, and Merio Scattola, eds., *Politische Begriffe und historisches Umfeld in der Politica Methodice Digesta des Johannes Althusius* (Wiesbaden: Harrassowitz Verlag, 2002), 54.

republican thought, which relied on the central concept of consociation or cooperative rule (*Genossenschaft*).[8]

More recently, Christoph Strohm has acknowledged that earlier assumptions about Althusius' deviation from orthodox Reformed theology were misguided. However, Strohm maintains that Althusius' Reformed theological commitments – which he generally confines to beliefs about predestination and the continuing political relevance of Mosaic law – are of "no essential importance" to the political doctrines of popular sovereignty or the right to resistance. Since Althusius did not rely on these particular theological doctrines when outlining his distinctive political views, there is no reason to describe his theory as Reformed.[9] Even the appearance of the monarchomach doctrine of double covenant in Althusius' *Politica* is accidental to the fundamental structure of the work, Strohm contends.[10]

Recent Anglophone scholarship has made similar claims. I have already noted how the secular republican accounts of Skinner and others have employed a dichotomous view of the theological *foedus* and political *pactum*. Like Gierke, Skinner claims Althusius' *Politica* as one of the earliest representatives of modern "secularized political science."[11] Following in this vein, Robert von Friedeburg has suggested that the covenant theology developed by Olevianus, Ursinus, and others at Heidelberg and Herborn was both a deviation from orthodox predestinarian Reformed theology and minimally influential on Althusius' conception of politics. For Althusius, von Friedeburg maintains, the "'pactum' with God has to be distinguished from the 'foedus' of Federal theology." The former regards the obligation of the supreme and lesser magistrates to "secure the true faith in the regnum, understood as similar to collective responsibility in the Roman Law of obligations."[12] It is unclear what von Friedeburg considers the distinctive purpose of the *foedus* to be, since he does not provide analysis of the theological concept. It simply falls off the radar, since it is assumed to be politically irrelevant.

Other Anglophone scholars posit that Althusius was, in some sense, a failed secularist. For instance, Ian Hunter has argued that Althusius *attempted* to articulate a properly secular legal relationship between various political

---

[8]   Heinz Schilling, "Calvinismus und Freiheitsrechte," in *Civic Calvinism in Northwestern Germany and the Netherlands* (Kirksville, MO: Sixteenth Century Journal Publishers, 1991), esp. 89–104.

[9]   Christoph Strohm, *Calvinismus und Recht* (Tübingen: Mohr Siebeck, 2008), 189–92.

[10] Strohm, *Calvinismus und Recht*, 259–62.

[11] Quentin Skinner, *The Foundations of Modern Political Thought*, vol. 2 (Cambridge: Cambridge University Press, 1978), 350.

[12] Robert von Friedeburg, *Self-Defence and Religious Strife in Early Modern Europe. England and Germany, 1530–1680* (Burlington, VT: Ashgate, 2002), 112.

orders, but – due to the influence of Zanchi, Martinius, Alsted, and other early Reformed thinkers – fell back on an outmoded "confessional" or "metaphysical conception of political community."[13] Likewise, Brian Tierney has written that Althusius intended to offer a "rational" theory of the state independent of theological commitments. However, Tierney notes that if we look at the way in which he actually argues for his consociational conception of political life, "it is *disconcerting* ... to open Althusius's own work and find endless legal and scriptural quotations scattered over almost every page" (emphasis added).[14]

Despite this broad spectrum of scholarly opinion – which could be extended even further[15] – there is one feature that most of these accounts have in common. While scholars differ over where the fault line lies between the "secular" and "religious" elements of Althusius' thought, they generally agree that we can – and should – identify this fault line. This process often involves a re-signification of what counts as "Reformed" or as "covenant theology." If we can reduce Reformed or covenantal theology to a set of discrete propositional doctrines, it seems possible (and quite desirable) to isolate the theological concepts from their political counterparts. For instance, if Reformed theology is reducible to a particular doctrine of predestination or unique applications of the Mosaic Law, then we may identify the aspects of Althusius' political thought that have no direct connection to these doctrines. By a process of elimination, we are able to pinpoint and extract certain secular concepts that remain unsullied by theology.

On these grounds, for many scholars, it is the consociation that stands out here as Althusius' principle contribution to secular political theory. Heinz Schilling identifies the consociation or corporation as the center of Althusius'

---

[13] Ian Hunter, *Rival Enlightenments: Civil and Metaphysical Philosophy in Early Modern Germany* (Cambridge: Cambridge University Press, 2001), 59–60.

[14] Brian Tierney, *Religion, Law, and the Growth of Constitutional Thought 1150–1650* (Cambridge: Cambridge University Press, 1982), 72.

[15] For instance, although influenced by Skinner, Martin van Gelderen contradicts the reading of Althusius found in volume two of *Foundations.* van Gelderen describes Althusius as "one of the most radical theorists of the *Politica Christiana*," a genre which, he argues, assumed that "the study of political institutions and constitutions was intertwined with religion and theology." Far from looking to free-standing rational principles, Althusius relied on theological and scriptural arguments for his foundational ideas about political association. While I agree with van Gelderen about the theological sources of Althusius' political thought, van Gelderen assumes that Althusius' theological views stand in opposition to republican accounts of liberty and the common good. This is simply untrue: Theological and republican conceptions are not at all mutually exclusive. In fact, they often exist in a symbiotic relationship, as I argue below. See Martin van Gelderen, "Aristotelians, Monarchomachs and Republicans: Sovereignty and *respublica mixta* in Dutch and German Political Thought," in *Republicanism: A Shared European Heritage*, vol. 1 (Cambridge: Cambridge University Press, 2002), 205.

civic republicanism in explicit contrast to what he calls the "prophetical perspective" of Reformed theology and resistance theory.[16] Strohm makes a similarly sharp distinction between the consociational aspects of Althusius' political thought and the vestigial theological elements.[17] Dreitzel acknowledges the theological legacy of Althusius' use of the double covenant, but also claims that this doctrine was only an afterthought in Althusius' consociational theory.[18] The recent analysis of Althusius' consociation provided by Dreitzel, von Friedeburg, and Seidler omits any theological sources.[19] Add to this list Martin van Gelderen's definition of the consociation as "voluntary association," according to which the "foundation of politics and society" for Althusius and the monarchomachs was the principle of consent.[20] It is this consensual aspect of Althusian or monarchomach thought – the consociation – that appears detachable from whatever overarching theological structures supported early theories of resistance.

While there are notable exceptions, German and Anglophone scholarship generally assumes the secular character of Althusius' consociation. This majority opinion, however, does not stand up to close analysis of Althusius' own use of theological sources and commitments in his theorization of the concepts of covenant, law, and consociation.

ALTHUSIUS IN CONTEXT: THE ROOTS OF CONSOCIATION

Althusius' scholarly career began during the initial years of intense conflict between the monarchomachs and absolutists. Details about his early life are sparse, but we know that he began his studies by 1581, when he was reading Aristotle in Cologne.[21] While he trained in theology under several eminent Reformed thinkers, Althusius' primary studies were in jurisprudence. His dissertation, belatedly published in 1602, was a relatively standard work of jurisprudence, reflecting the influence of Jean Bodin, Pierre Gregoire, and Justus Lipsius, among others. As Merio Scattola has demonstrated quite convincingly, Althusius' political thought develops in significant ways from the 1602 dissertation through the three editions of the *Politica* (1603, 1610, and

---

[16] Schilling, "Calvinismus und Freiheitsrechte."
[17] Strohm, *Calvinismus und Recht*, 231ff.
[18] Dreitzel, "Althusius in der Geschichte des Föderalismus," 54.
[19] Friedeburg and Seidler, "The Holy Roman Empire of the German Nation," 136–7.
[20] van Gelderen, "Aristotelians, Monarchomachs and Republicans," 205–8.
[21] See Friedrich's account of Althusius life and career in Carl J. Friedrich, ed., *Politica Methodice Digesta of Johannes Althusius* (Cambridge, MA: Harvard University Press, 1932), xxiii–xli.

1614). Various jurisprudential concepts – including the concept of sovereignty (*iura maiestas*) itself – saturate his early work. However, after his move to Emden in 1604 and the publication of the second edition of the *Politica* in 1610, the *de rigueur* jurisprudential tropes and structures recede while Althusius' innovative conception of consociation becomes more central.[22] Scattola suggests that this is potentially due to the fact that Althusius' early writings were designed for legal instruction at the university, while his later work was written for a broader audience, as Althusius served as both a church and town elder in Emden.[23]

Several features of Althusius' career and context are important to underscore. The first pertains to the unique intellectual culture of the Herborn Academy, where Althusius served on faculty beginning in 1586, including two stints as rector.[24] Herborn was founded in 1584 by John VI of Nassau-Dillenburg at the request of his brother, William I of Orange. Herborn quickly became a hub of Reformed theological and political influence in the region, due in large part to internecine Protestant conflict during this period. Several years before the Academy was founded, Frederick III – a formidable sponsor of Reformed Protestantism in the Palatinate – died. After his death, Frederick's rigorously Lutheran son removed hundreds of Reformed scholars and pastors from their posts. A Reformed diaspora ensued, as prominent theologians such as Zanchi, Ursinus, and Olevianus were forced to find new institutional homes.[25] Olevianus became rector of the new academy at Herborn. While he died soon after assuming his post, he managed to recruit many prominent – and recently unemployed – Reformed scholars. Herborn quickly became known for the covenantal theology of Johannes Piscator, Matthias Martinius, Philippus Hoenius, and Olevianus, whose classic work on the topic was published in 1585. As Gerhard Menk, Joachim Wienecke, and Howard Hotson have noted, Herborn also had a distinct political reputation during its early years for generating theories of resistance.[26]

---

[22] Merio Scattola, "Von der Maiestas zur Symbiosis," in *Politische Begriffe*.

[23] Scattola, "Von der Maiestas zur Symbiosis," 217. Cf. Richard Tuck, *Philosophy and Government, 1572–1651* (Cambridge: Cambridge University Press, 1993), 157–8.

[24] See Gerhard Menk's classic work on Herborn, *Die Hohe Schule Herborn in ihrer Frühzeit* (Wiesbaden: Selbstverlag der Historischen Kommission für Nassau, 1981).

[25] Euan Cameron, *The European Reformation* (Oxford: Clarendon Press, 1991), 380–2; Daniel Toft, *Shadow of Kings: The Political Thought of David Pareus, 1548–1622* (PhD diss., University of Wisconsin-Madison, 1970), 67–8.

[26] See Menk, *Die Hohe Schule Herborn*, 233–4, 260–3; Howard Hotson and Maria Rosa Antognazza, *Alsted and Leibniz on God, the Magistrate, and the Millennium* (Wiesbaden: Harrassowitz, 1999), 101–4.

Before his death in 1586, Olevianus' efforts at recruitment brought Althusius to Herborn. H. H. Esser describes Olevianus as Althusius' "intellectual and spiritual sponsor," and a theological mentor as early as 1577. Other scholars, primarily German and Anglophone political and legal historians, have been puzzled by the connections between Althusius and the Reformed intellectual culture that surrounded him throughout his career. After all, Althusius was trained by Reformed theologians and jurists, formed close professional and personal relationships with many renowned Reformed scholars of his day, taught law at one of the most prominent Reformed academies at the turn of the seventeenth century, and gave up his academic career to take an active role in ecclesial and civic life in the community of Reformed exiles at Emden – while also allegedly writing one of the first theories of modern "secularized political science." The cognitive dissonance is telling.

The juxtaposition of Althusius' theological context with modern assumptions about his *Politica* is revealing. Robert Kingdon, John Witte, and others have noted the pervasive influence of Reformed theologians on Althusius, which is manifest through his countless citations of the works of John Calvin, Philip Melanchthon, Theodore Beza, David Pareus, Franciscus Junius, Girolamo Zanchi, Wilhelm Zepper, and others.[27] While most of these theological references are bracketed in the footnotes of modern editions of the *Politica*, the original Latin editions – which lacked footnotes – included them in long paragraphs replete with ancient, medieval, and contemporaneous citations.[28] It is common to find appeals to Zanchi and Junius interspersed among references to jurists such as Gregoire and Andrea Alciato, and ancient and medieval thinkers such as Aristotle and Thomas Aquinas. Together, the writings of theologians, jurists, and philosophers comprise a treasury of authoritative norms, maxims, and practices relevant to Althusius' conception of political life.

Here we must return to Althusius' consociation, allegedly his principal contribution to modern secular political theory. Recall that one of the

---

[27] Robert Kingdon, "Althusius' Use of Calvinist Sources," *Rechtstheorie* 16 (1997): 19–28; John Witte, *The Reformation of Rights: Law, Religion and Human Rights in Early Modern Calvinism* (Cambridge: Cambridge University Press, 2007), 143–207; Stephen Grabill, *Rediscovering the Natural Law in Reformed Theological Ethics* (Grand Rapids, MI: Eerdmans Publishing, 2006), 122–50.

[28] Like many contemporaneous works, Althusius' *Politica* was structured so that it could be employed in university instruction. It alternates between summary paragraphs, which offer a claim about the topic at hand, and paragraphs of reference material, which characteristically cite a series of authoritative biblical, theological, philosophical, and jurisprudential sources. The latter paragraphs are often printed in smaller type. In modern editions, the differentiation between summary and source paragraphs is lost.

challenges raised by early and late modern critics of monarchomach theory is the claim that the covenants are essentially legal fictions with no basis in actual historical practice.[29] Mornay and others tried to demonstrate that covenantal relations among God, the ruler, and the ruled constitute the political order. This monarchomach claim was vigorously contested, especially with respect to pagan kings and peoples, as we have seen. Writing twenty to thirty years after the *Vindiciae* and other monarchomach treatises, Althusius was keenly aware of the absolutist counterarguments of James VI, Alberico Gentili, William Barclay, and others.

Althusius explicitly adopts the monarchomach doctrine of the double covenant in later sections of the *Politica*. Some scholars have argued that this placement of the double covenant indicates that the doctrine is ancillary to Althusius' fundamental political theory. In the next section, I will show how this fails to account for the rationale underlying the structure of the *Politica*. At present, I merely want to acknowledge that Althusius' discussion of the monarchomach covenant, per se, follows upon his discussion of the consociation, and that this is an important detail.

Etymologically, consociation (*consociatio*) is a noteworthy term in Althusius' immediate context. It is extremely rare in classical and medieval texts. In a handful of Roman sources, the term may refer to an alliance,[30] or a legal bond constituting a public association. Cicero occasionally refers to *consociationes* that bind a community together and conform individual pursuits or desires to a common purpose.[31] After Cicero, ancient and medieval references are rather sporadic until the sixteenth century.[32] Aquinas occasionally uses the term. In his discussion of friendship, he defines consociational fellowship as a "reason for love" of self and neighbor insofar as the consociation is ordered to one's relationship with God.[33] It is through consociational

---

[29] In addition to this charge, Jürgen Habermas criticizes Althusius' theory for failing to provide reasons for which people would enter into covenant in the first place, let alone for continuing to support the ruler of the covenanted commonwealth: "Althusius cannot explain why individuals should enter into contracts at all, nor can he explain why they should respect the contracts once in force; and above all why the sovereign power, though it is conceived as originating in such contracts, should then, as constituted force, stand uncontested by the parties to the contract." According to Habermas, Hobbes helps to resolve some of Althusius' theoretical incoherence. *Theory and Practice* (Boston, MA: Beacon Press, 1973), 62–4.
[30] Livy, *History of Rome*, XL.5.10.
[31] Cicero, *De Officiis*, I.44 (157).
[32] See Conor Zwierlein, "Consociatio," in Francesco Ingravalle and Corrado Malandrino, eds., *Il Lessico Della Politica di Johannes Althusius* (Firenze: L.S. Olschki, 2005), 143–68.
[33] Thomas Aquinas, *Summa Theologiae*, II.II q26a4–5; cf. II.II q25a12.

relationships, Aquinas argues, that we can have "full participation" in the happiness of the union.

In the sixteenth century, the term has a specific theological and even sacramental gloss in early Protestant writings. Here, the recent work of Conor Zwierlein is an important corrective to much of the older German scholarship on this matter. Contrary to Dreitzel and others, Zwierlein has pointed out that references to *consociatio* are scattered throughout the writings of Protestant theologians such as Melanchthon, Ursinus, and Pierre Boquin. In these theological writings, the term does reflect a Ciceronian legacy, but is also used to signify the sacred fellowship that arises between God and God's people. Union with God involves a consociation of members who are bound together in recognition of the great love that is intrinsic to God's own nature, and which God extends to his human creatures. Consociation, Zwierlein writes, is best described as the Latin correlate for the theologically freighted Greek term *koinonia*.

We can find evidence for this claim in the writings of many of Althusius' theological sources, often in an ecclesiological or sacramental context. Ursinus defined the "spiritual fellowship" (*spiritualis consociatio*) between Christ and the church as participation in certain common goods.[34] The term also appears in the eucharistic debates between the orthodox Lutherans and crypto-Calvinists.[35] Melanchthon referred to the eucharistic meal as the means by which individuals enjoy fellowship (*koinonia*) or consociation (*consociatio*) with the body of Christ.[36] Similarly, as Zwierlein notes, Lambert Daneau in his 1596 *Politices Christianae* refers to the ecclesial body as a society of Christians that has been assembled and consociated (*consociatus*).[37]

The term has applications beyond ecclesiology and eucharistic theology as well. Three Reformed theologians, Theodore Beza, Franciscus Junius, and Immanuel Tremellius, produced a new Latin Bible translation between 1569 and 1580, which was widely used among Protestants through the seventeenth century.[38] In their marginal notes on Ecclesiastes, Junius and Tremellius use

---

[34] Zacharias Ursinus, *Commentary on the Heidelberg Catechism*, trans. G. W. Williard (1851), reprint of second American edition (Columbus, OH: Scott & Bascom, 1852), q. 77.

[35] Friedrich Bente, *Historical Introductions to the Book of Concord* (St Louis, MO: Concordia, 1965 [1921]), 180.

[36] Quoted in Philip Schaff, *History of the Christian Church*, vol. 8 (New York, NY: Charles Scribner's Sons, 1910), §133.

[37] Conor Zwierlein, "Reformierte Theorien der Vergesellschaftung: römisches Recht, föderaltheologische koinonia und die consociatio des Althusius," in Frederick Carney et al., eds., *Jurisprudenz, politische Theorie und politische Theologie* (Berlin: Duncker and Humblot, 2004), 215.

[38] For the greater part of a century, the Beza-Junius-Tremellius Bible – sometimes called the "Protestant Vulgate" – was the preferred edition of British and continental Protestants. It was used extensively by figures from Philip Sydney to John Donne to John Milton.

consociate as a verb. Commenting on the proverbs, "Though one may be over-powered, two can defend themselves. A cord of three strands is not quickly broken,"[39] the theologians write, "stronger are those who consociate the work among themselves." The consociation is taken to be a form of relationship in which members are bound together such that they are able to participate in certain common goods that cannot be enjoyed in isolation. Put simply, the consociation is greater than the sum of its parts.[40]

In addition to the Ciceronian references to *consociatio*, we have to account for the theological context of the term, which surrounded Althusius during the period he was writing the *Politica*. As Zwierlein argues, the concept provides Althusius with the means to merge a set of Aristotelian axioms about human sociality with jurisprudential forms and theological beliefs.[41] Through the consociation and its covenantal law, as we will now see, Althusius is able to construct what Zwierlein calls a "formal analogy" (*Strukturanalogie*) between political forms of consociation, on one side, and the covenantal fellowship of God and the people of God, on the other.

With this, we have our first reason to doubt the covenant-versus-consociation dichotomy that underlies a good deal of German and Anglophone scholarship. The dichotomy posits a sharp distinction between the secular and the religious that the concept simply could not support in Althusius' intellectual context. Althusius' consociationalism cannot be autonomous of his theological commitments, or his conception of covenant in particular. Rather, the consociation is the means by which Althusius is able to offer a sophisticated account of the covenant-as-fellowship conception that was *already* widely used by Reformed theologians to describe the relationship between God and God's people, as well as the ruler and the ruled. In this sense, we should be wary of attempts to reduce what counts as "Reformed" to discrete beliefs about soteriology (e.g. the doctrine of predestination), hermeneutics (e.g. an emphasis on the relevance of the Hebrew Bible or Mosaic Law), or political doctrine (e.g. the double covenant idea in isolation from a broader conception of covenant). The intellectual context of Althusius and his Reformed colleagues is too wide-ranging to admit for these sorts of reductions.

---

[39] Immanuel Tremellius and Franciscus Junius, eds., *Testamenti Veteris Biblia Sacra*, notes on Ecc 4: 8 (in modern English, 4:12).

[40] Also of interest is the 1541 Latin-German dictionary of Petrus Cholinus and Johannes Frisius which defines *consociatio* along covenantal or contractual lines as a *Vereinbarung* (covenant) or *Zusammenfügung, Dictionarium latinogermanicum* (Zurich, 1541).

[41] Zwierlein, "Reformierte Theorien," 217.

CONSOCIATIONAL COVENANT AND LAW

In contrast to earlier monarchomach treatises, Althusius' *Politica* was written during a time of relative peace in Western Europe. By the time that Althusius published his revised second edition in 1610, the political crises in France and the Netherlands had largely abated. A ceasefire between the United Provinces and the Spanish crown began in 1609, and lasted over a decade. Meanwhile, in France, the converted Catholic king, Henri IV, published the Edict of Nantes in 1598, establishing tenuous peace terms between warring Huguenot and Catholic parties. At the same time, as Scattola has written, the three editions of the *Politica* clearly reflect Althusius' wariness about political and military threats posed by royal and imperial Catholic powers, on one side, and provincial Lutheran ones, on the other. The Herborn Academy, after all, had served as a refuge for Reformed scholars ousted by Lutheran rulers. Similarly, when Althusius moved to Emden in 1604, he assumed a position of civic and ecclesial leadership in a community of Reformed exiles that had recently declared its independence from the Lutheran Count Edzard II and his son Enno III of East Frisia. The citizens of Emden, no less than the academics at Herborn, took themselves to be engaged in resistance to unjust and tyrannical powers. As Scattola notes, each edition of the *Politica* manifests Althusius' intent to provide a theoretical justification for Reformed resistance, and a decisive refutation of the crop of absolutist theories that appeared in the first decade of the seventeenth century.[42]

While the anti-absolutist aims of Althusius are present even in his first edition, the most innovative aspects of Althusius' work begin to emerge in the second edition of 1610. The first edition was a sort of *digestum*, a compilation of authoritative maxims that attempted to summarize, arrange, and occasionally improve upon traditional political doctrines.[43] In the subsequent editions, Althusius provided a more comprehensive account of the symbiotic relations within the consociation, which includes the exchange of services, goods, and rights that constitute the political community.[44]

The later editions of Althusius' *Politica* provide a philosophical account of the sorts of antecedent relationships that give rise to norms and obligations. Politics, as Althusius defines it in the first sentence of the first book, is the "art of consociating persons to the end of establishing, cultivating, and conserving social life among them." Subsequently, Althusius describes politics as a form

---

[42]   Scattola, "Von der Maiestas zur Symbiosis," 248–9.
[43]   Scattola, "Von der Maiestas zur Symbiosis," 215.
[44]   Scattola, "Von der Maiestas zur Symbiosis," 220.

of "symbiotics" in which members (*symbiotici*) of the political community "obligate themselves reciprocally to each other, by explicit or tacit covenant (*pactum*), to mutual communication of whatever is useful and necessary for the shared exercise of social life."[45]

What follows throughout the rest of the *Politica* is an elaboration of what this consociational conception of rightly ordered politics might look like. The structure of the final edition of the *Politica* is not readily apparent on first glance at the table of contents. Althusius, who was trained in Ramist pedagogy, characteristically uses an extensive table containing a series of binary distinctions to distinguish the elements of politics. It is these tables that provide the key to understanding the overall structure of the *Politica*.[46]

Following his general account and definition of consociational politics, Althusius begins making a series of increasingly meticulous distinctions among the forms, functions, and offices of political community. After accounting for various forms of "simple" private consociations, such as the family and *collegium* (books 2–4), and "particular" public consociations, such as cities and local provinces (books 5–8),[47] Althusius proceeds to consider what he calls the *universalis maior consociatio* – namely, the commonwealth. His analysis of the commonwealth takes up the majority of the *Politica*. Following his schema, we can outline his analysis in three main parts plus two appendices:

- Books 9–17 describe the symbiotic fellowship of a well-ordered consociation, and the rights[48] that constitute it.
- Books 18–27 concern the "who" of the consociation: the offices and officeholders authorized to oversee and preserve the rights of the commonwealth. This includes discussion of what constitutes these offices

---

[45] Unless otherwise noted, I have used the third edition of Althusius' *Politica methodice digesta* (Herborn, 1614); see I.1, 2.

[46] What may have been a useful pedagogical tool for Althusius and his students is no longer intuitive to modern readers. The modern abridged English edition of the *Politica* helpfully supplies a schema of the extensive tables that Althusius uses to outline the components of politics.

[47] Althusius' analysis of these intermediary consociations is added in the second edition. Scattola, "Von der Maiestas zur Symbiosis," 214.

[48] In Althusius' intellectual context, the term *ius* does not correspond directly to the modern English concept of right or rights. I briefly address this matter below. The literature on this topic is vast, but representative analyses include Brian Tierney, *The Idea of Natural Rights: Studies on Natural Rights, Natural Law and Church Law 1150–1625* (Grand Rapids, MI: Eerdmans, 1997); Annabel Brett, *Liberty, Right, and Nature: Individual Rights in Later Scholastic Thought* (Cambridge: Cambridge University Press, 1997); Kenneth Pennington, "The History of Rights in Western Thought," *Emory Law Journal* 47 (1998): 237–52; and Oliver O'Donovan, "The Language of Rights and Conceptual History," *Journal of Religious Ethics* 37:2 (June 2009): 193–207.

and what sorts of knowledge and virtues are required to administer the
rights of the consociation properly.

- Books 28–37 concern the "what" of the consociation: the goods and
  services of the commonwealth over which officeholders have administrative oversight. This includes discussion of the public functions and
  relationships that the rights of the consociation are meant to preserve, via
  two modes of administration – ecclesial and civil.
- Books 38 and 39 are, functionally, appendices on the species of tyranny,
  the forms of legitimate resistance, and the administrative types of political rule.

In response to the consociation-versus-covenant interpretation, we should
observe that Althusius' primary analysis of the monarchomach double covenant occurs at the outset of book 28. This is significant, insofar as Althusius'
discussion of the particular terms of covenantal relations takes place *subsequent* to his discussion of the symbiotic nature and offices of consociational
life. The reasons for this ordering will become apparent as we turn to
Althusius' analysis of consociational law and covenant.

Althusius on Law

Scholars often describe Althusius' consociation as a theoretical innovation,
and they have good reasons for doing so. At the same time, Althusius' consociational politics relies extensively on many traditional political beliefs and
practices. In fact, as we have seen, Althusius took himself to be providing an
accurate empirical description of the way that human beings consociate
together. He did not intend to construct what he calls a top-down "utopian"
theory of political life. In fact, he faults some of his close colleagues, and even
(somewhat unfairly) Thomas More, for pursuing those goals.[49]

Althusius' conception of law shares many traditional, often Aristotelian or
Thomistic, commitments about the nature of justice and political obligation.
In order to grasp what is new or distinctive about Althusius' consociation, we
first need to outline the broad contours of Althusius' conception of law.

---

[49] Althusius writes: "Nor can I here approve the opinion of Bartholomaeus Keckermann and
Philip Hoenonius, who suppose that in politics the types of supreme magistrate are first to be
taught, then the mixed state constituted from the three types that we have discussed, and only
then the provinces and cities. This conflicts with the law of method." The methodological law
to which Althusius refers is his principle that one ought to start with the most basic forms of
consociation and built up, so to speak, to the heights of consociational politics – the
"universal" commonwealth, *Politica*, XXXIX.84, 966.

For Althusius, as for many of his Reformed theological colleagues, the fellowship between God and human persons provides determinate content for the norms and relations of the political community. Political life was natural, or creational, in a distinctive theological sense. It is perhaps somewhat surprising that, on this particular point, Althusius sounds rather more Aristotelian than Augustinian: human persons are always already in consociation with each other; the governing structures of the political community are expressions of this fundamental reality. As E. H. Kossmann put it, for continental Reformed theorists in Althusius' context, "the transition from natural to civil society occurred calmly since the state was actually little more than the institutionalization of what had always existed since man was created."[50]

As in the theological writings of his pupil Johann Heinrich Alsted, Althusius believes that various relations of command and obedience are built into the framework of God's creation, ordered to their respective common goods. Ecclesial relations ought to bring forth and sustain "pious, learned, wise, and good persons." Likewise, the ordered relations of the political nobility and middle-class burghers ought to produce individuals equipped with the virtues needed to preserve the common goods of their vocation and community.[51] We can see evidence of this in all varieties of human relations, he says, insofar as "in every consociation and form of symbiosis some persons are rulers ... others are subjects, or inferior." Althusius, like the vast majority of his contemporaries, assumes this is true for the domestic as well as the political sphere: Husbands occupy an office of rule, while wives take up an office of subjection,[52] just as there exist roles of rule and subjection in the political community.

The anti-egalitarianism of Althusius' thought is as unexceptional in his context as it is problematic in ours. Still, two qualifying features stand out. First, Althusius consistently analyzes these relationships in terms of role and social obligation. That is to say, he believes that certain public offices and duties (*officia*) exist for the common good of the relationship; insofar as a person fails to perform the duties that obtain to the office they occupy, the corresponding party may no longer be obligated to obey. The implications of

---

[50] E. H. Kossmann, *Political Thought in the Dutch Republic* (Koninklijke Nederlandse. Akademie van Wetenschappen; Amsterdam, 2000), 29.

[51] *Politica*, VIII.48, 149.

[52] He writes: "The conjugal consociation and symbiosis is one in which the husband and wife, who are bound each to the other, communicate the advantages and responsibilities of married life," *Politica*, II.38, 23. And: "The director and governor of the common affairs pertaining to this consociation is the husband. The wife and family are obedient, and do what is commanded," II.40, 24. Cf. Anna Becker, "Gender in the History of Early Modern Political Thought," *The Historical Journal* (2017): 1–21.

this view of social roles and obligations becomes clear not only in Althusius' discussion of resistance to tyranny, but in his engagement with William Barclay on the matter of divorce, and its relevance for political relations.

Althusius points out that Barclay's paternalist view of political rule – discussed in the last chapter—is directly related to his view of marriage and the duties that obtain in these analogous consociations. According to Barclay, an equal cannot have *imperium*, or the authority to command, over another equal. Therefore, Althusius remarks, "Barclay says that as the husband who is constituted over his wife is her superior, so the king is superior to the commonwealth and realm." However, this involves a fundamental confusion about the nature of command and obedience, according to Althusius:

> I say that the superiority and power the husband has over his wife he derives from the marriage. And this is only for a time and with a condition, namely, that it lasts as long as the marriage endures, that is, as long as the marriage is not dissolved by adultery, desertion, or death. When the marriage is dissolved, every marital power he exercises over his wife is ended. Of equal seriousness with desertion is the intolerable cruelty of a husband that makes it impossible to live with him. Because of incurable cruelty, and its hazard to life and health, theologians concede dissolution of marriage, and defend divorce by the authority of sacred scripture.[53]

On these terms, it becomes clear that while Althusius does take the office of husband to be one of rule over the office of wife, he believes that the power derives from the relationship itself. A person comes to acquire the power to rule over a particular (marital) consociation through participation in the relationship, and obedience to its terms. This opens up the possibility for moral and legal conditions, and even communal accountability, since – as many of Althusius' Protestant theological colleagues would affirm[54] – the wife of an absent or abusive husband could appeal to civil or ecclesial authorities for support and retributive justice. The political analogies of this view are equally clear for Althusius, who introduces the idea of a lawful "divorce" between political rulers and their subjects on account of "the intolerable and incurable tyranny of a king by which all upright cohabitation and consociation with him are destroyed." If a marital consociation, which is "ordained by divine authority to be indissoluble," may be dissolved because of a serious breach of covenant, why not the political consociation? After all,

---

[53] *Politica*, XVIII.105, 313.
[54] Althusius specifically cites Beza in this passage. He could have appealed to many other Protestant authorities as well, including the well-known writings of Martin Bucer on this matter.

he argues contra Barclay, consociational relations of command and obedience are constituted by the relationship, not vice versa.

Althusius similarly recognizes that the orders of rule and obedience entail mutual recognition of virtue, excellence, and spiritual gifts. God provides consociational forms of life for his people so that individuals may learn to live well in community. In fact, the diversity and disparity of talents and goods only serves to strengthen the consociational bonds. It is for this reason, Althusius writes, that "God willed to train and teach human persons not through angels, but through our fellows."[55] Althusius here alludes to Calvin's statement that "God might have acted, in this respect, by himself, without any aid or instrument, or might even have done it by angels; but there are several reasons why he rather chooses to employ men." Strikingly, while Calvin is referring to the conditions under which God governs the ministry of the church, Althusius applies this dictum to consociational life more broadly. Just as God blesses his people, the church, through spiritual gifts, Althusius writes that God also scatters his gifts among all members of the consociation: "He did not confer all things to one person, but some to one and some to others, so that you have need for my gifts, and I for yours." Drawing on the Pauline image of the church as a body with many parts, Althusius describes the origin of consociational life: Since God spread his gifts unevenly through the consociational body, "so was born, as it were, the need for communicating necessary and useful things, which communication was not possible except in social and political life." Through this means, we can see that God desires

> that each person need the service and aid of others in order that friendship would bind all together, and no one would consider another to be valueless. For if each did not need the aid of others, what would society be? What would reverence and order be? What would reason and humanity be? Every one therefore needs the experience and contributions of others, and no one lives to himself alone.[56]

This leads directly to a second qualifying feature of Althusius' consociational understanding of command and obedience, which regards his claim in I.28–9 that consent (*consensus*) is an essential cause of consociation. As I noted earlier, scholars such as Martin van Gelderen and Daniel Lee have, quite legitimately, emphasized the consensual nature of Althusius' consociation. Althusius repeatedly calls consent the "efficient cause" of political consociation. In order for a consociation, including a marital one, to endure, it must

---

[55] *Politica*, I.26, 8.
[56] *Politica*, I.25–6, 8.

involve the ongoing consent, support, or agreement of its members. To this extent, at least, we can see that there are clear (although, by contemporary standards, still insufficient) consensual limits on Althusius' conception of natural relationships of command and obedience.

However, attention to what Althusius calls the efficient cause is not enough. While van Gelderen and Lee, among others, focus on this particular cause of consociation, they neglect to mention the *other* three causes. According to Althusius, the efficient cause is necessarily related to: the formal cause, which is the communicative and institutional practices of the fellowship; the material cause, which is the aggregate of precepts for communicating things for the common good; and perhaps most importantly, the final cause, which is the communal enjoyment of the good life, piety, and justice.[57]

Apart from these causes, Althusius does not believe that the ongoing agreement of the people to the terms of the consociation is sufficient. Certainly, if members of the consociation did not continue to support or consent to the terms of the relationships, the consociation would disintegrate. But this is one consideration among others: Without the formal cause, the consociation would lack the necessary rational, communicative, and institutional structures for its existence. Without the material cause, the consociation would not have the norms or exemplary practices by which its members could make judgments about, or regulate, their common forms of life. Without the final cause, the political consociation would lack an ordering purpose.

Notice that Althusius' use of fourfold causation is related to Beza's earlier discussion of the tyranny of Minos – although presented in a more nuanced manner. Like Beza, Althusius believes that that consent is an insufficient criterion for rightly ordered political relations. This would be a fundamental misconception of the nature and purpose of law, since people might agree to all sorts of unjust and impious terms, perhaps under threat of violence. To prevent these sorts of unjust social relations and political orders, we must be able to articulate a better conception of law in general.

Althusius' most concentrated analysis of the nature and ends of law appears in book 21, which begins his account of the cardinal virtue of political prudence that is required in the magistrate's administration of the commonwealth. Althusius believes that political prudence may be divided and subdivided into various species and kinds, which fall under the categories of understanding (*intellectus*) and judgment (*delectus*). For our purposes, what matters most is his three-part account of political knowledge (*scientia*) in particular: the rule of living and administering (that is, law), the nature of the people, and the nature of rule or *imperium*.

Like Beza, Mornay, and other Reformed theologians, Althusius states that "norm of living, obeying, and administering" is the will of God, which instructs us about the way of life (*via vitae*), what ought to be done and not done.[58] Citing more than a dozen biblical passages, Althusius writes that the magistrate who has oversight over the consociation is obligated by his office to use this law as a measure and touchstone in his political judgments. Laws in general, therefore, are like "hedges, walls, guards, or boundaries" that direct us along the way to "wisdom, happiness, and peace in human society."[59] Without law, human consociations devolve into a bestial form of life (*belvina vita*).

Althusius' account of natural law follows upon this general definition. Much like Zanchi, from whom he borrows extensively, Althusius frames his analysis of natural law within a broader description of the virtues needed for members of the commonwealth to flourish in society. Law in general, of which natural law is one species, is required so that individuals may identify the characteristic forms of human flourishing that pertain to them in their social context. Without these sorts of laws, the symbiotic goods of the community would disintegrate.

Natural law, which Althusius sometimes calls common law,[60] regards the natural forms of knowledge and inclination that God "implanted" in all human persons. Through this natural law, human beings may specify the sorts of reasons (*rationes*) and means (*media*) that direct them toward right relations with God and neighbor; namely, God is to be honored, and the neighbor to be loved.[61] Following Zanchi and other Reformed Thomists, Althusius states that by this "natural inclination, or secret impulse of nature, we are urged to perform what we understand to be just, and to avoid what we recognize to be wicked." Also

---

[58] *Politica*, XXI.16, 403.

[59] *Politica*, XXI.18, 406.

[60] The conflation of terms is occasionally problematic, and probably due to the composite influences of the theologians and jurists in Althusius' corpus. For the jurists, *lex communis* could refer to the common judgments and practices of various peoples. Althusius occasionally uses the term in this way, although in his more theoretical passages, he hews closer to the theological valence of natural law, as seen in Zanchi and others. See Jean Porter on the differences between scholastic canon and civil law, *Natural and Divine Law* (Grand Rapids, MI: Eerdmans, 1999), 25–61.

[61] "Quoad notitiam et inclinationem, quibus media et rationem Dei colendi et proximi diligendi, omnibus hominibus praescribit, indicat, et ad illa impellit," *Politica*, XXI.19, 406–7. Quoting the Reformed theologian Benedict Aretius, Althusius calls natural law "nothing other than the general theory and practice of love, both for God and for one's neighbor," XXI.20, 407. Althusius appears to cite the wrong passage in Aretius' *Problemata Sacra*. The comments on natural law and its relation to Christian love appear in locus 149, in which Aretius argues against the Anabaptist claim that the *ius naturae* is at odds with the Christian *regula charitatis*.

like Zanchi, Althusius argues that the efficacy of this law – that is, the extent to which it does in fact "propel" individuals toward what is truly good and the just – varies greatly.[62] There are different grades (*gradus*) of this natural inclination, as God enlivens or "excites" this internal law in different ways in different individuals. In this sense, natural law is not a set of determinate judgments that any rational individual can make. Rather, like Zanchi, Althusius describes natural law as the means by which human beings, reliant on the grace of God, are able to recognize that which is good or evil.[63]

At the same time, Althusius does not follow Zanchi in providing a detailed theoretical explanation of how natural law is conceptually distinct from the moral law of the Decalogue. He clearly recognizes the difference between the two species of law in many passages, while in others he uses natural, common, and moral law as synonyms. In terms of his theory of law, this latter practice can be misleading, since it is not always immediately clear whether Althusius is referring to the *principia* of natural law or to the further elaboration of these *principia* that God reveals in the Hebrew Bible and New Testament.[64]

Like many Reformed theologians, Althusius believes that the Mosaic Law in particular was a summary and elaboration of the moral *principia* that God gave to humanity in creation. This helps to explain the lack of a consistent and precise distinction between natural and moral law in the *Politica*. Althusius takes the moral precepts of the Decalogue to be effective pedagogical starting points for his political analysis. In fact, he faults other political thinkers for failing to account for the ways that the precepts of the Decalogue "infuse a vital spirit" into consociational life, since they "constitute a way, rule, guiding star, and boundary for human society."[65] While specific theological

---

[62] Cf. Althusius, *Dicaeologicae* (Frankfurt, 1618), 1.13.11, 36–7.

[63] For this reason, as Merio Scattola argues, Althusius stands within the tradition of premodern natural law discourse, which is distinct from the modern theories that begin appearing later in the seventeenth century, "Models in the History of Natural Law," in *Ius commune. Zeitschrift für Europäische Rechtsgeschichte* 28 (2001), 91–159. See also the comments from Annabel Brett and others on Althusius' objective, rather than subjective, view of natural law: Brett, *Changes of State: Nature and the Limits of the City in Early Modern Natural Law* (Princeton, NJ: Princeton University Press, 2011), 162; "The History of Contract as a Motif in Political Thought," *The American Historical Review* 84:4 (Oct. 1979), 925–6; Scattola, "Von der maiestas zur symbiosis," 224.

[64] My own judgment on this matter is that Althusius' conceptual confusion is the result of his attempt to combine two related but distinct discourses on law: one drawn from the theologians and the other from the jurists. While Althusius cites liberally from both, the influence of the latter is particularly notable when he reverts to talking about common law as a synonym of natural law.

[65] *Politica*, preface to the second and third editions. Interestingly, it was this pedagogical use of the Decalogue that sparked controversy even among his colleagues at Herborn. Althusius cites

and theoretical distinctions between natural and divine moral law are often present in the *Politica*, they are not always made explicit, as in the theological writings of Zanchi, Junius, and others.[66]

Despite the conceptual slippage in Althusius' references to natural, common, and the moral law of the Decalogue, he is rather more precise about the relationship between natural and positive law.[67] This is likely no accident, since it is this distinction that he regards as essential to his anti-absolutist conception of law and political order.

On the matter, Althusius affirms many of the maxims and theological commitments of earlier Augustinian, Thomist, Reformed, and monarchomach thinkers. Accounting for the particular circumstances of his people, a prudent magistrate must make particular political judgments from the general *principia* of natural and moral law. In this way, positive law is "nothing other than the practice of this natural law as adapted to a particular polity." Citing Zanchi, Althusius notes that the *principia* of natural law do not immediately give us the "particular conclusions [that are] suitable to the nature and condition of an action and its circumstances." Nor does natural law prove sufficient to restrain evil and promote the good. It is important to note that for Althusius even the Decalogue provides only further *general* moral categories (do not murder, do not steal); it offers "no certain, special, and fixed" set of conclusions about how those moral norms ought to be adapted to particular contexts and communities.[68]

Rather, positive law ought to instruct individuals how they might seek after and achieve natural justice: "for which reason it is called the servant and handmaiden of common law, and a teacher leading us to the observance of common law."[69] All species of law – natural, moral, and positive – are based on right reason (*recta ratio*) and are ordered to the same end: "justice and piety ... and the same equity and common good in human society."[70] They

---

Zanchi in support of the claim that the moral precepts of the Decalogue are binding insofar as they "agree and explain" the law of nature common to all peoples, XXI.29.

[66] Compare Althusius' later work on jurisprudence, *Dicaeologicae*, in which he distinguishes between the various species of law in a slightly different manner. He claims that many theorists erroneously describe various species of law – such as the law of nations or common law – as "effects" of law. It is more accurate, he claims, to call these "efficient causes of law," since all law is collected from the precepts of right reason. In this sense, all law is rational judgment about the good, *Dicaeologicae*, 1.13.9, 36.

[67] Althusius also calls positive law *lex propria*. In order to avoid confusion, I have adopted a consistent terminology.

[68] *Politica*, XXI.33, 416.

[69] *Politica*, XXI.30, 414.

[70] *Politica*, XXI.32, 415.

differ with respect to contingency, or what Althusius calls "the possibility and necessity of just changes." Positive law is distinctly "adaptable to time and circumstance." Therefore, while Althusius notes that the moral law requires that God be worshipped, "positive law determines that this is to be done each seventh day."

In this way, the obligations of natural law (e.g. avoid evil) and the moral law of the Decalogue (e.g. do not murder) remain general precepts. It is positive law that makes these general obligations determinate, and "accommodates them to the experience and usefulness of the commonwealth and the circumstances of each activity." This points to the vital need for magistrates who possess the intellectual virtues necessary to understand the conditions of their people, and the moral virtues required to act justly toward them. This last claim, in fact, provides the rationale for Althusius' entire discussion of law.

On these terms, it can hardly be the will of the ruler *simpliciter* that makes a law morally or politically binding. As with Zanchi, Mornay, and other Reformed thinkers, Althusius affirms that an unjust law is no law at all. All positive civil law must be "mixed" with "something of natural and divine immutable justice."[71] Positive law "can obligate no one against natural and divine equity." There is no authoritative power (*potestas*) for evil. Rather, as Althusius cites the Salamancan theologian Fernando Vazquez, the nature and character of rule (*imperium*) and authority will be that they respect and care for the genuine utility and advantage of subjects.[72] On this same point, Althusius quotes the same passage from Augustine's *Civitas Dei* found in the *Political Education*: "to rule is nothing other than to serve the utility of others."

While Augustine and other earlier figures in the Christian tradition claimed that authoritative rule must be rightly ordered, Althusius provides an additional justification for this conception of law and authority. His conception entails a form of natural justice under the law: "administrators . . . regard their subjects not as slaves and bonded servants, but as brothers" (*sed suorum fratrum loco habere tenentur*). While fulfillment of their administrative duties will require rulers to issue directives to their subjects, this relationship of command and obedience does not rest simply on a pre-relational inequality. In fact, "before assuming this administration, and after resigning it," rulers are "equal and similar to all other private persons" (*rector et administrator par et similis est reliquis privatis hominibus*).[73] Again, it is important to see that Althusius *does* believe that individuals of "superior" talents and wisdom will

---

[71] *Politica*, IX.21, 177.
[72] *Politica*, IX.25, 179.
[73] *Politica*, XVIII.15, 180.

naturally rise to offices of rule, and that this is for the common good of the consociation.[74] However, we can distinguish this belief about the *propensity* and *capacity* for ruling office from the belief that the authority of the ruling office derives *simpliciter* from these "natural" propensities (a view that Althusius does not hold). This distinction helps to explain, for example, the apparent tension between Althusius' objectionable views about gender and his more innovative views about marital authority arising from the relationship, rather than the natural superiority of the male, per se.

This supplies further reasons for holding that the positive laws issued by the ruler must accord with natural and divine standards of justice in order to have moral and political force. Like Mornay and others, Althusius supports this claim theologically, by recourse to an *a fortiori* argument: If even God cannot sin by breaking his immutable law, how much more is the earthly ruler bound to norms of natural and divine justice? This hardly undermines the authority of the ruling office, rightly understood. This conception of law and authority stands against any rival view that entails "absolute power, or what is called the plenitude of power." In fact, it would be a misapplication of terms to ascribe this sort of power to any ruler, earthly *or divine*:

> Therefore, for an emperor to be unable and forbidden to do iniquitous and prohibited things does not detract from his power (*potentia*) or his liberty, but defines the ends and deeds in which his true power and liberty consist. For it is not the nature of rule (*imperium*) that it is able to rule in any manner whatever, nor is it the nature of power (*potestas*) that it can do anything whatever, but only what is fitting to nature and right reason. So God is not able to lie, as the Apostle [Paul] said, nor can he make two different things, such as light and darkness, exist at the same time in the same place. Nevertheless, he is not said to be less omnipotent. Nor is the king said to be impotent because he cannot ascend into the heavens, touch the skies with his hand, move mountains, or empty the ocean.[75]

All forms of power, Althusius argues, are "established for the utility of those who are ruled, not of those who rule, and the utility of the people or subjects does not in the least require unlimited power." This claim about the nature of rule and law derives quite directly from Althusius' theological beliefs about the way that God relates to his creation and creatures. Absolute power, he argues,

---

[74] *Politica*, I.37–8, 11.

[75] *Politica*, XXXIX.8, 946. Althusius repeats versions of this *a fortiori* argument in multiple passages: "Even almighty God is said not to be able to do what is evil and contrary to his nature," XIX.11, 330. Further, we do not consider God "to be less powerful because he is intrinsically unable to sin," XXXVIII.72, 914.

is not only unnecessary for the welfare of the people, it is "wicked and prohibited." This is true insofar as *absoluta potestas* refers to a species of power whose exercise is unjust by its very definition. Absolute power contradicts the principle, "we cannot do what can only be done injuriously," since it is unable to make the necessary moral distinctions between just and unjust acts.[76] In other words, absolutist conceptions of authority and law suffer from a normative deficiency.

In summary, Althusius' *a fortiori* argument regards two related matters: How can we countenance earthly *rulers* who claim prerogatives that transgress God's own norm of justice? Why should we obey *laws* that run contrary to the historical and covenantal conditions that obtain between the perfectly good God and his people?

Gentili and Barclay both draw Althusius' attention on this matter, the former with respect to the voluntarist conception of divine and regal authority, and the latter with respect to the nature of covenantal political agency. The first matter pertains to our earlier discussion of consent as the efficient cause of consociation. Althusius entertains the possibility of a people that has chosen to subject itself to a magistrate without protective "laws or conditions." In such cases, he notes, Gentili argues that the power of the magistrate is free and unlimited in accordance with the original consent of the people. Althusius answers that even in these cases, the people may avail themselves of other means of resistance. Original consent is insufficient justification for absolute power. The political relationship between the ruler and the ruled remains bound by "whatever things are holy, equitable, and just." These normative standards are determinative whether or not they were made explicit in the original election of the ruler or not. This is true, Althusius argues, because "there is no instance in which a people has conceded power to accomplish its own destruction."[77] To describe any political relationship in these terms would be to make a categorical mistake. How could a people ever truly agree to bestow someone with power to accomplish its own ruin? This runs contrary to the way that human beings reason about their own goods and ends.

This is doubly true insofar as Althusius argues that the power of the people is antecedent to the power of the prince. On this account, the political ruler is not the paterfamilias familiar to absolutist theory, but an administrative figure who, rather than "supporting his subjects, is supported by them."[78] The ruling office

---

[76] Along similar lines, Merio Scattola provocatively comments that modern theories of natural law run suffer from this normative deficiency, and introduce the possibility of the "end of tyranny," "Models," 43–7.

[77] *Politica*, XIX.33, 341–2.

[78] *Politica*, XXXVIII.78, 916–17.

is brought into existence for the common good of the consociation. The ruling person issues authoritative commands insofar as he or she does so in accordance with the antecedent norms and relations that order consociational life.

In this regard, the antecedent relationship between the people and their God is directly relevant. As Althusius argues, contra Gentili, the consociated people enjoy a relationship with God prior to any political structures or commands given by earthly sovereigns. Attendant to this antecedent relationship are certain norms that obligate the people of God to act in certain ways. Even if we did consider the earthly ruler as paterfamilias, Althusius argues, we would still be bound by Christ's claim, "whoever loves father or mother more than me is not worthy of me." As with the absolutist theorists, piety to God therefore conditions piety to earthly superiors. While Barclay appealed to the example of God the Father's absolute dominion over creation to defend the earthly sovereign's *imperium* over his people, Althusius appeals to our antecedent obligations to God in order to restrict and determine what the people owes to its ruler.

It is with respect to these terms that Althusius makes a corresponding appeal to the covenantal relations between God and his people – relations that provide determinate normative standards for political agency and obligation.

Althusius on Covenant

For Althusius, the claim about the relational nature of administrative authority rests on his underlying account of consociational power. Here, we arrive at one of Althusius' most widely recognized political doctrines: The rights of sovereignty, over which the ruler has administrative oversight, arise from the consociated people – *jura majestatis vero ut a corpore consociatio inceperunt*.

Annabel Brett has argued that Althusius' consociational power is emblematic of a new turn in early modern political thought. According to an earlier view, Brett argues, the figure with the authority to direct the community toward its common good was the regnant political ruler. He (and it was generally a *he*) was the "head" of the political body. Traditional political thought, with some notable exceptions, did not generally explain the origins of this political headship; it was simply assumed. In early modern thought, the political analogy of head and body took on a new meaning. Althusius – drawing on the work of sixteenth-century jurists such as Pierre Gregoire – speaks of the "spirit" (*spiritus*) or "soul" (*anima*) of the political body, which serves to bind the community together.[79] This spirit has a unitive as well as

---

[79] Brett specifically calls attention to the influence of Pierre Gregoire, *Changes of State*, 128–31. Cf. *Politica*, II.4.

directive function – it is that which "makes the body the specific body that it is." While granting that every political body, or consociation, has a figurative head, Althusius believes that there is a spirit in the body itself that serves to unite and constitute the community *qua* political community.[80] Brett suggests that this innovation marks an important break with traditional Aristotelian political thought, by making political rule a matter of unified *imperium* as well as power directed toward an end (the scholastic concept of *potestas*).

At the same time, Brett recognizes that Althusius maintains the new language of spirit and *imperium* alongside traditional analyses of power. Although she does not make this argument herself, this should suggest to us that we can better understand Althusius' conception of consociation as *both* traditional and modern: traditional with respect to his account of law and social order, and modern with respect to his theoretical attention to the origins of law and social order.

Here, Brett's attention to Althusius' language of spirit helps us understand what he says about the consociation and its covenants. As he explains in the preface to his first and third editions, the rights of sovereignty (*jura majestatis*) belong to the political consociation, rather than the supreme magistrate. It is these rights that he calls the "vital spirit, soul, heart, and life by which, when they are sound, the republic lives, and without which the commonwealth crumbles and dies, and is considered unworthy of the name."[81]

This statement needs some clarification on two conceptual points. First, with respect to the "rights" of the republic or consociation, we must note that Althusius is trading on a concept of rights distinct from that assumed by most modern theories. Brett helpfully underscores that for early modern Protestants and Aristotelians like Althusius, "the central sense [of *ius*] is neither an individual right nor a commanding law, but an intersubjective rightfulness or lawfulness, or the body of norms that governs a particular domain of such inter-subjectivity."[82] Rights and right-order are therefore fundamentally interrelated: A rightly ordered consociation is one in which the rights are preserved, and rights are preserved insofar as they rightly order the consociation. Althusius later explicitly defines the rights of sovereignty by reference to the Greek concepts of *eutaxia* and *eunomia*.[83] On these terms, when the ruler arrogates certain powers that rightly belong to the consociated people, he violates the *iura* that bind the community together.

---

[80]   Brett, *Changes of State*, 130.
[81]   *Politica*, preface to the first edition.
[82]   Brett, *Changes of State*, 91.
[83]   *Politica*, IX.15. Althusius refers to *eutaxia* in the second edition, *eunomia* in the third.

This leads to the second clarification. Althusius' use of the language of *ius* relates to his head-body-spirit metaphor. Just as a disordered consociation reflects the perversion or disintegration of its *iura*, it also reflects the failure of the spirit to unite the body together toward a common good. As Althusius clarifies in the preface to his third edition, it is the rights of sovereignty that are the consociation's spirit, and these are "so proper" to the consociation that "even if [the consociated people] wishes to abdicate them, to transfer and alienate them to another, it would by no means be able to do so, any more than one can communicate the life one enjoys to another." On these terms, the directive role of the political ruler, or "head," functions in service of the "spirit" of the consociational body. Althusius recognizes the ruler "as the administrator, overseer, and governor of these rights of sovereignty." However, the commonwealth, which itself is "consociated in one symbiotic body from many smaller consociations," retains the usufruct of sovereignty (*usufructuarium majestatis*). For this reason, when a mortal prince dies, his administrative power reverts to the consociated people, "which is called immortal because its generations perpetually succeed one after the other."[84]

In light of this, the foundation of Althusius' consociation does not appear to entail a rejection of Aristotelian teleology, or the Thomistic view that the head of the political body has directive power. Rather, Althusius retains the conceptual apparatus of the traditional conception of law and social order, but incorporates it within his innovative account of the consociation and the consociational origins of law and social order. The right of the realm, which is the unifying *spiritus* of the community, has as its purpose (*proposita*) the preservation of the good order of the consociation. Further, it is this *ius* that "directs the actions of all its members" toward these ends by means of "appropriate duties" and obligations.[85] Far from rejecting the traditional teleological structure of political order, Althusius confirms it, while locating the source of *imperium* and its *ius* in the consociated body itself.[86]

---

[84] *Politica*, preface to the third edition.

[85] *Politica*, IX.15, 173. This claim also clarifies that, for Althusius, the good of the community is prior to the establishment of specific laws and rights. This provides a useful revision to John Witte's view that "Althusius' theory of society and politics helped to actualize and implement his theory of law and rights." Without getting caught up in semantics, it is important to remember that it is Althusius' account of consociational political life that gives rise to his account of law and the rights of sovereignty. See the preface to the third preface: "Since the jurist receives information, instruction, and knowledge about matters from those arts to which such matters belong, and about the right and merit of fact from his own science, it is not surprising that he receives knowledge of some matters from political science." The account of politics and political *ius* precedes the application of that *ius* in law.

[86] It is interesting to note that absolutists also used the head-body-spirit metaphor at various times. For instance, as Brett mentions, Arnisaeus argues that the political body is constituted

This, at last, gives us the context needed to understand the role that covenants – and the doctrine of double covenant in particular – play in Althusius' theory. It would be a mistake, however, to think that the concept of covenant, or the influence of covenant theology, has been absent until this point. As we have seen, the concept of covenant has multiple valences. While Althusius certainly employs the terms *pactum* and *foedus* to refer to covenants-as-contracts, particularly in book 28, his account of the *consociatio* itself reflects a view of covenant-as-fellowship. The consociation is Althusius' political correlate for the spiritual fellowship that Reformed theologians ascribed to the covenantal relationship between God and God's people. It involves the mutual recognition of certain common goods in which members may participate through the relationship. It entails specific conditions that exist for the preservation of the fellowship. Further, it details the penalties for breaking covenant, and obligates its members to take responsibility for correcting those who have imperiled the fellowship.

On these terms, we can distinguish two modes of covenants in Althusius' *Politica*: first, the consociational covenant, which is rightly ordered fellowship in the common good; second, the contractual covenant, which articulates terms of agreements appropriate to this fellowship. These two covenantal modes should not be decoupled, just as right order and the rights of sovereignty are fundamentally interrelated for Althusius. Corrado Malandrino makes the excellent point that for Althusius the covenant-as-contract "serves these purposes: to enlarge, enrich, make it stronger and safer symbiotic *consociatio*."[87] At the same time, Althusius' account of consociation relies on an antecedent relationship with God, which itself involves both covenantal fellowship and conditions.[88]

Althusius' use of contractual covenants appears throughout the *Politica*. Two instances are particularly relevant. First, and most fundamentally, contracts of this sort attend the constitution of magisterial rule. Althusius uses different Latin terms for this phenomenon. His most descriptive term, however, is the *contractum mandati*, or contract of commission. This contract obtains to "both of the contracting parties," the consociated people and the supreme magistrate.[89] Within this reciprocal obligation, however, we may distinguish between the party that issues the terms – the consociated people –

---

not around goods conducive to common (and eternal) life, but through order, per se, *Changes of State*, 132.

[87] Corrado Malandrino, "Foedus (confoederatio)" in *Il Lessico Della Politica di Johannes Althusius*, 193.

[88] Cf. Malandrino, "Foedus," 191.

[89] *Politica*, XIX.7, 329.

and the party that receives the terms – the magistrate. It is the magistrate who "binds himself to the consociational body to administer the realm or republic according to divine laws, right reason, and the body of the republic." Here, Althusius cites an anti-absolutist *locus classicus* from Deuteronomy 17, in which future kings of Israel are bound to obey God's law and to refrain from exalting themselves "above other members of the community." According to Althusius, the proper response of the consociated people is to "bind itself in obedience" to the magistrate who "administers the commonwealth according to the prescribed laws." As we have seen throughout Reformed covenantal discourse, it is the fellowship that gives rise to covenantal terms and conditions.

This foundational analysis of contractual covenants occurs in book 19, near the beginning of Althusius' account of the offices and officeholders of the commonwealth. In this context, the *pactum* or *contractum mandati* provides the formal structure of consociational life. That is to say, the contractual covenant articulates the normative relationships and practices of the political community, and the penalties that attend breach of faith.

In book 28, Althusius turns from the offices and officeholders of the consociation to the goods and services that they are authorized to administer. He notes that administration of the consociation's public functions is either *civil* or *ecclesial* in nature. This distinction has proved problematic for readers of Althusius who assume that he has in mind a strict dichotomy between the "secular" and the "religious." It is important to remember that for Althusius that which is civil or secular (he uses the terms interchangeably) pertains to the political life that members of the consociation share in common. That which is ecclesial or religious pertains to the functions and goods of the kingdom of God (*regnum Dei*) as it is inaugurated and sustained in the political consociation. In other words, both civil and ecclesial matters comprise symbiotic life in the commonwealth. Ecclesial or religious matters are distinguished from civil or secular matters by the fact that they explicitly refer to that which Christians owe as debts of piety to God in their public affairs.

It is in this latter context that Althusius introduces the monarchomach doctrine of the double covenant. By identifying the double covenant as part of the ecclesial or religious administration of the commonwealth, Althusius addresses one of the problematic aspects of Mornay's original account. Mornay was concerned to show how covenantal relations constitute all political orders, but did not sufficiently explain how this could be true of pagan communities. According to Althusius, all political orders are still covenantal in nature, but they are covenantal first and foremost in the consociational mode. That is, Althusius believes that all commonwealths – Jewish, Christian, or pagan – have a consociational origin and form of life, but he does not assume that all commonwealths have entered into explicit contractual covenants between God and the people, or the king and people.

Far from being an instance of secularization – in the modern sense of the term – this development in Althusius' theory allows him to make the theological terms of the covenant even more explicit and precise. By describing political life as consociational, Althusius provides *general* terms for the norms and practices of the community. By applying the double covenant to political life, he gives determinate content and norms to *Christian* social orders.

In what Althusius calls the religious covenant (*pactum religiosum*), members of the consociated body commit themselves to render due obedience and reverence to God "as subjects and vassals."[90] According to these covenantal terms, God retains proprietary right (*ius*) over his creation and creatures. Remarkably, Althusius claims that this is analogous to the manner in which the *consociated body* and its lesser magistrates retains its *ius* over the realm even after it recognizes the administrative authority of the supreme magistrate. While religious and civil covenants pertain to distinct ends, they function in parallel.

Althusius also makes it clear that the religious covenant entails both piety and justice, insofar as it regards that which members of the consociation owe to God and each other. This point stands in direct opposition to Barclay. Recall that Barclay's conception of covenant lacked any sort of mutual accountability, or common surety, between the king and the people in their respective covenants with God. The king *ought* to render piety to God, but if he failed to do so, the people had no authority to intervene. Althusius notes that Barclay's covenantal doctrine "merely makes both debtors to God alone."[91] According to Althusius, Barclay offers a half-truth that is all the more objectionable and dangerous for its semblance of the real thing:

> In fact, no one can doubt that such a covenant, or contract, constitutes the right and obligation both to God and between the promising debtors, namely,

---

[90] *Politica*, XXVIII.15, 575.

[91] Barclay also claims that, since the magistrate and subjects enter into the covenant simultaneously, it makes no sense to say that the *populus* is prior to the magistrate. Althusius counters this claim by making an appeal to traditional trinitarian doctrine: the Father "begets" the Son from all eternity. This causal relationship of "begetting" does not impute any temporal priority to the Father, since the three persons of the Trinity are eternally co-substantial. And yet, it is still true – in a meaningful sense – that the Father is the (eternal) cause of the Son. As with the Father and the Son, Althusius argues, so with the people and the magistrate. Even if we grant Barclay's point about (the lack of) temporal priority, he claims, this does not mean that the *populus* are not the cause of the magistrate, *Politica*, XXXVIII.114, 930.

between the people and the king. What is at stake in this obligation is not only the public practice of orthodox religion and the sincere worship of God, but also the second table of the Decalogue, of the right and honest administration of justice. This is, both tables are involved.

According to Althusius, therefore, these religious obligations entail some covenantal form of mutual accountability. The consociation, of which the supreme magistrate is the head, is obligated *as a body* to render piety to God and justice to neighbor. It is the consociation that stands in relationship to God prior to any individuated relationship between the king and God, or the king and the people. If either the ruler or the ruled violate these covenantal terms, all parties are mutually implicated and responsible for restoring right-relations.[92] According to the terms of the covenant, he argues, "one debtor is held responsible for the fault of the other, and shares his sins if he does not hold the violator of this covenant to his duty, and resist and impede him so far as he is able." God stands as vindicator of this covenant: "He will cast Israel down because of the sins of Jeroboam."

This understanding of covenantal accountability cuts in both directions. The covenantal agency of the consociated people involves a set of implicit or explicit conditions and responsibilities. These responsibilities are particularly demanding for lesser magistrates – Althusius, following Calvin and others, often calls them ephors – who have been granted representative authority to hold the supreme magistrate to account. In other words, lesser magistrates may sin by commission or by *omission*: "by remaining silent, defaulting, dissembling, permitting, or enduring" the sins of a covenant-breaking lord. They are positively bound "to remind a deviating magistrate of his duty, and to resist him," or otherwise suffer divine judgment.

Althusius' doctrine of consociational political agency is a strenuous one. He recognizes this fact, and argues that the demands of political agency are in fact compulsory. Since the consociation cannot "alienate" the right of sovereignty, its members cannot evade their covenantal obligations to God, magistrate, or fellow members –*symbiotes* – in the community. To describe this symbiotic social order, Althusius employs a rival metaphor to Barclay's paterfamilias. Rather than conceiving of the supreme magistrate as a patriarch, and his subjects as children or slaves, Althusius describes the political relationship as one of guardian and ward. When a guardian is chosen, he or she is in some sense "over" the ward, and acquires a certain authority to command and direct the ward toward some good end. However, the guardian "does not for this

---

[92] *Politica*, XXVIII.23–4, 582.

reason have greater authority and power than the proprietor who does the constituting." On these terms, the consociated people "has committed to the king, under certain conditions and restrictions, power and authority to rule it, and has preserved for itself, under certain conditions, power and authority over a degenerate king."[93]

As in his account of the nature and ends of law, Althusius argues that the authoritative power of the ruler is not absolute, but "limited and circumscribed" by the wellbeing of the consociation. Therefore, just as *lex iniusta non est lex*, an unjust ruler is not a ruler. In such cases, the obligation to resist lies upon the consociational community as a whole.

CONCLUSION: CONSOCIATIONAL IMMORTALITY

Althusius' anti-absolutism involves both a critique of voluntarism, in its twin forms, and of paternalism. His criticism of the absolutists, as well as his constructive consociational theory, is more adequately understood by accounting for Althusius' theological commitments. His understanding of the character of God, the ways in which God relates to his people, the conditions and penalties that God provides in covenants with humanity – all these commitments find expression in Althusius' account of political norms and relations. His rejection of regal voluntarism is parallel to his rejection of theological voluntarism; his objections to earthly tyranny double as reasons for rejecting a tyrannical conception of God; his reading of the Jewish law and prophets supports his belief in covenant accountability. The theological resonances have many echoes, politically speaking.

One of the most theologically resonant features of Althusius' political theory is one that often goes unnoticed. Here we come full circle, returning to one the earliest insights of Reformed covenantal theology: that the covenanted *populus* is the eternal inheritance of God.

Recall the early-sixteenth-century theological reflections of Johannes Oecolampadius, who wrote that it is through the covenantal relationship that God places his law in our hearts and thus prompts us to recognize him as our lord. As a pledge of his faithfulness, God the Father offers Christ as both surety and sacrifice. By this means, we are drawn into fellowship with God, "insofar as we are loved by him and are moved to love in return." This is our blessed bond, the *felix nexus*, which keeps us fast to him and his laws. The provision of the covenant and its laws is therefore an expression of God's favor and a revelation of God's election of his people as his eternal inheritance.

---

[93] *Politica*, XVIII.94, 310.

This theme runs throughout Reformed covenant theology, as we have seen. It is also reflected, I want to suggest in conclusion, in Althusius' emphasis on the immortality of the consociation.

The belief that the political community somehow partakes of immortality, and is therefore antecedent to the mortal king, does not originate in Althusius' *Politica*, nor is it the exclusive province of theologians. As we already noted, Mornay makes a version of this claim in the *Vindiciae* when he writes that the "commonwealth never dies, although kings be taken out of this life one after another." He compares this phenomenon to the way in which "the continual running of the water gives the river a perpetual being, so the alternative revolution of birth and death renders the people immortal." Likewise, the Reformed theorist and historian François Hotman – whom Althusius cites on this matter – intimated that the king is mortal, while the kingdom is perpetual.[94] Similar ideas populate late medieval conciliarist writings.

In addition to all these considerations, however, it would be a mistake to ignore the theological connotations of Althusius' own claim that it is not the king or his office that is immortal, but the commonwealth itself.[95] Kings pass away, but social relationships and the goods they communicate abide throughout the succession of generations. In order to make this claim about the commonwealth's immortality, Althusius must also be committed to a certain conception of the consociation, as we have seen – along with its diverse forms, practices, and goods. That is to say, he must believe that consociational life does in fact permit individuals to participate in common goods that they could not enjoy or engender in isolation. Strikingly, this consociational form of life does appear to have something like a sacramental character, as Zwierlein suggested. It is this consociational form of life that creates and sustains the conditions by which individuals may enjoy the sorts of common goods for which God created them. By participating in the consociation, individuals who would otherwise stand in alienation are drawn together to satisfy "the needs of body and soul." Further, through the consociation they come into collective possession of the inalienable sovereign right of the commonwealth.

Consociational life therefore ought to exist in many forms, on many scales, but always already ordered to a common end: enjoyment of a just and pious life together. When Bullinger, Oecolampadius, Calvin, Zanchi, and others referred to the one and eternal covenant of God as an expression of divine favor, they marveled that God would offer fellowship through such a human

---

[94] François Hotman, *Francogallia*, Latin text by Ralph Giesey, trans. J. H. M. Salmon (Cambridge: Cambridge University Press, 1972), 400–1.

[95] *Politica*, XIX.18, et al.

custom. The covenant provided for fellowship with the divine, and rational participation in God's providential rule over creation. Althusius' consociation provides an analogous account of covenantal fellowship, law, and right order, yet in distinctly political terms. He transposes spiritual fellowship into the political community, noting the harmonies that result when persons with complementary gifts and virtue "communicate" those things among each other. These are the gifts of God for the *polis* of God.

It is this perpetual communicative exchange that gives the consociation its life and its immortality. It is through Althusius' description of this process that we can see the distinctive cross-patterns of his theological and political influences. The virtues, norms, and relations of the theologians apply to political phenomena, just as the terms, maxims, and schemata of the jurists apply to theological doctrines and relationships. For Althusius, this all happens quite organically, since the work of the theologian, the jurist, and the political philosopher ought to be coordinated to the shared ends of the community: In the end, "all arts are unified in practice."[96] It is perhaps fitting that the concept of covenant itself serves a symbiotic role in this regard for Althusius' theory – as the nexus of early Reformed theology and political thought.

---

[96]   This statement is offered in the prefaces to both the 1603 and 1614 editions of his *Politica*.

6

Resisting the Devil

Early Modern Resources for Late Modern Times

Resistance, we have seen, was the practical corollary of early modern Protestant thinking on the nature of authority, law, and covenantal accountability. Around the turn of the seventeenth century, Reformed political thinkers and agents assumed the capacity for, and the legitimacy of, certain acts of resistance in response to the violation of covenantal fellowship. In fact, the consociated political body may even be *divinely* obligated to resist severe instances of unjust rule. For these Protestant figures, this was a modern addendum to the traditional maxim *lex iniusta non est lex*. The terms of the covenant entailed nothing less.

In previous chapters, I focused on the sorts of acts or states of affairs that provide justification for lawful resistance, and the way that failure to render justice to fellow members of the covenant was also considered failure to render justice to God. As we saw in the writings of Johannes Althusius, these social obligations are ordered to various common goods of consociational life that have their origin in God's covenantal love for his people. Althusius and other Reformed political thinkers believed that divine justice would be meted out to those who imperil these common goods of fellowship, whether in this life – ostensibly through authorized political representatives – or the next.

Up to this point, my historical analysis has focused on the possible rationale and justification for lawful resistance. Now we must ask: Once covenantal fellowship has been broken, what remains to order political acts of resistance? In other words, after considering the conditions that occasion acts of resistance, we must address their lawful *means* and *ends*. How might resistance be carried out rightly? By whom? And to what end?

In what follows, I have two interrelated tasks to fulfill: first, to describe the moral virtues and conceptual distinctions that early Protestant theorists employed to evaluate acts of resistance to tyranny; and second, to reemploy these early modern concepts for reflection on rightly ordered resistance in our own day.

The first task involves properly accounting for the theological commitments and moral intuitions of Reformed resistance theorists, based on what they could accurately be said to believe in their own historical context.

The second task is less historical and more constructive. It involves asking whether some of these early modern Protestant claims, commitments, and distinctions can be repurposed in our own context.[1] Many recent works in political theology and Christian ethics invoke the theme of resistance as central to the work of social criticism. However, many of these accounts reflect the disciplinary influence of recent social theory rather than theological ethics. As a result, they often lack the orienting normative concerns that have historically motivated Christian ethicists and moral theologians. I wish to use the resources of Althusius' political thought and this neglected radical strand of the Protestant tradition to revive an account of resistance that is internal to the Christian theological tradition – an account that relies on a broader conception of divine justice, covenantal responsibility, and mutual accountability. Simply put, Bullinger, Beza, Althusius and their contemporaries can offer us something that social theorists like Walter Benjamin, Michel Foucault, and Judith Butler – for all their insights – cannot: an account of radical politics that is both theologically rich and historically grounded in the Protestant tradition.

LAWFUL RESISTANCE

The Swiss theologian Heinrich Bullinger published his seminal work on covenant theology in 1534. The previous year, his only extant dramatic work was staged in Basel, on a Sunday in March.[2] We do not know much about the play's reception at the time, although several twentieth-century works on early modern theater mark it as significant.[3] There are few recorded productions of the play after its initial staging. The only known production in modern times

---

[1] In this sense, I am proposing a reconstruction or retrieval of aspects of this tradition similar to John McCormick's work on the neglected democratic aspects of Machiavelli's thought, Eric Gregory's work on Augustine's relevance for political liberalism, and Luke Bretherton's own attempt to recover an Althusian consociationalism for broad-based community organizing. McCormick, *Machiavellian Democracy* (Cambridge: Cambridge University Press, 2011); Gregory, *Politics and the Order of Love: An Augustinian Ethic of Democratic Citizenship* (Chicago, IL: University of Chicago Press, 2008); Bretherton, *Resurrecting Democracy: Faith, Citizenship, and the Politics of a Common Life* (Cambridge: Cambridge University Press, 2015).

[2] See Susannah Jill Martin's unpublished dissertation "Heinrich Bullinger's *Lucretia and Brutus*" (PhD diss., University of California, Davis, 2003). Martin notes the possibility that Bullinger wrote a second play, although we have no record of it, 49.

[3] Martin, "Heinrich Bullinger's *Lucretia and Brutus*," 5–19. Cf. Hildegard Elisabeth Keller, "God's Plan for the Swiss Confederation: Heinrich Bullinger, Jakob Ruf and Their Uses of Historical Myth in Reformation Zurich," in Randolph Head and Daniel Christensen, eds.,

took place, again in Basel, in the autumn of 1939, when an amateur collegiate group staged the play as the Swiss Confederation mobilized for a potential war with Germany.

Bullinger's play, *Lucretia and Brutus*, concerns the overthrow of a tyrant and the tenuous aftermath of political resistance. As Bullinger makes clear in the play's introductory address, it is a historical drama with an explicit contemporary lesson. Drawing on the histories of Livy and Dionysius, Bullinger recounts the familiar story of Sextus Tarquin's rape of Lucretia, Lucretia's subsequent suicide, and the rebellion led by Junius Brutus in response. In ancient and medieval Christian thought, the narrative of Lucretia, Brutus, and the Tarquins had a long and complicated reception history. Often, the central consideration of the story was the moral status of Lucretia's suicide. In Bullinger's drama, however, Lucretia's violation and Brutus' rebellion take up only the first act of the play. The greater part of the work concerns the difficulties that attended a political community's act of resistance.

Bullinger tells the audience that the "play presents a model how freedom once achieved may be maintained against all tyranny and oligarchy."[4] After the citizens of Rome overthrow the Tarquin's perverse monarchical regime, sending the king into exile, Brutus becomes the pivotal figure. He proposes that the community enter into a covenant, or oath, to reject all unjust rule from now on and "refuse to take any gifts from princes or any other lords." Whoever breaks this promise, he announces, should be "slaughtered like this goat."[5] Here, if we recall the linguistic history in Bullinger's 1534 treatise on covenant theology, the resonance is quite striking. As in the relationship between God and humanity, the covenant (*foedus*) is attended by grotesque (*foede*) ritual sacrifice. The whole community swears the oath, appeals for divine aid, enters into a sacred bond, and acknowledges the attendant penalty of law. Bullinger comments that they have "extracted freedom by force" from the Tarquins, and now "also determined how they might preserve it."

Almost immediately, a threat to the newly liberated republic arises. The exiled king returns and asks the city council to be readmitted as a citizen. When this request is denied, he asks for the return of his possessions, hoping

---

Orthodoxies and Diversities in Early Modern German Culture: Order and Creativity 1550–1750 (Leiden: Brill, 2007), 139–67; Detlef Metz, *Das protestantische Drama: Evangelisches geistliches Theater in der Reformationszeit und im konfessionellen Zeitalter* (Köln, Weimar, Wien: Böhlau Verlag, 2013), 264–5.

4 The German text is found in Horst Hartmann, *Heinrich Bullinger – Hans Sachs: Lucretia Dramen*, 39. An English translation, which I have used with minimal modification, is provided in Martin's unpublished dissertation.

5 Hartmann, *Heinrich Bullinger*, 63; Martin, "Heinrich Bullinger's *Lucretia and Brutus*," 89–90.

the people will take pity on him and that his wealth might be the means to regain his influence in the city. There is disagreement in the city council over the right response. The terms of the oath prohibited just this sort of concession. However, doubts begin to arise among some of the citizens, including – it turns out – Brutus' own sons. Soon, there is an active conspiracy to readmit the king and confess that the community made a mistake in overthrowing the previous regime. A slave named Vindices brings word of this plot to Brutus, who makes the critical decision to execute the conspirators, including his own sons. A good ruler, he tells the council, cannot make the rich, the powerful, or even family immune to justice. Those who break the oath and destroy the very foundations of the commonwealth must be held to account. Otherwise, the liberators become no better than the tyrant they overthrew. "The law that was bent by him / Must be made straight again through time and a commitment to fairness." In the end, the punitive justice meted out to Brutus' sons is contrasted with the reward offered to the honorable slave Vindices, who is freed from servitude, granted full citizenship, and given resources to establish himself in the community.

While Bullinger's drama faded into obscurity after its initial staging, it offers insight into some of the motivations and fears of an early Protestant community that was still coming to terms with shifting ecclesial and political allegiances. Once you have begun the process of reformation and resistance, how can you ensure that these processes do not devolve into anarchy or re-entrenched forms of injustice and oppression?

To answer this question, early Protestants had to consider not just *whether* resistance is legitimate in a particular circumstance, but also what *means* of resistance are lawful, and what *ends* these acts of resistance seek to attain.

Much of the scholarship on Protestant resistance has focused on the first matter – the causes of legitimate resistance.[6] In what follows, however, I want to address the subsequent matters. First, what are the virtues that ought to

---

[6]   Representative works include Robert Kingdon, "Calvinism and Resistance Theory: 1550–1580," in J. H. Burns and Mark Goldie, eds., *The Cambridge History of Political Thought 1450–1700* (Cambridge: Cambridge University Press, 1991), 193–218; Quentin Skinner, *The Foundations of Modern Political Thought*, vol. 2 (Cambridge: Cambridge University Press, 2006 [1978]), 189–348; Tim Hochstrasser, "The Claims of Conscience: Natural Law Theory, Obligation and Resistance in the Huguenot Diaspora," in J. C. Laursen, ed., *New Essays on the Political Thought of the Huguenots of the Refuge* (Leiden: Brill, 1995), 15–51; Martin van Gelderen, "'So meerly humane': Theories of Resistance in Early Modern Europe," in Annabel Brett and James Tully, eds., *Rethinking the Foundations of Modern Political Thought* (Cambridge: Cambridge University Press, 2006), 149–70; Robert von Friedeburg, *Self Defence and Religious Strife in Early Modern Europe: England and Germany, 1530–1680* (Aldershot: Ashgate, 2002).

attend these acts such that the common good is preserved? Second, what are the conceptual distinctions that help virtuous individuals identify tyranny in the first instance? And third, how might virtuous individuals identify the proper remedies for different types of tyranny?

The Virtues of Resistance

There are two contrasting examples of political rule in Bullinger's play. When the drama begins, Collatinus, the husband of Lucretia and cousin to the Tarquins, has oversight of the city. Bullinger's introductory address portrays him as a leader who "lacked courage," and was "always lingering, delaying and whitewashing." At key moments, he fails to recognize the danger posed to the city, or if he does recognize it, he shrinks back from the right sort of action. When the king demands his possessions back, Collatinus worries that a refusal would damage the city's reputation. By contrast, the play presents Brutus as an exemplar of courage and prudence. While Brutus does not figure prominently in the first act, once Lucretia's death has unsettled the political community, he springs into action. In Brutus, Bullinger says, the audience will find "an example of how a courageous / And faithful man handles power."[7]

This virtue of courage is a recurring theme in many Reformed writings on resistance. In particular, we can identify two traditional species of courage – patience and perseverance – that dispose individuals to respond appropriately to injustice.

Emphasizing patience as a virtue needed for resistance may seem counterintuitive. After all, patience in the face of injustice could be construed as passive, or even a failure of courage. Some have read early Protestant writings on tyranny in exactly these terms. John Calvin, for instance, seems to offer textual support for this reading of the early Reformed tradition. He typically shrinks back from endorsing stronger, more active forms of political resistance. While he permits lesser magistrates to challenge tyrannical rulers, the people as a whole do not have the right to resist civil rulers. Popular rebellion would be an irresponsible and impious form of human agency. Calvin does mention the possibility of God raising up an avenger (*vindex*) to defend the people against a tyrant.[8] However, such cases are quite rare, he thinks. As John Thompson notes, Calvin does not seem to allow "any real latitude for such

---

[7] Hartmann, *Heinrich Bullinger*, 40, and repeated in the second act, 62; Martin, "Heinrich Bullinger's *Lucretia and Brutus*," 62, 88.

[8] John Calvin, *Institutes of the Christian Religion* (1559), IV.20.30. See the discussion of this claim in William Stevenson, *Sovereign Grace: The Place and Significance of Christian Freedom in John Calvin's Political Thought* (Oxford: Oxford University Press, 1999), 34–5; and chapter

avengers." This is unsurprising, considering "Calvin's dislike for both enthusiasts and conspirators."[9] Apart from the unlikely appearance of such an extraordinary liberator, popular political agency is quite limited. If the people are afflicted by an oppressive regime, they ought to pray to the divine sovereign for help, rather than resist earthly rulers themselves.

If this is this all that can be said about the virtue of patience, then it does seem irrelevant, if not directly contrary, to acts of resistance. Patience appears apolitical.

If this is true, however, it is strange to note that exhortations to Christian patience do not fade away in the later, ostensibly more "radical," political works of Reformed resistance theorists. In fact, such exhortations figure quite prominently in Theodore Beza, Philippe de Mornay, and Johannes Althusius. Again, this may seem counterintuitive, until we consider how these thinkers actually describe the virtue and its role in political life.

While some of Calvin's statements do appear to cast the virtue of patience in apolitical terms, there is another way to conceive of it. When Beza, Mornay, Althusius, and other Reformed thinkers refer to patience, they generally describe it as the virtuous response to affliction. On these terms, patience is passive only insofar as it is *responsive* to some unjust act or state of affairs. While the virtue of patience often entails abstention from a certain sort of action, it would be misguided to describe it as intrinsically apolitical in nature. Close readings of Mornay and Beza will explain why this is the case.

In the *Vindiciae contra tyrannos*, Mornay notes that proponents of absolute royal power often pointed to biblical statements that appear to obligate Christians to obey all magisterial commands, no matter their impropriety or injustice. He refers to 1 Peter 2: "Fear God. Honor the King. Servants, obey your masters, even the corrupt (*discolus*)." While maintaining that Christians are not obligated to obey unjust commands, Mornay acknowledges that many of the commands of the corrupt king should be obeyed. This concession seems to indicate an uneasy tension in Mornay's argument. How is it possible for Christians to endorse both Mornay's doctrine of resistance to tyranny and this Petrine doctrine of obedience?

We might begin to resolve this tension by distinguishing between a command that is *itself* unjust and a command that issues from a corrupt or

---

three of Ruben Rosario Rodriguez, *Racism and God-Talk: A Latino/a Perspective* (New York, NY: New York University Press, 2008).

9   John L. Thompson, "Patriarchs, Polygamy, and Private Resistance," *Sixteenth-Century Journal* 25 (1994), 18n48. Quentin Skinner likewise points out that for all of Calvin's feints in the direction of resistance, he fails to provide a "clear and unequivocal theory of revolution." *Foundations*, vol. 2, 192.

unjust *source*. In the former case, as we have already noted, Mornay claims that political subjects have no prima facie obligation to obey. In the latter case, matters are more complicated. On this point, Mornay's analysis is less precise than at other moments in his treatise, but his argument follows these lines: A corrupt king may issue many sorts of commands that are burdensome or objectionable in some way. Setting aside idolatrous commands, which must never be obeyed, there may be cases in which it is fitting for virtuous citizens to endure patiently the whims of a corrupt ruler. However, obedience to these objectionable commands arises not from "fear of penalty," but out of love and "service to God." In this sense, the act of obedience is not performed in accordance with the political command, which arises out of the magistrate's desire to dominate his subjects, but rather referred to God. While the tyrant assumes that he has successfully bent the will of his subjects, God, "who cannot be deceived," recognizes their actions as just and patient service to himself.[10] The virtue of patience in this sense disposes the wronged party to refrain from responding with evil, and to re-describe acts of political obedience as acts of faithful service to God, not the corrupt magistrate.[11]

Beza addresses a similar tension, but makes a clearer case for the compatibility of patience and virtuous resistance. In question four of *De jure magistruum*, he reflects on the example of Christ and the martyrs, who have by "example clearly shown that injustices should be patiently borne."[12] He writes that this is the greatest glory of Christians (*summa Christianorum gloria*). Along similar lines, we might recall Girolamo Zanchi's comments about the divine law to walk the second mile or turn the other cheek. The patient person bears affliction without returning injustice for injustice.

However, Beza questions whether all injustices must be borne in the manner of Christ and the martyrs. He asks: Is there no other remedy for injustice?[13] Many of his absolutist rivals, he acknowledges, believe that political subjects must always respond with patient obedience. Prayer, penitence,

---

[10] *Vindiciae contra tyrannos* (Edinburgh, 1579), 30. Cf. George Garnett, ed. and trans., *Vindiciae contra tyrannos* (Cambridge: Cambridge University Press, 1994), 33.

[11] Throughout this passage, Mornay seems primarily concerned with political commands that entail improper religious observance. He believes that impiety and idolatry must never be committed or endured, on the grounds that it is impossible to refer these sorts of acts to God. Mornay does not clarify in this passage whether there are *other* forms of injustice the endurance of which cannot be referred to God. That said, immediately following this passage, Mornay turns to his analysis of the double covenant. It is implicit that through the establishment of this covenant (specifically, its second part) that the people institute legal means to protect itself from regal injustices of various forms, not only idolatry.

[12] Theodore Beza, *De Jure Magistratuum* (Ioannem Mareschallum Lugdunensem, 1576), 11.

[13] Beza, *De Jure Magistratuum*, 11.

and the cultivation of patience are all that remains to an oppressed people. Beza offers the usual affirmations in response. Like Mornay, he grants that Christian patience is "praiseworthy before all other virtues," since it is a "great impetus toward attaining eternal blessedness." He also acknowledges the possibility that tyranny may be an occasion of God's chastening of a disobedient people, and commends spiritual disciplines such as prayer and penitence as "true and necessary remedies for the overthrow of tyranny." And yet, he pivots, "I deny that all these considerations make it illicit for a people oppressed by obvious tyranny to protect themselves from their enemy by just remedies, *in addition to* prayer and penitence" (emphasis added).[14]

On these terms, it becomes clearer that the Christian virtue of patience is not the disavowal of political agency per se. Acts of patience are ordered to the common good, since the endurance of some injuries is generally required in any community populated by sinful individuals. In such cases, prayer and other forms of political agency are quite fitting. However, severe forms of moral injury and social corruption often require remedies alongside prayer and repentance. The virtue of patience inhibits individuals from returning evil for evil. As such, the prohibition of evil is a moral absolute for both the ruler and the ruled. But this in no way rules out additional *righteous* remedies for evil. In fact, failure to pursue these other remedies may be a failure of prudence or moral resolve. Failure of this sort is not a manifestation of the virtue of patience, we should say, but rather its semblance. As Roland Bainton glossed Beza on this matter, the entrenchment of tyranny, and the very need for what Calvin called the extraordinary liberator, might be explained by the community's failure to address wrongs at an earlier time. God finally has to provide a special command to overthrow the tyrant because the people "were too stupid to see that they might have resisted tyranny without it."[15] The liberator is only necessary because the people have misidentified docility as the virtue of patience.

The virtue of courageous perseverance[16] plays a complementary role in resistance writings. In Bullinger's play it is one of Brutus' most prominent characteristics. His actions demonstrate "How authority ought to be used / For

---

[14] Beza, *De Jure Magistratuum*, 17. Notably, the Henry-Louis Gonin translation describes this in terms of a "right" to resist, but this vocabulary is absent from the original Latin passage.

[15] Roland Bainton, "The Immoralities of the Patriarchs According to the Exegesis of the Late Middle Ages and of the Reformation," *Harvard Theological Review* 23.1 (January 1930), 48. Bainton suggested that this was one way for Beza to disagree respectfully with his mentor Calvin, who had written that tyrannicide was only licit by an exceptional divine command.

[16] In the Thomist moral tradition that underlies much of Protestant resistance theory, perseverance was, like patience, a species of courage. Aquinas defined perseverance as that which "makes someone persist firmly in good, against the difficulty that arises from the very

the common use and virtue / For freedom and justice / That there ought to be a man of perseverance / The like of whom has not been seen."[17] In the face of external challenges, and at great personal cost, Brutus remains constant and faithful to the oath. Emidio Campi connects this emphasis on perseverance with Bullinger's contemporaneous concerns about the Swiss confederation. In his early political writings, Campi notes, Bullinger often worries that an influx of foreign mercenaries and money has made the Swiss feckless.[18] They had grown weary in the pursuit of the common good:

> You have no democracy any more. Rather, oligarchy and the pension lords rule over the people, who receive no pensions. All others remain silent, and no one is honorable, pious, and true as he should be for his community and nation. No one takes this disastrous situation seriously and no one will do anything for the common good.[19]

In this political context, then, virtuous acts of perseverance are those in which citizens, over time and at great difficulty, stand firm in pursuit of the common good. They are not deterred by external challenges or temptations. They do not shirk the demands of citizenship; like Brutus, they keep the covenant.

For Beza, Mornay, and other theorists of resistance, it is important to distinguish these virtuous acts of courage from rashness. They emphasize that acts of resistance must not undermine the entire purpose of the endeavor. That is to say, we have to consider whether a particular act of resistance may actually destroy the fellowship that it was intended to save. Mornay offers one illustration of this, and Beza another.

Mornay, like Calvin, considers the possibility that God may send his people an "avenger." Individuals with this "extraordinary vocation" are "for the most part lacking to us in this age." We might expect this to be cause for regret, but Mornay turns the sentiment around. He warns that the people should look out,

---

continuance of the act." He further distinguished perseverance from constancy, defining the latter as perseverance in the good against *external* hindrances. While this conceptual distinction between extrinsic and intrinsic difficulty is useful, it is not – to my knowledge – in evidence in Protestant political thought. Cf. Thomas Aquinas, *Summa Theologiae*, II.II q137a3.

[17] Here, I have opted for Emidio Campi's translation of the German text, in "Brutus Tigurinus: Heinrich Bullinger's Early Political and Theological Thought," in *Shifting Patterns of Reformed Tradition* (Gottingen: Vanderhoeck & Ruprecht, 2014), 46. The original text is in Hartmann, *Heinrich Bullinger*, 62.

[18] Andries Raath and Shaun de Freitas similarly connect Bullinger's historical drama with his own sixteenth-century concerns. Just as Brutus' Roman "democracy is saved because of the council's virtuous reliance on the oath," there is hope for the Swiss cantons. "Rebellion, Resistance, and a Swiss Brutus?" *The Historical Journal* 48.1 (March 2005), 18.

[19] See Campi, "Brutus Tigurinus," 50.

"lest, while seeking an avenger against tyranny, it by chance follows after someone who, after expelling the tyrant, transfers this same tyranny to himself." This is a common phenomenon, he argues. Imprudent attempts to avoid present evils bring about even worse oppression in the long term.[20]

Beza makes an analogous point with respect to oath-keeping. As we saw in chapter three, he believes that oaths are only binding insofar as they accord with the norm of justice. At the same time, Beza notes that breaking an oath – even an objectionable one – is a grave matter. In fact, the moral seriousness of the oath is one of the reasons why he believes it is illicit for private persons to resist an unjust authority when they have previously pledged to obey it. Just as we keep our word in private contracts and agreements, even when they lead to our loss, how much more serious are the political terms we have agreed to keep. In other words, the common project that we have agreed to pursue may sometimes require us to submit to terms that we would rather not. We do so, not out of fear, but for the sake of the common good. If we serially break our oaths to each other, social trust breaks down, and the fellowship we hoped to preserve withers away through our rashness.[21]

It is important to note that both of these examples entail practical wisdom in answering certain questions: Is this the right time or place to resist? What sort of resistance is called for? Will an act of resistance yield a worse injustice than the present circumstances? What previous commitments and promises are relevant? To resist lawfully, we must be ready to make judgments on these matters. Doing so entails the proper recognition of tyranny and the criteria of lawful resistance. Here, we need to turn back to Johannes Althusius' *Politica*, which offers us an extensive taxonomy of tyranny, and an analysis of its remedies.

Identifying Tyranny

In the debates between political absolutists and the monarchomach theorists, the former charged the latter with impiety and sedition – not only on political but also theological and biblical grounds. If everyone is to be subject to the governing authorities, as Paul categorically claimed in his epistle to the Romans, then those who resist earthly sovereigns simultaneously resist the divine sovereign. By arguing for the legitimacy of resistance to civil rulers, the monarchomachs condoned the sin of striking down the Lord's anointed.

---

[20] *Vindiciae*, 214 (Garnett, 171–2).
[21] Beza, *De Jure Magistratuum*, 29.

As we have seen, the response of Protestant resistance theorists had two steps: first, they made a normative distinction between a true ruler and a tyrant.[22] Resistance is prohibited in the former case, but permitted – potentially – in the latter. Second, they claimed that certain persons, whether individual magistrates or an authorized assembly, are "public" figures invested with the authority to resist the unjust actions of other public figures. We need to address these two steps in turn.

For Althusius, as we have already seen in some detail, tyranny is defined as the contrary of just and morally upright political rule. In other words, it is the privation of good rule: "Through tyranny, the foundations and bonds of the consociation are obstinately, persistently, and incurably destroyed and overthrown, against the ruler's pledged faith and professed oath."[23]

Althusius, like earlier proponents of resistance, denies that a ruler who perpetrates these tyrannical conditions is the sort of ruler that Paul has in mind in the epistle to the Romans. A tyrant is not a minister of God, but is better described as an instrument of the devil (*sed diaboli instrumentum dicitur*).[24] What is owed to this sort of ruler?

For Althusius, this is not just a rhetorical question and his answer is not as straightforward as we might have expected. We might expect Althusius to authorize any and all acts of resistance to someone he describes as diabolical.

---

[22] A number of excellent scholarly works have addressed the political importance of theological debates over Paul's claim in Romans chapter thirteen and other scriptural *loci classici*. In addition to the general bibliography in note 6, other notable works on this topic include Daniel Toft, *Shadow of Kings: The Political Thought of David Pareus, 1548–1622* (PhD diss., University of Wisconsin-Madison, 1970), G. Sujin Pak, "Luther, Melanchthon, and Calvin on Romans 5 and 13," in Kathy Ehrensperger and R. Ward Holder, eds., *Reformation Readings of Romans* (New York, NY: T&T Clark, 2008), and the critical edition of Peter Martyr Vermigli's influential "Commentary on Romans 13," in *The Political Thought of Peter Martyr Vermigli*, Robert M. Kingdon, ed. (Geneva: Librairie Droz, 1980), as well as the later works contained in that edition. To provide one example of these heated debates, we might look to the Heidelberg theologian David Pareus. Between the appearance of the first and second editions of Althusius' *Politica*, Pareus published a commentary on Paul's epistle to the Romans (*In divinam ad Romanos S. Pauli ap. Epistolam Commentarius*). It was a prodigious work, approximately 1,700 pages in length. However, it was Pareus' commentary on the thirteenth chapter, a small fraction of the tome, that earned him notoriety (*Quaestiones Controversae Theologicae, de Jure Regum et Principum*). In 1612, an excerpt on chapter thirteen began to circulate on the continent and in Britain. Pareus advocated a doctrine of resistance that resembled those of Beza, Mornay, and Althusius, and was similarly identified as a monarchomach. After it came to the attention of James I, copies of the book were burned publically at Paul's Cross. Cf. I. W. S. Campbell, "Calvinist Absolutism: Archbishop James Ussher and Royal Power" *Journal of British Studies* 53.3 (July 2014), 588–610; Cyndia Susan Clegg, *Press Censorship in Jacobean England* (Cambridge: Cambridge University Press, 2004), 85.

[23] Johannes Althusius, *Politica methodice digesta* (Herborn, 1614) XXXVIII.1, 883.

[24] Althusius, *Politica*, XXXVIII.1–2, 884.

Or perhaps we might assume that the existence of tyranny puts an end to preexisting social commitments and moral norms, in essence, authorizing popular revolution. But Althusius' answer is more complex.

In an appendix to the *Politica*, added in the second edition in 1610, Althusius analyzes the various species of tyrannical rule so that his readers can better identify the right response in particular cases. Tyrants may be instruments of the devil, but not all diabolical agents are the same, nor should they be resisted each in the same way.

Here, Althusius reminds his readers that not all failures or imperfections of rule are tantamount to tyranny – or, to be more precise, tyranny in its absolute or paradigmatic sense. In less extreme cases, Althusius cautions, virtuous citizens should not act rashly. Some rulers may be unjust in one aspect of their office, but not others. Some rulers may suffer from a failure of will in performing their duties. And others may have started down a tyrannical path, but may still be turned away from their destination by wise counselors. Many individual sins and imperfections can and should be tolerated in order to preserve political fellowship. Althusius draws an analogy between political and marital covenantal relationships: the individual sins of a magistrate do not necessarily abrogate his authority, *in se*, "just as a marriage is not dissolved by every misdeed committed by one spouse against another, except for adultery, since this is directly contrary to the nature" of the fellowship.[25]

To determine the right responses to political injustice, therefore, we have to consider tyranny in its various forms. Borrowing from earlier Protestant and medieval sources, Althusius distinguishes between "fundamental" and "administrative" tyranny. The former concerns the foundational laws, religious oaths, and social bonds that make the community a cohesive political body.[26] We might describe this as constitutional tyranny, or tyranny *in extremis*, in which the tyrant breaks the oath they made to the political community – and to God – and so destroys the social order, and impedes the relevant public figures from the performance of their duties.[27] If a ruler were to commit treason, for instance, or plot against their own people, such actions would violate the very foundation of the political order.

The second form of tyranny concerns the unjust or impious administration of the community's goods. It is much more common, and takes more complicated forms, than the first. In this species of tyranny, the ruler is still technically

---

[25] Althusius, *Politica*, XXXVIII.4, 885.

[26] Althusius, *Politica*, XXXVIII.6, 886. He identifies the biblical Omride queen Athaliah, the French king Charles VI, and Philip II of Spain as examples of this form of rule.

[27] Althusius, *Politica*, XXXVIII.7, 886. The English translation strangely drops Althusius' characterization of the oath as ordered to "religion."

fulfilling their office, serving as administrator of the goods of society, but doing so in a perverse way – at the expense of their people. The improper administration of goods might be general in nature, as in the exercise of absolute power, or more specific. Althusius here provides a catalog of vices and behaviors that characterize this latter form of administrative tyranny. This catalog provides examples to help his readers to recognize injustice when it is cloaked under some other description. Among other things, the tyrant is one who corrupts social practices, luxuriates in material comforts at public cost, permits crimes to go unpunished, and nourishes factions and wars to weaken the collective strength of his subjects.[28] If this list sounds familiar to us today, Althusius would not be surprised: Tyranny is a perennial condition that encroaches wherever a community has become vicious or unvigilant.

Identifying Tyranny's Remedies

It is one thing to claim that it is legitimate for the people to resist an unjust ruler. It is another matter to have the practical wisdom to identify a tyrannical ruler and the forms of systemic injustice that give rise to such a figure.

Besides articulating the distinction between a true ruler and a tyrant, Althusius and others made a second breakthrough in early modern political thought: a new conception of popular political agency, supported by a theological account of divine power and goodness. The political community, as a whole, is authorized by God to hold the ruler to account. It may recognize certain persons, whether individual magistrates or an authorized assembly, as "public" figures with the authority to resist the unjust actions of a tyrant.

In previous chapters, I noted that the premodern theological tradition had abundant conceptual resources to distinguish between just rule and tyrannical rule. Tyrants, demagogues, and oligarchs are not a modern invention, of course. What then should Christians do when confronted by tyrants and their perverted systems of governance? Premodern theologians argued that, while political subjects are generally obligated to obey the command of a political superior as if it came from God, the command is only morally binding if it is just and lawful. A magistrate's command to commit theft, murder, or any other act prohibited by the moral law must not be obeyed. In this sense, what I have called a passive, or *indirect*, form of resistance would be considered legitimate. Aquinas even goes so far as to suggest the legitimacy of

---

[28] See Althusius, *Politica*, XXXVIII.10–20. This catalog is not translated in the modern English edition.

some sort of political resistance to tyranny: "A tyrannical government is not just, because it is directed, not to the common good, but to the private good of the ruler ... Consequently, there is no sedition in disturbing a government of this kind."[29] Aquinas does not, however, provide an account of the mechanism for popular resistance, nor does he articulate a doctrine of popular sovereignty that would support such a collective undertaking.[30] Althusius and his fellow Reformed resistance theorists do.

We now need to consider these *mechanisms* for resistance. In other words, how might a people go about resisting a tyrant and various forms of structural injustice? More precisely, how might a people resist tyranny in a *just* and *righteous* manner, so that they do not fall prey to the temptations of absolute and arbitrary power?

Early modern theologians like Althusius and Beza were fully conscious of the temptations that often accompany acts of social and political resistance. The tyrant is an existential threat to the political community, but some acts of resistance may themselves threaten to undermine the common good of fellowship, if carried out imprudently, rashly, or maliciously. Oftentimes, it is better to endure unjust conditions in patient hope that acts of forbearance, rather than resistance, may better serve the common good of the community. If we resist wrongly, social trust breaks down, and the fellowship we hoped to preserve may instead wither away through our rashness.[31]

With these temptations in mind, it is important to consider the practicalities of resistance – a moral task that the early modern Protestants took quite seriously. This involves considering a series of practical, prudential questions of the following sort: Is this the right time or place to resist? What sort of resistance is called for? Will an act of resistance result in greater injustice than the present circumstances? What previous commitments and promises are relevant? To resist lawfully, we must be ready to make judgments on these matters.

Here, is it crucial to emphasize that for Althusius and even the most radical of his Reformed contemporaries, acts of resistance do not occur in anything like a Schmittian state of exception. Preexisting moral norms are not suspended, nor are the principles, institutions, and communal bonds that made

[29] Thomas Aquinas, *Summa Theologiae*, II.II q42a2.
[30] Compare also Aquinas' claim that the subject of civil friendship (that is, the subject in which we find the fundamental good of the fellowship) is the ruler of the people, not the people itself, *Summa Theologiae*, II.II q26a2. This is the reason, he thinks, why citizens owe the ruler obedience. For early moderns like Althusius, as I argue below, Aquinas' account would need to be significantly altered.
[31] See Beza's discussion of this in *De Jure Magistratuum*, 29.

the political community something valuable in the first place. That is to say, acts of resistance are not acts of revolution, but rather restoration. In fact, as I will argue in the next section, acts of resistance may be judged as legitimate, in part, insofar as they aim at protecting the common good of fellowship in the community.

How then should we go about identifying the proper criteria of lawful resistance to various species of tyranny? To make these sorts of judgments, Althusius directs us toward a traditional form of moral inquiry: The criteria of lawful resistance are the *who, what, where, when,* and *why* of the action.[32] When considering the legitimacy of political resistance, as in traditional accounts of just war theory, each of these considerations bears on the rightness of the undertaking.

First, the *who:* There must be an authorized representative of the political community. Althusius, following Calvin and others, refers to this officer as an *ephor,* a lesser magistrate, or some authorized public agent. This public agent is someone who bears responsibility for resistance to injustice, and to whom the people ought to join themselves, adding their own strength, resources, and counsel.[33] Here, it is crucial to note that when Althusius restricts acts of resistance to this class of public agents he is not explicitly identifying a particular legal or political office. He is referring, rather, to a general species of public office that holds the supreme ruler to account for his or her actions. This species of public office may occupy a different place in the social hierarchy across different constitutional systems.[34] In other words, the people may look to any number of public figures – a prince, a duke, a city elder, or any authorized assembly of the people – for vindication. The democratic

---

[32] The following summary is taken from Althusius, *Politica,* XXXVIII.46 904ff.

[33] Althusius, *Politica,* XXXVIII.49.

[34] Some of Althusius' recent interpreters have jumped too quickly from this political analysis to particular jurisprudential claims. Althusius' *Politica* is fundamentally a work of politics, not jurisprudence (cf. his later work *Dicaeologicae*), and the point of talking about the "ephors" is not to identify the ephorate with specific German imperial estates, but to make the more general point: In political communities, it is the right of those who justly represent the *populus* to defend it against tyrants for the sake of the common good. Robert von Friedeburg offers a contrasting interpretation in *Self Defence and Religious Strife,* 116–18. He repeats this interpretation of Althusius' ephorate in *Luther's Legacy: The Thirty Years War and the Modern Notion of 'State' in the Empire* (Cambridge: Cambridge University Press, 2016), 175, 177n37, and 281 relying on what I take to be Henning Arnisaeus' critical misreading of Althusius. While von Friedeburg and I differ on whether Althusius' ephors necessarily identify a determinate constitutional office, we agree that for Althusius the right to resist does not come from heredity (as in earlier resistance literature, such as Philip of Hesse), but by virtue of the office one holds.

implications of this last option may be more obvious to us than it was to Althusius, but it is worth underscoring.

Second, and immediately related to the first point, the *what and where:* Jurisdiction matters when determining the right course of action. "What is to be done collectively by the public agents," Althusius argues, is best done through a deliberative process of mutual consent between the people and its authorized administrators. Deliberation must be careful, patient, and arrive at some sort of practical consensus. In other words, public figures must take care not to overstep their own authority and prosecute a tyrant in ways that go beyond their administrative purview or are disagreeable to the community's representatives.[35] In straightforward terms, this means that public administrators must not act "beyond the boundaries" of the scope or scale of their office. At the same time, Althusius' comments about jurisdiction reflect his belief that authoritative public action must arise from *within* the community. Correction and resistance are internal matters.

Third, the *when:* As the people go about identifying the right occasion to resist, and what measure of force should back up the act of resistance, several things must be considered. How serious and inflexible is the tyranny? Have all other remedies been exhausted? And how have the injustices of the tyrannical ruler been made public to the political community? On this final point, Althusius indicates that three forms of public recognition are central: recognition of tyranny's existence, its extent, and the means by which the tyrant has previously been challenged. This last point is crucial for Althusius, since there must be a record of admonishment and public correction prior to any formal act of forcible resistance. If these conditions are satisfied, as I detailed earlier, the unjust ruler must be held to account. Ideally, the public agents will call an assembly, but if they fail to do so, Althusius grants that "public avengers and deliverers should be constituted ad hoc by the people itself."

Finally, the *why:* the rationale for lawful resistance – the restoration of fellowship. Althusius writes that a tyrant must be resisted so long as the unjust conditions endure, whether in words, deed, or dissembling, and so long as "he acts contrary to the declared covenant." On these terms, lawful acts of resistance must continue "until the republic is returned to its original condition."[36] The remedy of resistance aims at the restoration of health to the political body, and perseveres until this end is accomplished. In other words, the people, having diagnosed the disease that plagues the body, may prescribe the

---

[35] Althusius, *Politica*, XXXVIII.53, 906.
[36] Althusius, *Politica*, XXXVIII.63, 910.

appropriate remedy – even if that means deposing a tyrant, or calling for forcible resistance to unjust power.

In his own context, these last two points are related in a crucial way for Althusius' consociational account of political life. Althusius was no modern democrat, and his assumptions about social statuses and political hierarchies reflect the mores of his own time. However, the way in which he links popular political agency with the responsibility of resistance to tyranny is quite significant. I noted earlier that Protestant resistance theorists countered absolutist readings of Romans 13 with a two-step argument. The second step, in which public persons are authorized by the community to hold other public persons to account, is given a new meaning in Althusius' consociational account of political life.

Here, we arrive at Althusius' primary innovation, the point at which he is willing to go beyond what I have termed the doctrine of indirect resistance that had long been part of the premodern theological tradition.[37] In effect, Althusius identifies the *people* themselves – and not their rulers and magistrates – as the principal human party of the covenant, the party who bears the primary responsibility for preserving right order. As a collective, covenanted body, the people have authority – given to them by God himself – to hold tyrannical princes to account. They may hold an unjust ruler responsible, name his sins publically, call for repentance, and even authorize public "vindicators" to mount an armed resistance to an "incurable" tyrant. According to these terms, magistrates and rulers are merely administrators or stewards of the political community and its common goods. And as administrators, they may be deposed as the people see fit.

At the turn of the seventeenth century, this transferal of political agency to the people did not go unnoticed. We have seen how figures such as Alberico Gentili and William Barclay argued that this conception of political life and power entailed blasphemy, impiety, and sedition. In addition to the absolutists discussed in chapter four, we could add Hugo Grotius, who tried to temper the radical potency of monarchomach thought in the early days of the Dutch Republic. After the Dutch acquired freedom, the doctrine of resistance found

---

[37] My distinction between direct or active resistance, on one hand, and indirect or passive resistance, on the other, is not absolute. There may, of course, be actions which seem to fall somewhere on the spectrum between the two categories. I find the distinction helpful, however, in distinguishing between direct popular contestation of the existing social order and forms of resistance in which the people ask for the intercession of other authority-bearing figures (e.g. God or lesser magistrates). I address some aspects of this distinction in my essay, "Rights, Recognition, and the Order of Shalom," *Studies in Christian Ethics* 27:4 (November 2014), 453–73.

in the *Vindiciae* and other texts seemed problematic, as Grotius worried that "the comments of Brutus turn all commonwealths into democracies."[38] A people, once vested with covenantal political agency via its relationships with the divine sovereign, may become its own vindicator. This broad-based conception of political responsibility seems as radical and decidedly more potent than Calvin's description of the single extraordinary liberator. After all, it is one thing to find a rare figure with the courage – or rashness – to overthrow a prince. It is another matter for the community as a whole to foster the virtues of patience, perseverance, and prudence among its citizens so that they are able to resist injustice, not as individuals (*singuli*), but as a consociated body.

EARLY MODERN RESISTANCE AND LATE MODERN PROBLEMS

What does this mean for contemporary theological ethics? Are there reasons to view these early modern ideas as something more than just historical relics? Is there still life in these traditional, white, European, Calvinist bones?

I want to draw out two practical, and I think increasingly relevant, implications of early Reformed resistance theory for contemporary Christian ethics. The first implication concerns covenantal responsibility and arises out of Althusius' doctrine of mutual accountability. As I argued above, if we read Althusius carefully, we will encounter a strenuous moral exhortation: Individuals cannot stand idly by when they witness systemic injustice in the church or political society. This may seem a trite moral maxim, easily endorsed by any right-thinking citizen. But I believe that Althusius' point runs deeper than this. He means to implicate us in the deepest, most complicated sins of our communities – simply by virtue of our membership in these communities. In effect, he tells us, insofar as you take yourself to be – and are recognized as – a member of a particular community, you bear a covenantal responsibility for its goods and ills, its virtues and vices, its justice and injustice. By participating in the life of whatever community you belong to (by choice or by birth), you are under a relentless obligation to seek its good, and to ensure that other members of the community are able to do likewise.

We often fail to fulfill this obligation, and in multiple ways. It may be relatively easy to identify the occasions in which we fall short by actively committing injustice against neighbor. It is more difficult, but no less

---

[38] See Peter Borschberg's work on Grotius' overlooked early political writings, *Hugo Grotius "Commentarius in Theses XI": An Early Treatise on Sovereignty, the Just War, and the Legitimacy of the Dutch Revolt* (Bern: Peter Lang, 1994).

important, to identify the occasions in which we sin not only by *commission*, but also by *omission*: "by remaining silent, defaulting, dissembling, permitting, or enduring" the sins and crimes of an unjust ruler or institution. Again, he stresses, the obligation to resist injustice and to set things right obtains to the community as a whole. Factions or parties within the political community cannot simply shirk responsibility or shift blame to their rivals; all are co-debtors before God. If anyone stands by while Jeroboam worships idols and slaughters the innocent, they partake in his sin – and his judgment. If we are truly going to claim popular political agency, we must also have a keen sense of our personal and collective responsibility for the shared life of the political community.

If Althusius is right about this, there are two related issues that must be addressed. First, acts of resistance must be regarded as *internal* to the community itself. In other words, resistance arises from within the community, for the sake of the community. Such acts may only be regarded as righteous and just if they are duly authorized, and this authorization comes from the political community that God has called into being. If someone claims to be a liberator, but does not derive their authority from the community, nor make themself accountable to the community, they lacks the authority to act justly on its behalf. The second related issue regards complicated questions about self-identity, mutual recognition, and the status of liminal persons who may not be fully recognized – or valued – by the communities they find themselves in. Whose voice *counts* in the community? I raise this issue here not to solve it once and for all, but rather to suggest that Althusius' discussion of broad-based political agency may be more democratic than he would have cared to admit. If everyone has a responsibility to care for the common good, and to ensure that every other member of the community is also able to participate in this fellowship, then the boundaries of inclusion may be more expansive and more porous than Althusius himself may have realized. It is possible to see glimmers of this possibility in some surprising niches of Althusius' writings.[39] The work that remains for contemporary Christian ethicists is to make explicit what was only implicit in the best parts of this

---

[39] For instance, in his discussion of religious freedom (not a topic on which Althusius is usually considered open-minded), the careful reader can find evidence of a broadly prudential defense of toleration. Althusius cautions magistrates against enforcement of orthodox religion in ways that would imperil the commonwealth (particularly a commonwealth with no homogenous religious identity). In these circumstances, the civil ruler "ought to tolerate the dissenters for the sake of public peace and tranquility, winking (*conniveo*) his eyes" for the sake of the political and ecclesial communities, XXVIII.66, 602–3. The common good of peaceful fellowship takes priority, to the extent that dissent can and should be tolerated.

strand of early modern thought. Protestant political thought is not a closed canon, and the heirs of Augustine, Aquinas, Calvin, Beza, and Althusius should feel authorized to direct the tradition toward new places and to address questions that would not have occurred to their theological forebears.

There is a second implication of early modern resistance theory, which builds on the first. If the demanding responsibilities of political life are to be carried out faithfully, members of the community will need to find ways to cultivate a set of discrete political virtues to sustain these efforts. Early moderns like Althusius paid a great deal of attention to the virtues that must be in evidence among a people and its rulers if a republic is going to survive, let alone flourish. These virtues, Althusius argues, must be cultivated in homes, congregations, civic communities, and workplaces before they can do the work on a larger political or electoral stage. While it may seem quixotic to campaign on an exhortation to virtue – for good reason these days – I think Althusius is correct. Perhaps ironically, it is on this point that Althusius falls back on the wisdom of the ancients and the medievals: A rightly ordered republic, one in which all members are able to pursue the common good, needs virtuous citizens and exemplars. And what are some of these virtues? They include the *prudence* to recognize the difference between justice and injustice, the *tolerance* to live well with those we find objectionable, the *piety* to honor the people, institutions, and traditions that made us who we are, and the *courage* to sacrifice for the sake of fellowship and call tyrants to account.

It is also important to account for the flipside of this matter: All too often, acts of resistance are undertaken by the vicious or those ill-equipped to rightly order the means and ends of these acts. Those lacking in prudence will misjudge their circumstances, or the conditions needed for successful resistance. Those lacking the virtue of tolerance will not be prepared to respond appropriately to those actions or people they find objectionable. Those lacking in piety may become demagogues. Those lacking in courage will habitually conform to the demands of individuals or institutions that exercise undue economic power or social pressure. In many of these cases, vicious agents of resistance and their fellow social critics might turn out to be a remedy more pernicious than the disease.

If we are to recover this early modern doctrine of resistance for contemporary purposes, we need to take note of Althusius' anxiety about the ways that resistance can go wrong. But at the same time, it is important to remember that righteous acts of resistance can often be identified by examining their primary ends and means. Do acts of resistance aim to preserve or restore the fellowship of the community? Or do they instead aim to shore up private goods and partisan interests? Are acts of resistance being carried out virtuously by representative individuals who act with prudence, courage, and charity? Or are they being carried out carelessly, rashly, and with ill intent?

These questions are not easily answered. And in a political context like our own, consensus answers will be even harder to come by. I find this reality regrettable – perhaps even cause for lament – but not paralyzing, nor sufficient grounds for resentment. The temptation to despair or to resort to some form of apocalyptic impatience may seem quite strong to us now. But insofar as political fellowship is still recognized as valuable, whether by our fellow citizens or by God, we have cause to hope. So long as there are those who devote themselves to cultivating the virtues needed to live well with each other, to pursue just relations, despite the personal cost, there is reason to continue to look for restoration.

If we want to repurpose an early modern doctrine of resistance for our own late modern troubles, this is where we must start: doing the hard, slow work of moral formation, correction, and confrontation. The work of virtuous, rightly-ordered resistance could begin on the smallest of scales: in homes, classrooms, congregations, or similar civic communities. Perhaps from those seedbeds we will see the outgrowth of something more expansive. However, regardless of the context, we can hope to see the public work of resistance being carried out by virtuous citizens who recognize themselves as co-debtors before God and neighbor for the common good of fellowship with each other. This invaluable good is something worthy of our attention, our struggle, and our sacrifice.

Bibliography

Agamben, Giorgio. *The Kingdom and the Glory: For a Theological Genealogy of Economy and Government*, trans. Lorenzo Chiesa. Stanford, CA: Stanford University Press, 2011.

Leviathans Rätsel, trans. Paul Silas Peterson. Tübingen: Mohr Siebeck, 2014.

Allen, J. W. *A History of Political Thought in the Sixteenth Century*. London: Methuen, 1928.

Alsted, Johann Heinrich. *Encyclopaedia septem tomis distincta*. Herborn, 1630.

Theologia Naturalis. Frankfurt, 1615.

Althusius, Johannes. *Civilis Conversationes libri duo*. Hanoviae, 1601.

Dicaeologicae libri tres. Frankfurt, 1618.

Politica Methodice Digesta. Herborn, 1603, 1610, 1614.

Politica Methodice Digesta, ed. Carl Friedrich. Cambridge, MA: Harvard University Press, 1932.

Politica Methodice Digesta, trans. Frederick Carney. Indianapolis, IN: Liberty Fund, 1995.

Alting, Johann Heinrich. *Methodus theologiae didacticae*. Amsterdam, 1656.

Armstrong, Brian. *Calvinism and the Amyraut Heresy: Protestant Scholasticism and Humanism in Seventeenth-Century France*. Madison, WI: University of Wisconsin Press, 1969.

Aquinas, Thomas. *Summa Theologiae*, 1265–74.

Arnisaeus, Henning. *De Autoritate Principum in Populum Semper Inviolabili*. Frankfurt, 1612.

De Jure Majestatis Libri Tres. Strasbourg, 1673 (1610).

De Jure Majestatis Libri Tres, trans. John Eliot (1628–30). London, 1882.

De Republica. Strasbourg, 1615.

Backus, Irena. "Calvin's Concept of Natural and Roman Law." *Calvin Theological Journal* 38, 7–26.

Bainton, Roland. "The Immoralities of the Patriarchs According to the Exegesis of the Late Middle Ages and of the Reformation." *Harvard Theological Review* 23.1, 39–49.

Baker, Wayne. *Heinrich Bullinger and the Covenant: The Other Reformed Tradition*. Athens, OH: Ohio University Press, 1980.

Ball, John. *A Treatise of the Covenant of Grace*, 1645.

Ballor, Jordan J. *Covenant, Causality, and Law: A Study in the Theology of Wolfgang Musculus*. Göttingen: Vandenhoeck and Ruprecht, 2012.

Barclay, William. *De Regno et Regali Potestate*. Paris, 1600.

Barth, Karl. *Church Dogmatics*, vol. 4, Part 1. Edinburgh: T&T Clark, 1956.

Baschera, Luca. "Ethics in Reformed Orthodoxy." In *Companion to Reformed Orthodoxy*, ed. Herman J. Selderhuis. Leiden: Brill, 2013.

Bateza, Anthony. *Becoming a Living Law: Freedom and Justice in the Ethical Writings of Martin Luther*. PhD diss., Princeton Theological Seminary, 2017.

Baum, G. and Cunitz, E., eds. *Histoire ecclésiastique des églises réformées au royaume de France*, vol. 2. Paris, 1884 [1580].

Beach, J. Mark. *Christ and the Covenant: Francis Turretin's Federal Theology as a Defense of the Doctrine of Grace*. Göttingen: Vandenhoeck and Ruprecht, 2007.

"The Doctrine of the Pactum Salutis in the Covenant Theology of Herman Witsius." *Mid-America Journal of Theology* 13, 101–42.

Becker, Anna. "Gender in the History of Early Modern Political Thought." *The Historical Journal*, 1–21.

Benedict, Philip. *Christ's Churches Purely Reformed: A Social History of Calvinism*. New Haven, CT: Yale University Press, 2002.

Bente, Friedrich. *Historical Introductions to the Book of Concord*. St Louis, MO: Concordia, 1965 [1921].

Berman, Harold. *Law and Revolution: The Formation of the Western Legal Tradition*. Cambridge, MA: Harvard University Press, 1983.

Beza, Theodore. *De Jure Magistratuum*. Lyon: Jean Mareschall, 1576.

On the Rights of Magistrates, trans. Julian Franklin. New York, NY: Pegasus, 1969.

Propositions and Principles of Diuinitie. Edinburgh: Robert Waldegraue, 1591.

Bierma, Lyle D. "Covenant or Covenants in the Theology of Olevianus." *Calvin Theological Journal* 22.2, 228–50.

"Federal Theology in the 16th Century: Two Traditions?" *Westminster Theological Journal* 45.2, 304–21.

German Calvinism in the Confessional Age: The Covenantal Theology of Caspar Olevianus. Grand Rapids, MI: Baker, 1996.

"Law and Grace in Ursinus' Doctrine of the Natural Covenant: A Reappraisal." In *Protestant Scholasticism: Essays in Reassessment*, Carl Trueman and R. Scott Clark, eds. Carlisle: Paternoster, 1999.

"The Role of Covenant Theology in Early Reformed Orthodoxy." *The Sixteenth Century Journal* 21, 453–62.

Black, Antony. "The Juristic Origins of Social Contract Theory." *History of Political Thought* 14.1, 57–76.

Bodin, Jean. *De Republica Libri Six*. Paris, 1586.

On Sovereignty, trans. Julian Franklin. Cambridge: Cambridge University Press, 1992.

Borschberg, Peter. *Hugo Grotius "Commentarius in Theses XI": An Early Treatise on Sovereignty, the Just War, and the Legitimacy of the Dutch Revolt*. Bern: Peter Lang, 1994.

Bozeman, Theodore Dwight. "Federal Theology and the National Covenant: An Elizabethan Presbyterian Case Study." *Church History* 61.4, 394–407.

Bradley, William. *The Correspondence of Philip Sidney and Hubert Languet*. Boston, MA: Merrymount Press, 1912.

Bretherton, Luke. *Resurrecting Democracy: Faith, Citizenship, and the Politics of a Common Life*. Cambridge: Cambridge University Press, 2015.

Brett, Annabel. *Changes of State: Nature and the Limits of the City in Early Modern Natural Law*. Princeton, NJ: Princeton University Press, 2011.

Liberty, Right, and Nature: Individual Rights in Later Scholastic Thought. Cambridge: Cambridge University Press, 1997.

"Natural Right and Civil Community: The Civil Philosophy of Hugo Grotius." *The Historical Journal*, 45.1, 31–51.

"Scholastic Political Thought and the Modern Concept of the State." In *Rethinking the Foundations of Modern Political Thought*, Annabel Brett and James Tully, eds. Cambridge: Cambridge University Press, 2007.

Brett, Annabel, James Tully, and Holly Hamilton-Bleakley, eds. *Rethinking the Foundations of Modern Political Thought*. Cambridge: Cambridge University Press, 2006.

Bruce, James. Divine Choice and Natural Law: The Eudokian Ethics of Francis Turretin. PhD diss., Baylor University, 2008.

Rights in the Law: The Importance of God's Free Choices in the Thought of Francis Turretin. Gottingen: Vandenhoeck & Ruprecht, 2013.

Bucer, Martin. *De Regno Christi*. In *Melanchthon and Bucer*. Louisville, KY: Westminster John Knox Press, 1969.

Instruction in Christian Love, trans. Paul Traugott Fuhrmann. Eugene, OR: Wipf & Stock, 2008 (1523).

Metaphrases et Enarrationes Perpetuae Epistolarum D. Pauli Apostoli. 1536.

Buchanan, George. *De Jure Regni Apud Scotos*. Edinburgh, 1579.

Bullinger, Heinrich. *A Hundred Sermons upon the Apocalypse of Jesus Christ*. London: John Day, 1561.

De Testamento Seu Foedere Dei Unico et Aeterno. Zurich, 1534.

Sermonum Decades Quinque. Zurich, 1557.

Burgess, Glenn. *Absolute Monarchy and the Stuart Constitution*. New Haven, CT: Yale University Press, 1996.

Burns, J. H. *The True Law of Kingship: Concepts of Monarchy in Early-Modern Scotland*. Oxford: Clarendon Press, 1996.

Button, Mark. *Contract, Culture, and Citizenship: Transformative Liberalism from Hobbes to Rawls*. University Park, PA: Pennsylvania State University Press, 2008.

Calvin, John. *Commentaries on the Twelve Minor Prophets*, vol. 5, trans. John Owen. Edinburgh: T. Constable, 1849.

Institutes of the Christian Religion, 1559.

Commentary on Genesis, 1554.

Sermons on Job, trans. Arthur Golding. London: George Bishop and Thomas Woodcocke, 1580.

Cameron, Euan. *The European Reformation*. Oxford: Clarendon Press, 1991.

Campbell, I. W. S. "Calvinist Absolutism: Archbishop James Ussher and Royal Power" *Journal of British Studies* 53.3, 588–610.

Campi, Emidio. *Shifting Patterns of Reformed Tradition*. Gottingen: Vandenhoeck & Ruprecht, 2014.

Catarino, Ambrogio. *Omnes in Adam ex pacto dei*. Gottingen: Vandenhoeck & Ruprecht, 2010.

Cavanaugh, William. "A Fire Strong Enough to Consume the House: The Wars of Religion and the Rise of the State." *Modern Theology* 11.4, 397–420.

Chodorow, Stanley. "The Church as a Juridical Community." In *Christian Political Theory and Church Politics in the Mid-Twelfth Century*. Berkeley, CA: University of California Press, 1972.

Clark, R. Scott. *Caspar Olevian and the Substance of the Covenant: The Double Benefit of Christ*. Edinburgh: Rutherford House, 2005.

Clegg, Cyndia Susan. *Press Censorship in Jacobean England*. Cambridge: Cambridge University Press, 2004,

Cleveland, Christopher. *Thomism in John Owen*. Burlington, VT: Ashgate, 2013.

Coffey, John. "Quentin Skinner and the Religious Dimension of Early Modern Political Thought." In *Seeing Things Their Way: Intellectual History and the Return of Religion*, Alister Chapman, John Coffey, and Brad Gregory, eds. Notre Dame, IN: University of Notre Dame Press, 2009.

"The Language of Liberty in Calvinist Political Thought." In *Freedom and the Construction of Europe*, vol. 1, Quentin Skinner and Martin van Gelderen, eds. Cambridge: Cambridge University Press, 2013.

Collot, Claude. *L'école doctrinale de droit public de Pont-a-Mousson*. Paris: Librairie générale de droit et de jurisprudence, 1965.

Condren, Conal. *George Lawson's Politica and the English Revolution*. Cambridge: Cambridge University Press, 2002.

Condren, Conal, Stephen Gaukroger, and Ian Hunter, eds. *Philosopher in Early Modern Europe: The Nature of a Contested Identity*. Cambridge: Cambridge University Press, 2006.

d'Arbleste Mornay, Charlotte. *A Huguenot Family in the XVI Century: The Memoirs of Philippe de Mornay, Written by His Wife*, trans. Lucy Crump. London: Routledge, 1926.

Darby, Graham, ed. *The Origins and Development of the Dutch Revolt*. New York, NY: Routledge, 2001.

Decock, Wim. *Theologians and Contract Law: The Moral Transformation of the Ius Commune (ca. 1500–1650)*. Leiden: Brill, 2012.

Denlinger, Aaron. *Omnes in Adam Ex Pacto Dei: Ambrogio Catarino's Doctrine of Covenantal Solidarity and Its Influence on Post-Reformation Reformed Dogmatics*. Göttingen: Vandenhoeck & Ruprecht, 2010.

D'Entreves, Alexander. *Natural Law: An Introduction to Legal Philosophy*. New Brunswick, NJ: Transaction Publishers, 2009 [1951].

Diefendorf, Barbara. *Beneath the Cross: Catholics and Huguenots in Sixteenth-Century Paris*. Oxford: Oxford University Press, 1991.

Dreitzel, Horst. "Althusius in der Geschichte des Föderalismus." In *Politische Begriffe und historisches Umfeld in der Politica Methodice Digesta des Johannes Althusius*, Emilio Bonfatti, Guiseppe Duso, and Merio Scattola, eds. Wiesbaden, 2002.

Protestantischer Aristotelismus und absoluter Staat. Wiesbaden: Steiner, 1970.

"Reason of State and the Crisis of Political Aristotelianism: An Essay on the Development of Seventeenth-Century Political Philosophy." *History of European Ideas* 28, 163–87.

Duke, Alistair, Gillian Lewis, and Andrew Pettegree, eds. *Calvinism in Europe 1540–1610: A Collection of Documents.* Manchester: Manchester University Press, 1992.

Eire, Carlos. *War Against the Idols: The Reformation of Worship from Erasmus to Calvin.* Cambridge: Cambridge University Press, 1989.

Elazar, Daniel, and John Kincaid, ed. *The Covenant Connection: From Federal Theology to Modern Federalism.* Lanham, MD: Lexington Books, 2000.

Engster, Daniel. *Divine Sovereignty: The Origins of Modern State Power.* DeKalb, IL: Northern Illinois University Press, 2001.

Farthing, John. "Foedus Evangelicum: Jerome Zanchi on the Covenant." *Calvin Theological Journal* 29: 149–67.

Figgis, John Neville. *Divine Right of Kings.* Cambridge: Cambridge University Press, 1914.

———. *Studies of Political Thought from Gerson to Grotius, 1414–1625.* Cambridge: Cambridge University Press, 1907.

Filmer, Robert. *Patriarcha and Other Writings*, ed. J. P. Sommerville. Cambridge: Cambridge University Press, 1991.

Franklin, Julian, ed., *Constitutionalism and Resistance in the Sixteenth Century.* New York, NY: Pegasus, 1969.

———. *Jean Bodin and the Rise of Absolutist Theory.* Cambridge: Cambridge University Press, 1973.

Garcia, Mark A. *Life in Christ: Union with Christ and Twofold Grace in Calvin's Theology.* Carlisle: Paternoster, 2008.

Gardiner, Stephen. "Answer to Bucer." In *Obedience in Church and State: Three Political Tracts*, P. Janelle, ed. Cambridge: Cambridge University Press, 1930.

Garnett, George. "Law in the *Vindiciae, Contra Tyrannos*: A Vindication." *The Historical Journal* 49.3, 877–91.

Gentili, Alberico. *Regales Disputationes Tres.* London, 1605.

Gierke, Otto von. *Community in Historical Perspective: A Translation of Selections from Das Deutsche Genossenschaftsrecht*, trans. Mary Fisher. Cambridge: Cambridge University Press, 1990.

———. *Natural Law and the Theory of Society, 1500–1800*, trans. Ernest Barker. Cambridge: Cambridge University Press, 1934.

———. *The Development of Political Theory*, trans. Bernard Freyd. New York, NY: W.W. Norton, 1939.

Gillies, Scott. "Zwingli and the Origin of the Reformed Covenant 1524–7." *Scottish Journal of Theology* 54.1, 21–50.

Gordon, Bruce. *The Swiss Reformation.* Manchester: Manchester University Press, 2002.

Grabill, Stephen. *Rediscovering the Natural Law in Reformed Theological Ethics.* Grand Rapids, MI: Eerdmans Publishing, 2006.

Gregory, Brad. *The Unintended Reformation: How a Religious Revolution Secularized Society.* Cambridge, MA: Harvard University Press, 2012.

Gregory, Eric. *Politics and the Order of Love: An Augustinian Ethic of Democratic Citizenship.* Chicago, IL: University of Chicago Press, 2008.

Grotius, Hugo. *De Jure Belli ac Pacis.* Paris, 1625.

———. *The Rights of War and Peace*, ed. Richard Tuck. Indianapolis, IN: Liberty Fund, 2005.

The Truth of the Christian Religion, trans. John Clarke. Indianapolis, IN: Liberty Fund, 2012.

Haakonssen, Knud. *Natural Law and Moral Philosophy: From Grotius to the Scottish Enlightenment*. Cambridge: Cambridge University Press, 1996.

Habermas, Jürgen. *Theory and Practice*. Boston, MA: Beacon Press, 1973.

Haggenmacher, Peter. "Grotius and Gentili: A Reassessment of Thomas E. Holland's Inaugural Lecture." In *Hugo Grotius and International Relations*, Hedley Bull, Benedict Kingsbury, Adam Roberts, eds. Oxford: Clarendon Press, 1990.

Hamm, Berndt. *The Early Luther: Stages in a Reformation Reorientation*, trans. Martin Lohrmann. Grand Rapids, MI: Eerdmans, 2014.

Helm, Paul. "Equity, Natural Law, and Common Grace" in *John Calvin's Ideas*. Oxford: Oxford University Press, 2004.

John Calvin's Ideas. Oxford: Oxford University Press, 2005.

Henderson, G. D. "Dutch Influences in Scottish Theology." *Evangelical Quarterly* 5.1, 33–45.

Henreckson, David. "Rights, Recognition, and the Order of Shalom." *Studies in Christian Ethics* 27.4, 453–73.

Henshall, Nicholas. *The Myth of Absolutism: Change & Continuity in Early Modern European Monarchy*. New York, NY: Routledge, 2013 [1992].

Heppe, Heinrich. *Reformed Dogmatics*, trans. George Thomson. London: George Allen & Unwin, 1950 (1861).

Corpus Theologiae Christianae. Zurich, 1732.

Herdt, Jennifer. "Calvin's Legacy for Contemporary Reformed Natural Law." *Scottish Journal of Theology* 67, 414–45.

Hinlicky, Paul. *Paths Not Taken: Fates of Theology from Luther Through Leibniz*. Grand Rapids, MI: Eerdmans, 2010.

Hobbes, Thomas. *Leviathan*, ed. Richard Tuck. New York, NY: Cambridge University Press, 1996.

Hochstrasser, Timothy. *Natural Law Theories in the Early Enlightenment*. Cambridge: Cambridge University Press, 2000.

"The Claims of Conscience: Natural Law Theory, Obligation and Resistance in the Huguenot Diaspora." In *New Essays on the Political Thought of the Huguenots of the Refuge*, J. C. Laursen, ed. Leiden: Brill, 1995.

Hoekstra, Kinch. "Early Modern Absolutism and Constitutionalism." *Cardozo Law Review* 34, 1079–98.

Hoffmann, Tobias. "Intellectualism and Voluntarism." In *The Cambridge History of Medieval Philosophy*, ed. Robert Pasnau (Cambridge: Cambridge University Press, 2010).

Holifield, E. Brooks. *Covenant Sealed: The Development of Puritan Sacramental Theology in Old and New England, 1570–1720*. Eugene, OR: Wipf & Stock, 2002.

Höpfl, Harro. *Jesuit Political Thought: The Society of Jesus and the State, c. 1540–1630*. Cambridge: Cambridge University Press, 2004.

"Scholasticism in Quentin Skinner's Foundations." In *Rethinking The Foundations of Modern Political Thought*, Annabel Brett and James Tully, eds. Cambridge: Cambridge University Press, 2007.

The Christian Polity of John Calvin. Cambridge: Cambridge University Press, 1982.

"The Ideal of *Aristocratia Politiae Vicina* in the Calvinist Political Tradition." In *Calvin and His Influence*, Irena Backus and Philip Benedict, eds. Oxford: Oxford University Press, 2011.

Höpfl, Harro, and Martyn P. Thompson. "The History of Contract as a Motif in Political Thought." *The American Historical Review* 84.4, 919–44.

Hotman, François. *Francogallia*, 1574.

Francogallia, ed. Ralph Giesey, trans. J. H. M. Salmon. Cambridge: Cambridge University Press, 1972.

Hotson, Howard. *Commonplace Learning: Ramism and Its German Ramifications, 1543–1630*. Oxford: Oxford University Press, 2007.

Johann Heinrich Alsted 1588–1638: Between Renaissance, Reformation, and Universal Reform. Oxford: Clarendon Press, 2000.

Paradise Postponed: Johann Heinrich Alsted and the Birth of Calvinist Millenarianism. Dordrecht: Springer, 2000.

Hotson, Howard, and Maria Rosa Antognazza. *Alsted and Leibniz: On God, the Magistrate and the Millennium*. Wiesbaden: Harrassowitz, 1999.

Hueglin, Thomas. *Early Modern Concepts for a Late Modern World: Althusius on Community and Federalism*. Waterloo, ON: Wilfrid Laurier, 1999.

Hunter, Ian. "*Charles Taylor's A Secular Age* and Secularization in Early Modern Germany." *Modern Intellectual History* 8.3, 621–46.

"*Conflicting Obligations: Pufendorf, Leibniz and Barbeyrac on Civil Authority.*" *History of Political Thought* 25.4, 670–99.

Rival Enlightenments: Civil and Metaphysical Philosophy in Early Modern Germany. Cambridge: Cambridge University Press, 2001.

Idziak, Janine Marie. "In Search of 'Good Positive Reasons' for an Ethics of Divine Commands: A Catalogue of Arguments." *Faith and Philosophy* 6.1, 47–64.

Israel, Jonathan. *The Dutch Republic*. Oxford: Oxford University Press, 1995.

James VI of Scotland. *True Law of Free Monarchies*. Edinburgh, 1598.

James, Susan. *Spinoza on Philosophy, Religion, and Politics: The Theologico-Political Treatise*. Oxford: Oxford University Press, 2012.

Janz, Denis. "Late Medieval Theology." In *The Cambridge Companion to Reformation Theology*, David Bagchi and David Steinmetz, eds. Cambridge: Cambridge University Press, 2004.

Junius, Franciscus. *Opuscula Theologica Selecta*, ed. Abraham Kuyper. Amsterdam, 1882.

Kahn, Victoria. *Wayward Contracts: The Crisis of Political Obligation in England, 1640–1674*. Princeton, NJ: Princeton University Press, 2004.

Kantorowicz, Ernst H. *The King's Two Bodies: A Study in Mediaeval Political Theology*. Princeton, NJ: Princeton University Press, 1985.

Keckermann, Bartholomeus. *Systema Disciplinae Politicae*, 1606.

Systema Ethicae. Hanoviae, 1607.

Keller, Hildegard Elisabeth. "God's Plan for the Swiss Confederation: Heinrich Bullinger, Jakob Ruf and Their Uses of Historical Myth in Reformation Zurich." In *Orthodoxies and Diversities in Early Modern German Culture: Order and Creativity 1550–1750*, Randolph Head and Daniel Christensen, eds. Leiden: Brill, 2007.

Kendall, R. T. *Calvin and English Calvinism to 1649*. Oxford: Oxford University Press, 1979.

Kent, Bonnie. *Virtues of the Will: The Transformation of Ethics in the Late Thirteenth Century.* Washington, DC: Catholic University of America Press, 1995.

Kingdon, Robert. "Althusius' Use of Calvinist Sources." *Rechtstheorie* 16, 19–28.

"Calvinism and Resistance Theory, 1550–1580." In *The Cambridge History of Political Thought 1450–1700*, J. H. Burns and Mark Goldie, eds. Cambridge: Cambridge University Press, 1991.

Geneva and the Consolidation of the French Protestant Movement, 1564–1572. Madison, WI: University of Wisconsin Press, 1967.

Myths about the St. Bartholomew's Day Massacres. Cambridge, MA: Harvard University Press, 1988.

Klashorst, G. O. et al., eds. *Bibliography of Dutch Seventeenth Century Political Thought: An Annotated Inventory, 1581–1710.* Amsterdam: Holland University Press, 1986.

Klauber, Martin. "Continuity and Discontinuity in Post-Reformation Reformed Theology: An Evaluation of the Muller Thesis." *Journal of the Evangelical Theological Society* 33.4, 467–75.

Knaake, J. C. F et al., and eds. *D. Martin Luthers Werke.* Weimer: Hermann Bohlaus Nachfolger, 1911.

Knox, John. *A Godly Letter of Warning or Admonition to the Faithful.* Edinburgh, 1553. *The Appellation from the Sentence Pronounced by the Bishops and Clergy.* Geneva, 1558.

Kossmann, E. H. *Political Thought in the Dutch Republic.* Amsterdam: Koninklijke Nederlandse Akademie van Wetenschappen, 2000.

Kossmann E. H., and A. F. Mellink, eds. *Texts Concerning the Revolt of the Netherlands.* Cambridge: Cambridge University Press, 1974.

Kraye, Jill, and Risto Saarinen, eds. *Moral Philosophy on the Threshold of Modernity.* Dordrecht: Springer, 2005.

Lang, August. "The Reformation and Natural Law." trans. J. Gresham Machen, ed. William Park Armstrong, *Calvin and the Reformation.* Grand Rapids: Baker, 1980 [1909].

Lang, Brita. "An Unidentified Source of John Locke's *Some Thoughts Concerning Education.*" *Pedagogy, Culture & Society* 9.2, 249–78.

Laski, Harold. "Political Theory in the Later Middle Ages." in *The Cambridge Medieval History*, vol. 8. Cambridge: Cambridge University Press, 1911–36.

Lee, Brian J. *Johannes Cocceius and the Exegetical Roots of Federal Theology: Reformation Developments in the Interpretation of Hebrews 7–10.* Göttingen: Vandenhoeck & Ruprecht, 2009.

Lee, Daniel. Civil Law and Civil Sovereignty. PhD diss., Princeton University, 2010.

Popular Sovereignty in Early Modern Constitutional Thought. Oxford: Oxford University Press, 2016.

"Private Law Models for Public Law Concepts: The Roman Law Theory of Dominium in the Monarchomach Doctrine of Popular Sovereignty." *The Review of Politics* 70.3, 370–99.

"Roman Law, German Liberties, and the Constitution of the Holy Roman Empire." In *Freedom and the Construction of Europe*, vol. 1, Quentin Skinner and Martin van Gelderen, eds. Cambridge: Cambridge University Press, 2013.

Letham, Robert. "Amandus Polanus: A Neglected Theologian?" *The Sixteenth Century Journal* 21, 463–76.

"The Foedus Operum: Some Factors Accounting for Its Development." *Sixteenth Century Journal* 14.4, 457–67.

Lewis, Gillian. "The Geneva Academy." In *Calvinism in Europe: 1540–1620*, Andrew Pettegree, Alastair Duke, and Gillian Lewis, eds. Cambridge: Cambridge University Press, 1996.

Lillback, Peter. *The Binding of God: Calvin's Role in the Development of Covenant Theology*. Grand Rapids, MI: Baker, 2001.

"The Early Reformed Covenant Paradigm." In *Peter Martyr Vermigli and the European Reformations*, Frank James, ed. Leiden: Brill, 2004.

"Ursinus' Development of the Covenant of Creation: A Debt to Melanchthon or Calvin?" *Westminster Theological Journal* 43.2, 247–88.

Lipsius, *De Constantia*, 1584.

Politicorum sive Civilis Doctrine libri sex. 1589.

Little, David. *Religion, Order, and Law.* Chicago, IL: University of Chicago Press, 1984.

Loughlin, Martin. *The Foundations of Public Law.* Oxford: Oxford University Press, 2010.

Lugioyo, Brian. *Martin Bucer's Doctrine of Justification.* Oxford: Oxford University Press, 2010.

Luther, Martin. *The Bondage of the Will*, trans. J. I. Packer and O. R. Johnston. Grand Rapids, MI: Baker Academic, 2012 [1525].

MacIntyre, Alasdair. *A Short History of Ethics.* London: Routledge and Kegan Paul, 1967.

Malandrino, Corrado. "Foedus (confoederatio)." In *Il Lessico Della Politica di Johannes Althusius*, Francesco Ingravalle and Corrado Malandrino, eds. Firenze: L. S. Olschki, 2005.

Malcolm, Noel. "Alberico Gentili and the Ottomans." In *The Roman Foundations of the Law of Nations*, Benedict Kingsbury and Benjamin Straumann, eds. Cambridge: Cambridge University Press, 2010.

Manetsch, Scott. *Calvin's Company of Pastors: Pastoral Care and the Emerging Reformed Church, 1536–1609.* Oxford: Oxford University Press, 2012.

Martin, Susannah Jill. *Heinrich Bullinger's Lucretia and Brutus.* PhD diss., University of California, Davis, 2003.

Martinius, Matthias. *De Gubernatione Mundi Commentaries.* Bremen, 1613.

McCormick, John. *Machiavellian Democracy.* Cambridge: Cambridge University Press, 2011.

McCoy, Charles S. *Fountain of Federalism: Heinrich Bullinger and the Covenantal Tradition.* Louisville, KY: Westminster/John Knox, 1991.

McCoy, Charles, and Wayne Baker. *Fountainhead of Federalism.* Louisville, KY: Westminster John Knox Press, 1991.

McCullock, Matt. "Johannes Althusius' *Politica*: The Culmination of Calvin's Right of Resistance." *European Legacy* 11.5, 485–99.

McGiffert, Michael. "From Moses to Adam: The Making of the Covenant of Works." *Sixteenth Century Journal* 19.2, 131–55.

McIlwain, Charles Howard. *Constitutionalism: Ancient and Modern.* Ithaca, NY: Cornell University Press, 1940.

McLaren, Anne. "Rethinking Republicanism: *Vindiciae Contra Tyrannos* in Context." *The Historical Journal* 49.1, 23–52.

McLelland, Joseph C. "Covenant Theology: A Re-Evaluation." *Canadian Journal of Theology* 3.3, 182–8.

Menk, Gerhard. *Die Hohe Schule Herborn in ihrer Frühzeit (1584–1660)*. Wiesbaden: Selbstverlag der Historischen Kommission für Nassau, 1981.

Mesnard, Pierre. *L'essor de la philosophie politique au XVIe siècle*. Paris: Boivin, 1936.

Metz, Detlef. *Das protestantische Drama: Evangelisches geistliches Theater in der Reformationszeit und im konfessionellen Zeitalter*. Köln, Weimar, Wien: Böhlau Verlag, 2013.

Milbank, John. "Radical Orthodoxy and the Radical Reformation." *The Conrad Grebel Review* 23:2, 41–54.

Miller, Perry. *The New England Mind*. Cambridge, MA: Harvard University Press, 1982 [1939].

Moltmann, Jürgen. "Zur Bedeutung des Petrus Ramus für Philosophie und Theologie im Calvinismus." *Zeitschrift für Kirchengeschichte* 68, 295–318.

Moots, Glenn A. *Politics Reformed: The Anglo-American Legacy of Covenant Theology*. Columbia, MO: University of Missouri Press, 2010.

Mornay, Philippe de. *Vindiciae Contra Tyrannos*. Basel, 1580.

Vindiciae Contra Tyrannos, ed. and trans. George Garnett. Cambridge: Cambridge University Press, 1994.

Mousourakis, George. *Roman Law and the Origins of the Civil Law Tradition*. New York, NY: Springer, 2015.

Mouw, Richard. *The God Who Commands*. Notre Dame, IN: University of Notre Dame Press, 1991.

Muller, Richard. "Calvin and the 'Calvinists': Assessing Continuities and Discontinuities Between the Reformation and Orthodoxy," in *After Calvin: Studies in the Development of a Theological Tradition*. Oxford: Oxford University Press, 2003.

"Covenant and Conscience in English Reformed Theology: Three Variations on a 17th Century Theme." *Westminster Theological Journal* 42, 308–34.

"Not Scotist: Understandings of Being, Univocity, and Analogy in Early-Modern Reformed Thought." *Reformation and Renaissance Review* 14.2, 127–50.

Post-Reformation Reformed Dogmatics, vols. 1–4. Grand Rapids, MI: Baker, 2006.

"The Covenant of Words and the Stability of Divine Law in Seventeenth-Century Reformed Orthodoxy." *Calvin Theological Journal* 29, 75–101.

The Unaccommodated Calvin: Studies in the Foundation of a Theological Tradition. Oxford: Oxford University Press, 2010.

"Toward the Pactum Salutis: Locating the Origins of a Concept." *Mid-America Journal of Theology* 18, 11–65.

"*Vera Philosophia cum sacra Theologia nusquam pugnat*: Keckermann on Philosophy, Theology, and the Problem of Double Truth." *The Sixteenth Century Journal* 15.3, 341–65.

Musculus, Wolfgang. *Loci Communes sacrae Theologiae*. Basil, 1560,

Nelson, Eric. *The Hebrew Republic: Jewish Sources and the Transformation of European Political Thought*. Cambridge, MA: Harvard University Press, 2010.

Nicollier-De Weck, Beatrice. *Hubert Languet*. Geneva: Librairie Droz, 1995.

Oberman, Heiko, *Luther: Man Between God and the Devil*, trans. Eileen Walliser-Schwarzbart. New Haven, CT: Yale University Press, 2006.

"Some Notes on the Theology of Nominalism." *Harvard Theological Review* 53, 47–76.

The Dawn of the Reformation: Essays in Late Medieval and Early Reformation Thought. Grand Rapids, MI: Eerdmans, 1992.

The Harvest of Medieval Theology. Grand Rapids, MI: Baker, 2001.

O'Donovan, Oliver. *The Desire of the Nations: Rediscovering the Roots of Political Theology.* Cambridge: Cambridge University Press, 1996.

"The Language of Rights and Conceptual History." *Journal of Religious Ethics* 37.2, 193–207.

The Ways of Judgment. Grand Rapids, MI: Eerdmans, 2006.

Oecolampadius, Johannes. *In Epistolam Ioannis Apostoli Catholicam primam.* Basel, 1525.

In Iesaiam. Basel, 1525.

Oestreich, Gerhard. *Neostoicism and the Early Modern State.* Cambridge: Cambridge University Press, 1982.

Olevianus, Caspar. *De Substantia Foederis Gratuiti inter Deum et Electos.* Geneva, 1585.

Old, Hughes Oliphant. *The Shaping of the Reformed Baptismal Rite in the Sixteenth Century.* Grand Rapids, MI: Eerdmans Publishing, 1992,

Owen, John. "Dissertation on Divine Justice," in *The Works of John Owen*, vol. 10, ed. William Goold. New York, NY: Robert Carter and Brothers, 1852 [1652].

The Greater Catechism. 1645.

Pagden, Anthony, ed. *Languages of Political Theory in Early-Modern Europe.* Cambridge: Cambridge University Press, 1987.

"'Making Barbarians into Gentle Peoples': Alberico Gentili on the Legitimacy of Empire." In *Burdens of Empire.* Cambridge: Cambridge University Press, 2015.

Pak, G. Sujin. "Luther, Melanchthon, and Calvin on Romans 5 and 13." In *Reformation Readings of Romans*, Kathy Ehrensperger and R. Ward Holder, eds. New York, NY: T&T Clark, 2008.

Panizza, Diego. "Political Theory and Jurisprudence in Gentili's *De Iure Belli*: The Great Debate Between 'Theological' and 'Humanist' Perspectives from Vitoria to Grotius" in *The Roots of International Law.* Leiden: Brill, 2014.

Pareus, David. *In divinam ad Romanos.* Stephanus Gamonetus, 1609.

In divinam ad Romanos S. Pauli Apostoli Epistolam Commentarius. Heidelberg, 1613.

Parker, Geoffrey. *The Dutch Revolt.* New York, NY: Penguin, 1984.

Pennington, Kenneth. "The History of Rights in Western Thought." *Emory Law Journal* 47, 237–52.

Pentland, Elizabeth. "Philippe Mornay, Mary Sidney, and the Politics of Translation." *Early Modern Studies Journal* 6, 66–98.

Pettegree, Andrew. *Emden and the Dutch Revolt: Exile and the Development of Reformed Protestantism.* Oxford: Oxford University Press, 1992.

Pictet, Benedict. *Theologia Christiana.* Geneva, 1696,

Pocock, J. G. A. *Ancient Constitution and the Feudal Law: A Study of English Historical Thought in the Seventeenth Century.* Cambridge: Cambridge University Press, 1987.

Machiavellian Moment: Florentine Political Thought and the Atlantic Republican Tradition. Princeton, NJ: Princeton University Press, 2003.

"Perceptions of Modernity in Early Modern Historical Thinking." *Intellectual History Review* 17.1, 79–92.

Polanus, Amandus. *Syntagma Theologiae Christianae.* Hanau, 1615.

Porter, Jean. *Natural and Divine Law.* Grand Rapids, MI: Eerdmans, 1999.

Pufendorf, Samuel. *De Jure Naturae et Gentium.* Lund, 1672.

Elementorum Jurisprudentiae Universalis. Frankfurt and Jena, 1660.

The Divine Feudal Law: Or, Covenants with Mankind, Represented, trans. Theophilus Dorrington. Indianapolis, IN: Liberty Fund, 2002.

Raath, A. W. G. "Heinrich Bullinger, Political Covenantalism and Vermigli's Commentary on Judges." *In Die Skriflig* 39.2, 311–24.

Raath, A. W. G. and Shaun De Freitas. "Rebellion, Resistance, and a Swiss Brutus?" *The Historical Journal* 48.1, 1–26.

"Theologico-Political Federalism: The Office of Magistracy and the Legacy of Heinrich Bullinger (1504–1575)." *Westminster Theological Journal* 63.2, 285–304.

Rist, John. *Augustine Deformed: Love, Sin, and Freedom in the Western Moral Tradition.* Cambridge: Cambridge University Press, 2016.

Rivet, Andre. *Instruction du prince chrestien.* Leiden, 1642.

Rodriguez, Ruben Rosario. *Racism and God-talk: A Latino/a Perspective.* New York, NY: New York University Press, 2008.

Rollock, Robert. "De Foedere Dei." In *Analysis dialectica Roberti Rolloci Scoti.* Edinburgh, 1594.

Rolston, Holmes. "John Calvin Versus the Westminster Confession." *Scottish Journal of Theology* 23, 129–56.

Rubinstein, Nicolai. "The History of the Word *Politicus* in Early-Modern Europe." In *The Languages of Political Theory in Early-Modern Europe,* Anthony Pagden, ed. Cambridge, Cambridge University Press, 1987.

Rutherford, Samuel. *Lex Rex.* London, 1644.

The Covenant of Life Opened. Edinburgh, 1655.

Salmon, J. H. M. "An Alternative Theory of Popular Resistance: Buchanan, Rossaeus, and Locke." In *Renaissance and Revolt: Essays in the Intellectual and Social History of Early Modern France.* Cambridge: Cambridge University Press, 1987.

"Bodin and the Monarchomachs." In *Jean Bodin: Verhandlungen der Internationalen Bodin Tagung in München,* Horst Denzer, ed. Munich: Beck, 1973.

"Catholic Resistance Theory, Ultramontanism, and the Royalist Response, 1580–1620." *The Cambridge History of Political Thought, 1450–1700,* J. H. Burns and Mark Goldie, eds. Cambridge: Cambridge University Press, 1991.

The French Religious Wars in English Political Thought. Oxford: Clarendon Press, 1959.

"The Legacy of Jean Bodin: Absolutism, Populism, or Constitutionalism?" *History of Political Thought* 17.4, 500–22.

Sanderson, John. *"But the People's Creatures": The Philosophical Basis of the English Civil War.* Manchester: Manchester University Press, 198.

Scattola, Merio. "Models in History of Natural Law." *Ius Commune* 28, 91–159.

"Von der Maiestas zur Symbiosis." In *Politische Begriffe und historisches Umfeld in der Politica Methodice Digesta des Johannes Althusius*, Emilio Bonfatti, Guiseppe Duso, and Merio Scattola, eds. Wiesbaden: Harrassowitz Verlag, 2002.

Schaff, Philip. *History of the Christian Church*. New York, NY: Charles Scribner's Sons, 1910.

Schilling, Heinz. "Calvinismus und Freiheitsrechte." In *Civic Calvinism in Northwestern Germany and the Netherlands*. Kirksville, MO: Sixteenth Century Journal Publishers, 1991.

Civic Calvinism in Northwestern Germany and the Netherlands. Kirksville, MO: Sixteenth Century Journal Publishers, 1991.

Religion, Political Culture, and the Emergence of Early Modern Society. Leiden: Brill, 1992.

Schmitt, Carl. *Political Theology*, trans. George Schwab. Chicago, IL: University of Chicago Press, 2005 [1922].

The Concept of the Political, trans. George Schwab. Chicago, IL: Chicago University Press, 2007 [1932].

The Leviathan in the State Theory of Thomas Hobbes: Meaning and Failure of Political Symbol, trans. George Schwab and Erna Hilfstein. Westport, CT: Greenwood Press, 1996 [1938].

Schneewind, J. B. "Modern Moral Philosophy: From Beginning to End?" in *Essays on the History of Moral Philosophy*. Oxford: Oxford University Press, 2010.

"The Divine Corporation and the History of Ethics." In *Philosophy in History*, Richard Rorty, J. B. Schneewind, and Quentin Skinner, eds. Cambridge: Cambridge University Press, 1984.

"The Misfortunes of Virtue." *Ethics* 101.1, 42–63.

Schreiner, Susan. *The Theater of His Glory: Nature and the Natural Order in the Thought of John Calvin*. Grand Rapids, MI: Eerdmans, 1995.

Schrenk, Gottlob. *Gottesreich und Bund im alteren Protestantismus*. Gütersloh: 1923.

Scott, Jonathan. *Algernon Sidney and the English Republic 1623–1677*. Cambridge: Cambridge University Press, 2005.

Sedinger, Tracey. "Sidney's 'New Arcadia' and the Decay of Protestant Republicanism." *Studies in English Literature 1500–1900* 47.1, 57–77.

Sinnema, Donald. "The Discipline of Ethics in Early Reformed Orthodoxy." *Calvin Theological Journal* 28, 10–44.

Skinner, Quentin. "From the State of Princes to the Person of the State." In *Visions of Politics*, vol. 2. Cambridge: Cambridge University Press, 2002.

Hobbes and Republican Liberty. Cambridge: Cambridge University Press, 2008.

Liberty Before Liberalism. Cambridge: Cambridge University Press, 1998.

Reason and Rhetoric in the Philosophy of Hobbes. Cambridge: Cambridge University Press, 1996.

The Foundations of Modern Political Thought. 2 vols. Cambridge: Cambridge University Press, 1978.

Visions of Politics: Renaissance Virtues, vol. 2. Cambridge: Cambridge University Press, 2002.

Skinner, Quentin, and Bo Strath, eds. *States and Citizens: History, Theory, Prospects*. Cambridge: Cambridge University Press, 2003.

Sommerville, Johann P. "English and European Political Ideas in the Early Seventeenth Century: Revisionism and the Case of Absolutism." *Journal of British Studies* 35.2, 168–94.

Soo Han, Byung. "The Academization of Reformation Teaching in Johann Heinrich Alsted." In *Church and School in Early Modern Protestantism*. Leiden: Brill, 2013.

Southworth, John. *Theodore Beza, Covenantalism, and Resistance to Political Authority in the Sixteenth Century*. PhD diss., Westminster Theological Seminary, 2003.

Spellman, W. M. *European Political Thought 1600–1700*. New York, NY: St Martin's, 1998.

Spencer, Stephen. "Francis Turretin's Concept of the Covenant of Nature." In *Later Calvinism: International Perspectives*. Kirksville, MO: Sixteenth Century Journal Publishing, 1994.

Strehle, Stephen. *Calvinism, Federalism, and Scholasticism: A Study of the Reformed Doctrine of Covenant*. Bern: Lang, 1988.

Stein, Peter. *Roman Law in European History*. Cambridge: Cambridge University Press, 1999.

Steinmetz, David. *Calvin in Context*, second edition. Oxford: Oxford University Press, 2010.

——— "Calvin and the Absolute Power of God." *Journal of Medieval and Renaissance Studies* 18.1, 65–79.

——— *Luther and Staupitz: An Essay in the Intellectual Origins of the Protestant Reformation*. Durham, NC: Duke University Press, 1980.

Stephens, W. P. *Theology of Zwingli*. Oxford: Oxford University Press, 1986.

Stevenson, William. *Sovereign Grace: The Place and Significance of Christian Freedom in John Calvin's Political Thought*. Oxford: Oxford University Press, 1999.

Stillman, Robert. *Philip Sidney and the Poetics of Renaissance Cosmopolitanism*. Burlington, VT: Ashgate, 2008.

Stoever, William. *A Faire and Easie Way to Heaven: Covenant Theology and Antinomianism in Early Massachusetts*. Middletown, CT: Wesleyan University Press, 1978.

Straumann, Benjamin. "The *Corpus iuris* as a Source of Law Between Sovereigns in Alberico Gentili's Thought." In *The Roman Foundations of the Law of Nations: Alberico Gentili and the Justice of Empire*, Benedict Kingsbury and Benjamin Straumann, eds. Oxford: Oxford University Press, 2011.

Strohm, Christoph. *Calvinismus und Recht*. Tubingen: Mohr Siebeck, 2008.

——— "Methodology in Discussion of 'Calvin and Calvinism.'" In *Calvinus Praeceptor Ecclesiae*, Herman Selderhuis ed. Geneva: Librairie Droz, 2004.

Sutherland, N. M. *The Massacre of St. Bartholomew and the European Conflict, 1559–1572*. London: Macmillan, 1972.

Thompson, John L. "Patriarchs, Polygamy, and Private Resistance." *Sixteenth-Century Journal* 25.1, 3–27.

Tierney, Brian. *The Idea of Natural Rights: Studies on Natural Rights, Natural Law and Church Law, 1150–1625*. Grand Rapids, MI: Eerdmans, 1997.

——— "'The Prince Is Not Bound by the Laws': Accursius and the Origins of the Modern State." *Comparative Studies in Society and History* 5.4, 378–400.

——— *Religion, Law, and the Growth of Constitutional Thought 1150–1650*. Cambridge: Cambridge University Press, 1982.

Timmerman, Daniel. *Heinrich Bullinger on Prophecy and the Prophetic Office (1523–1538)*. Göttingen: Vanderhoeck & Ruprecht, 2015.

Timpler, Clemens. *Philosophiae Practicae*, pars prima. Hanoviae, 1612.

Toft, Daniel. *Shadow of Kings: The Political Thought of David Pareus, 1548–1622*. PhD diss., University of Wisconsin-Madison, 1970.

Torrance, James B. "Covenant or Contract?" *Scottish Journal of Theology* 23.1, 51–76.

Treasure, Geoffrey. *The Huguenots*. New Haven, CT: Yale University Press, 2013.

Trueman, Carl, and R. Scott Clark, eds. *Protestant Scholasticism: Essays in Reassessment*. Carlisle: Paternoster, 1999.

Tuck, Richard. *Natural Rights Theories: Their Origin and Development*. Cambridge: Cambridge University Press, 1979.

———. *Philosophy and Government, 1572–1651*. Cambridge: Cambridge University Press, 1993.

Tuininga, Matthew. *Calvin's Political Theology and the Public Engagement of the Church: Christ's Two Kingdoms*. Cambridge: Cambridge University Press, 2017.

Turretin, Francis. *Institutio Theologiae Elencticae*. Geneva, 1688.

Ullmann, Walter. "Development of the Medieval Idea of Sovereignty." *English Historical Review* 64, 1–33.

———. *History of Political Thought: The Middle Ages*. Baltimore, MD: Penguin, 1965.

Ursinus, Zacharias. *Commentary on the Heidelberg Catechism*, trans. G. W. Williard. Columbus, OH: Scott & Bascom, 1851.

———. *Corpus Doctrinae Christinae*. Heidelberg edition, 1616.

Van Asselt, Willem J. "Amicitia Dei as Ultimate Reality: An Outline of the Covenant Theology of Johannes Cocceius (1603–1669)." *Ultimate Reality and Meaning* 21.1, 35–47.

———. *Federal Theology of Johannes Cocceius (1603–1669)*, trans. Raymond A. Blacketer. Leiden: Brill, 2001.

———. *Introduction to Reformed Scholasticism*. Grand Rapids, MI: Reformation Heritage Books, 2011.

Van Drunen, David. *Divine Covenants and Moral Order: A Biblical Theology of Natural Law*. Grand Rapids, MI: Eerdmans, 2014.

———. *Natural Law and the Two Kingdoms: A Study in the Development of Reformed Social Thought*. Grand Rapids, MI: Eerdmans, 2009.

———. "The Use of Natural Law in Early Calvinist Resistance Theory." *Journal of Law and Religion* 21.1, 143–67.

van Gelderen, Martin. "Aristotelians, Monarchomachs and Republicanism: Sovereignty and *Respublica Mixta* in Dutch and German Political Thought, 1580–1650." In *Republicanism: A Shared European Heritage*, 2 vols. Martin van Gelderen and Quentin Skinner, eds. Cambridge: Cambridge University Press, 2002.

———. "'So meerly humane': Theories of Resistance in Early Modern Europe." In *Rethinking the Foundations of Modern Political Thought*, Annabel Brett and James Tully, eds. Cambridge: Cambridge University Press, 2006.

———. *The Political Thought of the Dutch Revolt 1555–1590*. Cambridge: Cambridge University Press, 2002.

van Gelderen, Martin, ed. and trans. *The Dutch Revolt*. Cambridge: Cambridge University Press, 1993.

Veenstra, Jeffrey. "On the Law in General." *Journal of Markets & Morality* 6.1, 317–98.

Vermigli, Peter Martyr. *The Political Thought of Peter Martyr Vermigli*, Robert M. Kingdon, ed. Geneva: Librairie Droz, 1980.

Visser, Derk. "The Covenant in Zacharias Ursinus." *Sixteenth Century Journal* 18.4, 531–44.

von Friedeburg, Robert. "Buchanan and the German Monarchomachs." In *George Buchanan: Political Thought in Early Modern Britain and Europe*, Caroline Erskine and Roger Mason, eds. Farnham: Ashgate, 2012.

"Cuius regio, eius religio: The Ambivalent Meanings of State-Building in Protestant Germany, 1555–1655." In *Diversity and Dissent. Negotiating Religious Difference in Central Europe, 1500–1800*, Howard Louthan et al., eds. New York, NY: Berghahn, 2011.

"From Collective Representation to the Right to Individual Defence: James Steuart's Ius Populi Vindicatum and the Use of Johannes Althusius' Politica in Restoration Scotland." *History of European Ideas* 24.1, 19–42.

Luther's Legacy: The Thirty Years War and the Modern Notion of 'State' in the Empire. Cambridge: Cambridge University Press, 2016.

"*Persona* and Office: Althusius on the Formation of Magistrates and Councilors." In *The Philosopher in Early Modern Europe*, Conal Condren et al., eds. Cambridge: Cambridge University Press, 2006.

Self-Defence and Religious Strife in Early Modern Europe. England and Germany, 1530–1680. Aldershot: Ashgate, 2002.

von Friedeburg, Robert and Michael Seidler. "The Holy Roman Empire of the German Nation." In *European Political Thought 1450–1700*, Howell Lloyd, Glenn Burgess, and Simon Hodson, eds. New Haven, CT: Yale University Press, 2007.

von Friedeburg, Robert, Michael Seidler, and Horst Dreitzel. "The Holy Roman Empire of the German Nation." In *European Political Thought, 1450–1700*, Howell A. Lloyd, Glenn Burgess, and Simon Hodson, eds. New Haven, CT: Yale University Press, 2007.

Wallace, Peter J. "The Doctrine of the Covenant in the Elenctic Theology of Francis Turretin." *Mid-America Journal of Theology* 13, 143–79.

Walzer, Michael. *Revolution of the Saints: A Study in the Origins of Radical Politics*. Cambridge, MA: Harvard University Press, 1965.

Wansink, H., ed. *The Apologie of Prince William of Orange Against the Proclamation of the King of Spaine*. Leiden: Brill, 1969 [1581].

Weir, David. *The Origins of Federal Theology in Sixteenth Century Reformation Thought*. Oxford: Oxford University Press, 1990.

Wendelin, Marcus Friedrich. *Christianae theologiae*. Hanover, 1634.

William I of Orange. *The Apologie of Prince William of Orange Against the Proclamation of the King of Spaine*, ed. H. Wansink. Leiden: Brill, 1969 [1581].

Witsius, Hermann. *De Oeconomia Foederum Dei cum Hominibus*, 1677.

The Economy of the Covenants Between God and Man, trans. William Crookshank. London, 1822.

Witte, John. *God's Joust, God's Justice*. Grand Rapids, MI: Eerdmans, 2006.

The Reformation of Rights: Law, Religion and Human Rights in Early Modern Calvinism. Cambridge: Cambridge University Press, 2007.

Wollebius, Johannes. *Compendium Theologiae Christianae.* 1626.

Woolsey, Andrew. *Unity and Continuity in Covenantal Thought: A Study in the Reformed Tradition to the Westminster Assembly.* Grand Rapids, MI: Reformation Heritage Books, 2012.

Zanchi, Girolamo. *De Religione Christiana Fides*, Luca Baschera and Christian Moser, eds. Leiden: Brill, 2007 [1601].

De Natura Dei. Neustadt an der Weinstraße, 1598.

Operum theologicorum IV. Geneva: S. Gamonetus, 1613.

De Religione Christiana Fides, Luca Baschera and Christian Moser, eds. Leiden: Brill, 2007.

Tractatus de Praedestinatione Sanctorum, pos. 7, trans. Augustus Toplady. New York, NY: George Lindsay, 1811.

Zaret, David. *The Heavenly Contract.* Chicago, IL: University of Chicago Press, 1985.

Zwierlein, Conor. "Consociatio." In *Il Lessico Della Politica di Johannes Althusius.* Francesco Ingravalle and Corrado Malandrino, eds. Firenze: L. S. Olschki, 2005. "Reformierte Theorien der Vergesellschaftung: römisches Recht, föderaltheologische koinonia und die consociatio des Althusius." In *Jurisprudenz, politische Theorie und politische Theologie*, Frederick Carney et al., eds. Berlin: Duncker and Humblot, 2004.

Zwingli, Ulrich. *De Vera et Falsa Religione.* Zurich, 1525.

Refutation of the Tricks of the Catabaptists. In *Selected Works*, Samuel Macauley Jackson, ed. Philadelphia, PN: University of Pennsylvania, 1901 [1527].

Index